More Praise
Action-First Learning

"Karl Kapp's *Action-First Learning* is a must-read for anyone in L&D. It offers clear, actionable strategies to create learning experiences that truly resonate with participants and drive real-world results."
—**David Kelly,**
  Chairman, The Learning Guild

"Karl's latest book brilliantly combines learning with interactivity and fun. It ensures effective learning experiences and meaningful results in today's distracted, AI-driven world."
—**Christina Holloway, CPTD, SHRM-SCP,**
  Director, Learning and Development, NTT DATA

"Get ready to shake up traditional learning! This book is a valuable resource for anyone aiming to make learning more engaging. In addition to introducing the Action-First Learning Framework, it's packed with practical strategies, real-world case studies, and AI-powered tips. Discover a fresh approach to elevate how you teach and learn."
—**Jessica Briskin, PhD,**
  Associate Professor, Commonwealth University, Bloomsburg

"This is exactly the kind of idea book I like to keep handy. Another practical gem from Karl Kapp, *Action-First Learning* underscores just how important it is to engage learners up front and offers design guidelines for nine versatile game structures. It also contains inspiring examples that will spark your creativity. I highly recommend it!"
—**Catherine Lombardozzi,**
  Learning Strategy Consultant and Founder,
  Learning 4 Learning Professionals

KARL M. KAPP

ACTION-FIRST LEARNING

Instructional
Design Techniques
to Engage and Inspire

PRESS
ALEXANDRIA, VA

Illustrations by Kevin Thorn.

ATD Press is an internationally renowned source of insightful and practical information on talent development, training, and professional development.

ATD Press
1640 King Street
Alexandria, VA 22314 USA

Ordering information: Books published by ATD Press can be purchased by visiting ATD's website at td.org/books or by calling 800.628.2783 or 703.683.8100.

Library of Congress Control Number: 2024948539

ISBN-10: 1-95715-792-5
ISBN-13: 978-1-957157-92-4
e-ISBN: 978-1-95715-793-1

ATD Press Editorial Staff
Director: Sarah Halgas
Manager: Melissa Jones
Content Manager, Learning and Development: Jes Thompson
Developmental Editor: Shelley Sperry
Production Editor: Katy Wiley Stewts
Text Designer: Shirley E.M. Raybuck
Cover Designer: Rose Richey

Printed by BR Printers, San Jose, CA

Contents

Preface

When I reflect on my career in instructional design and educational technology, a memory from my early professional days often resurfaces. I was hired to train people to use a software tool that helped manufacturers with materials requirements planning. I knew nothing about manufacturing, so I signed up for a series of courses to learn about the industry, its terminology, and how products were produced. I thought it would make me a better trainer if I understood the purpose behind the software in addition to knowing which values to insert into which fields. I was highly motivated to learn, and I couldn't wait to get to the first session.

I arrived at the training center, located deep in an industrial park, on a sunny afternoon. I heard a lawn mower humming in the background as I took my seat near one of the windows. I saw an overhead projector at the front of the room next to a huge stack of slides the instructor would use to teach the class.

Immediately, I struggled to stay engaged. The instructor monotonously recited information directly from the slides and his dog-eared teacher's guide. He spoke with no emotion, as if unaware of the two dozen learners in the room. Slide after slide after slide.

I watched the clock and focused my mental energy to see if I could make the time pass more quickly—to no avail. My head hurt from listening to the instructor's dull drone. The sound of the lawnmower was musical in comparison. I contemplated leaving at the break and never returning.

"There has to be a more effective way to learn this material," I thought. As I stared out the window, I began to envision an environment in which this training could come alive through interactive activities, making the content tangible and relevant. In my head, I started to construct a game to bring the manufacturing floor into the classroom.

I ended up surviving to the end of the course—barely. But the lessons I took away had nothing to do with the content the instructor was trying to share. Shortly after that ordeal, I began pursuing the passion that has animated my whole career: making training experiences engaging, learner focused, and—dare I say it—fun.

I started by teaching and writing about using games and gamification in instructional design. After years of resistance and misunderstanding, the concept has now taken off, and I've published books on gamification and created gamification and interactive learning courses on LinkedIn Learning; gamification is now built into learning platforms as a matter of course and there are even gamification graduate certificates. The global push toward interactive learning has helped spread the gamification concept to many more people. What is most gratifying is that the gamification movement has saved so many learners from the mind-numbing experience I had early in my career.

But there was more to be done. My quest to transform the L&D landscape to make it more learner focused and meaningful continued. I realized that the words *game* and *gamification* often stood in the way of my students, executives, training managers, and readers understanding a more fundamental value: the need to encourage learners to *do something*—to *take action*.

Academic research, learner feedback, and my personal experiences all show that when learners do something right away during the learning process, they are more fully engaged. The immediate action seems to set the tone for the rest of the instruction period. Over the years, I gathered different methods, practiced different approaches, and honed my action-first techniques to ensure learners realize the greatest benefit. As a result, I've finally developed the Action-First Learning Framework you find in this book. Action for action's sake is not the goal of action-first learning. The goal is *purposeful* and *meaningful* action—always tied to learning. I can attest that participants are always more fully engaged in my workshops and graduate classes when I ask them to first take action. Even if I lecture later in a session, their enthusiasm and energy remain high.

When I began to use the term *action-first learning* regularly in the classroom, in online learning modules, and in designing training workshops, I immediately thought of Action Comics. Although it's now associated primarily with Superman, the first issue of Action Comics (which was published in 1938) was an anthology of 11 different stories—only one of which was about the Man of Steel.

When I began to codify my thinking about action-first learning experiences, I realized this book should also be an anthology bringing together the nine most successful techniques for creating action-focused learning that leads to better critical thinking, communication, and social interaction. The results are in your hands. Consider each action-packed technique, understand its value and purpose, and implement it in your designs using the step-by-step instructions presented here.

But I didn't write this book alone. Along the way, I've been lucky to work with some wonderful practitioners and vendors who have drawn on their own experiences in the field to contribute some of the case studies included here. Jessica Angove of Tipping Point Media, Anders Gronstedt of The Gronstedt Group, and Natalie Roth of Centrical all generously share fascinating case studies that allow you to learn how someone else has used an action-first technique to solve a real-world challenge.

I'm also indebted to Amy Pape, who shared her passion for making learning more accessible by writing chapter 11 on how anyone can make the action-first design process more accessible to all learners. I firmly believe that when we design with a multitude of abilities in mind, we design for everyone.

And of course, I couldn't produce a book about action-first learning without paying further homage to Action Comics. I asked my colleague Kevin Thorn to lend his expertise to the chapter on comics as an action-first learning technique. In addition to his work as an accomplished e-learning designer, Kevin is also an illustrator and contributed the comic-style artwork in each chapter to inject a bit of fun and whimsy—just as I suggest you do in your learning designs. I think everyone loves finding Easter eggs, nods to pop culture, and surprises mixed with more serious topics, so I hope you enjoy the ones I've sprinkled throughout *Action-First Learning*.

Reflecting again on my own experience daydreaming in that painfully dull training class years ago, I now know for certain how different it could have been. I also know how different—and better—all such learning experiences can be if we all take an action-first approach to their design.

I'm calling on everyone in our professional community to recognize that learning is a dynamic, ongoing process—and that we need new tools to take advantage of that. I wrote *Action-First Learning* as one such tool that can help you build compelling, effective, action-first experiences for the learners you serve. I hope you enjoy the techniques, tips, and examples I've honed over the years. Together, by taking action, we can transform learning.

Karl M. Kapp, EdD, Professor of Instructional Design and Technology
Commonwealth University

Introduction

 Let's do a memory-recall experiment. Close your eyes for a moment and envision the most boring, mind-numbing training or learning experience you've ever had. It can be an online learning experience in an e-learning module, an in-person classroom lecture, or even a virtual classroom experience. Jot down the attributes that made it boring and mind-numbing, as well as what could have been done to lessen the boredom. Now, write down a vow to never let anyone endure that kind of experience again. Not on your watch. Mind-numbing learning is a design decision. We can all do better. *(Find the explanation at the end of the chapter.)*

We've all been there. You walk toward a classroom with a group of fellow employees for mandatory training. The topic is evidently important to someone, maybe even you, but you're a bit fuzzy on the details of what's happening. You enter the fluorescent-lit room with coffee in hand. You see a stack of handouts, each 75 pages long. You brace yourself for a long day.

Or maybe you click on the link to the online learning module you've been assigned and immediately see a wall of objectives, slides with fancy bullet points, paragraphs of content spread out over five or six screens, some click-to-reveals, and the occasional multiple-choice question embedded in the module because . . . interactivity is good, right? As your head nods for the fifth or sixth time and you try to stifle a monumental yawn, you wonder if anyone gets anything out of this type of instruction. Spoiler alert: They don't.

Maybe you've designed, developed, and delivered experiences eerily similar to those I've described or those you wrote down in the action-first

activity that opened this chapter. These types of experiences need to end for you and your learners.

This book is a road map to a better place, with detailed instructions and tips intended to help you stop designing mind-numbing learning experiences. In these pages, you'll find a variety of what I call *action-first learning techniques*, which will engage, inspire, and educate your learners.

Action-first learning becomes especially important in this age of artificial intelligence (AI). In a world where typing a simple sentence into an online tool produces pages of AI-generated digital text, images, automated flashcards, or quiz questions, your learners aren't just looking for content. They're looking for learning experiences that reinforce what they know, test their comprehension, and help them practice the skills they've just been taught. That's action-first learning.

Our learners need these kinds of experiences. If, as L&D professionals, we are going to help develop our fellow employees' abilities to think critically, solve problems, negotiate, communicate, and lead others, we need to provide learning through action. We don't need more people who can only passively read, listen to a lecture, sit in front of a computer screen, and click *next* when prompted. We need to leverage what we know about the science of human learning and encourage learners to act, to learn by doing, and to apply problem-solving and critical thinking skills *during the learning process*—not just hope they will do all those things back on the job. As instructional designers and learning experience designers, we are competing with too many external stimuli—including smartphones, smartwatches, and even smartglasses—to create dull, actionless learning designs.

Actionless learning just doesn't work anymore (if it ever did). The alternative—based on research, personal experience, and common sense—is action-first learning design. As instructional designers, trainers, educators, facilitators, and learning experience designers, action should be our go-to tool.

It's our responsibility to encourage learners to engage actively and playfully with content, their peers, and difficult processes like critical thinking. Why "playfully"? Because research shows that children learn best and most naturally through play. Educators describe play-based learning as a highly effective model in which children explore, experiment, and engage with their environment in ways that are both enjoyable and educational.

If play works so well for young, developing minds, why not also design workplace training using this concept? It doesn't mean we should abandon traditional instructional design principles or ignore the fact that many of us are working on serious endeavors in which out-and-out play might not be practical. It means we, as designers and facilitators of instruction, need to work carefully, strategically, and methodically to include elements of play in our learning experiences—and action is a key element of play.

Few children play by sitting in a chair, facing forward, and listening passively to a friend read from a piece of paper or a slide. Rather, they explore, use their imaginations, interact with peers, create games with their own rules, try on roles (such as firefighter, dinosaur, astronaut, or teacher), race each other, take things apart, and manipulate language through made-up songs or rhymes. In short, they learn through action.

However, too few of our instructional design models or research studies in training and development are focused on action or engagement; instead, they focus on topics like learning objectives, the optimal length of videos, or the value that a talking-head video adds to instruction. In the traditional research and design models that are widely taught and disseminated, what is missing are practical, in-the-trenches tactics for encouraging action and practicing learning outcomes within learning experiences.

I've observed firsthand in classrooms how the atmosphere, energy level, and enthusiasm for instruction completely change when I start with action. The simple act of calling on learners to do something like solve a mystery, pick a card, take on a role, or explore a website changes the nature of the learning. It encourages peer-to-peer collaboration and exploration, and, dare I say, makes the learning more fun and meaningful.

Action is the missing piece in our design models, approaches to teaching, and academic theories. Unfortunately, the lack of widespread attention to action-first learning means that there aren't many resources for designers, developers, facilitators, and trainers to turn to when we need to create engaging, playful, active instruction. This is why I developed the Action-First Learning Framework. I've advocated for this approach for many years through gamification and game-based learning, but this is the first time I've gathered the most effective action-first techniques in one place and explained when they are most useful for designing meaningful instruction. This is an introduction to the Action-First Learning Framework and a guide to help you convert your actionless designs to action-first learning experiences.

Why Now?

Do we have to embrace action-first learning right now? Can't we just take it slowly?

In the coming years, learning designs that lean on uninspired, passive presentations of content will be replaced by various forms of artificial intelligence. Organizations won't need humans to design those kinds of experiences. However, employees and organizations will still need and crave richer, more compelling learning designs from human creators—designs that use imaginative techniques and strategies to transfer knowledge, teach and reinforce soft skills, change behavior, and add meaning and purpose to learning experiences.

If, as L&D professionals, we want to have a more profound impact on employees and organizations, we urgently need to rethink how we craft learning experiences. We must move away from simple designs, slides listing content in bullet points, and lectures. Now is the time to embrace the action-first learning mindset, philosophy, strategies, and techniques.

More Meaningful Learning

Crafting a worthwhile action-first learning experience requires that we infuse two kinds of meaning into all aspects of our action-first designs:

1. **Outcomes need to result in meaningful behavior changes that the organization values.** Through action-first strategies, designers can better engage learners' cognitive domain to improve their *analytical, evaluative,* and *creative* abilities to meet organizational goals. In addition, when physical skills and abilities are required, action-first approaches can improve

learners' mastery of physical movements, manipulation of tools and machinery, and other key skills.

2. **Learning experiences must be meaningful to the employees themselves.** Employees should want to undertake the experience and value the outcomes on both a personal and professional level. If we don't try to engage learners' emotions, or the *affective domain*, we may endanger our desired outcomes. Combining learning with a bit of fun, interactivity, and memorable experiences can make all the difference.

What's Ahead

In the chapters that follow, I'll first define my Action-First Learning Framework in more detail and share some of the educational theories supporting action-first learning. Then, we will explore nine distinct types of action-first experiences and why each is effective. I'll include compelling case studies that bring each strategy to life, plus learning design checklists and tips. Every chapter has a sample prompt or two to help you deploy AI tools as you design your action-first experiences, as well as links to resources you can use to improve your knowledge and implementation of action-first learning designs.

In an effort to put action-first learning into practice, even in the more passive medium of a book, each chapter begins with an action you need to take. You could just skip that action because no one is looking over your shoulder, but if you join in, the actions you take will not only increase your knowledge but also make reading the book more enjoyable.

The nine types of action-first learning experiences covered in the book are:

1. **Card games.** These are simple, easy to play, and almost universally understood. They can be configured in a variety of formats, both physically and digitally. These traits make them an ideal tool for delivering engaging and meaningful instruction.

2. **Board games.** These can deliver insights into systems thinking that are hard to achieve through conventional instructional

methodologies. They can be used to teach skills related to resource allocation, prioritization, and critical thinking.

3. **Escape rooms.** In a physical or virtual escape room, a learner must apply problem-solving and communication skills to a specific set of challenges. Escape rooms encourage critical thinking and higher-order problem solving.

4. **Comics.** These combine visual and textual storytelling in a sequential format that is engaging and informative. Comics help learners follow a logical progression of ideas, enhancing comprehension and retention while including the learner as an integral part of the experience.

5. **Branching scenarios.** A branching scenario offers learners an authentic context in which to make decisions and witness the consequences of those decisions for an especially robust learning experience.

6. **Live interactive experiences.** Traditionally, live classroom instruction has been a static, one-way exchange of information. With modern technologies, we can design an interactive two-way exchange that combines storytelling, learning, and real-time feedback tailored to the learning audience.

7. **Augmented reality.** AR allows a learning designer to superimpose an image or text on a learner's view of the real world. This composite view enhances the learner's experience of the content. AR demands that learners actively engage with content that is virtually right in front of them.

8. **Virtual reality.** Sometimes called "the metaverse," VR is a fully immersive, 360-degree experience that provides opportunities for a learning designer to work in both the cognitive and affective domains. All the learner's senses can be engaged in these high-fidelity experiences.

9. **AI-assisted coaching.** AI tools can create interactive conversations and highly reactive ad hoc training moments. They can be bundled to create a "coach in your pocket," allowing learners to take action and engage with the coach in any learning situation.

After exploring all these approaches, we will also consider how to improve action-first learning design by making it more accessible to all learners. And in the final chapter, I'll walk through how to plan and implement your own action-first design, and how to get buy-in from your organization.

By now, I hope that I've aroused your curiosity about the Action-First Learning Framework and that you're eager to discover the tools and techniques that can turn any learning session into an engaging, effective action-first learning adventure. I've designed this book so you can bounce around from chapter to chapter and don't need to progress in a linear fashion. If you're interested in making a specific type of action-first experience, go right there. If you want a comprehensive view, jump to the last chapter.

The important thing is that you take action. So, try the action-first activities at the beginning of each chapter and check out the QR codes, worksheets, and videos mentioned throughout the book. Implement some of the ideas and keep a journal of how they worked and what you might do differently next time.

You can't design action-first learning unless you take action.

To paraphrase Ferris Bueller, "You're still here? This chapter is over. Go to the next chapter . . . Go!"

EXPLANATION OF THE ACTION-FIRST ACTIVITY

Visualization can be an incredibly useful action-first learning technique. By envisioning the most boring learning experience and then thinking through how it could have been better, you are engaging in the first action needed to design and deliver a more engaging, action-first learning experience.

1
Actions Speak Louder Than Words

Take a moment to write down your own definition of action-first learning (no looking ahead!). As you read the chapter, see if yours matches the one I provide. What are the common attributes of the two definitions? What are the differences? Do you agree or disagree with my definition? *(Find the explanation at the end of the chapter.)*

At the end of this chapter, you should be able to answer these questions:

- Why is the term *action-first learning* valuable?
- Why is action-first learning so effective?
- What theoretical foundations and research support action-first learning?

Most children—including me—let their imaginations run wild while playing with action figures. As adults, we take pride in acting decisively at work when circumstances demand it. And we share our experience, knowledge, and skills by directing the action of others.

As designers and facilitators of instruction, we can take a cue from these near-universal experiences: action as play, action in the workplace, and action as education. Instead of passively taking in information, we can encourage learners to engage actively and playfully with content, their peers, and with difficult processes like critical thinking.

Providing passive learning experiences does little to foster engagement, spark creative thinking, or motivate learners. As passive, uninspired presentations of content are replaced by various forms of AI, organizations and employees will continue to value richer, more inspiring

learning designs created by humans. These learning experiences will transfer knowledge, teach and reinforce soft skills, change behavior, and add meaning and purpose to the content—not to mention helping to build culture and connections within organizations.

If, as L&D professionals, we want to have a more profound impact on employees and organizations, we urgently need to rethink how we craft learning experiences. We must move away from simple designs, basic slides listing content in bullet points, and passive online or face-to-face lectures. It's time to embrace an action-first learning mindset and philosophy. *(Cue dramatic music.)*

Why Action-First Learning?

The concept of *action-first learning*—or directly involving learners in the process of acquiring knowledge and skills in an active way—is not new. Instructional designers, facilitators, and teachers have long advocated for *learning by doing, action-based learning, active learning, learner-centric designs,* and *problem-based learning.* So, why do we need yet another term in the already crowded lexicon? I'm advocating that we adopt the term *action-first learning* for three reasons:

1. **Instructional designs should encourage each learner to act as soon as possible in a learning experience.** A long preamble or a ton of prework simply bogs down the process. Engaging learners from the beginning is crucial, and encouraging some form of action at the start of a learning experience draws everyone into the content. It's much harder to regain a learner's attention after they have disengaged than to initially grab their attention.

2. **The term action-first learning helps us avoid some preconceived notions about learning design.** Many of the terms I've mentioned already have specific definitions in an academic context. Purists usually won't stand for deviations or colloquial uses of terms they've relied on for years. For example, the term *action-based learning* was originally coined in the 1940s by professor and management consultant Reginald

"Reg" William Revans. He proposed more than 23 criteria for what does and does not constitute action-based learning (Willis 2004). Although such meticulous definitions are appropriate in an academic setting, saddling a learning practitioner with 23 markers to determine what is and isn't action-based learning is counterproductive and unnecessarily onerous. *Action-first learning* is a more flexible term that represents active, engaging learning design as an approach to developing meaningful instruction.

3. **Action-first learning allows the L&D community to make engaging, meaningful, active learning part of a broader design philosophy.** Like the well-known improvisational theater technique, the term *action-first learning* is based on saying, "Yes, and . . ." This response allows people to move forward and collaborate, regardless of the situation unfolding on stage or in a virtual or in-person classroom. In improv theater, when a suggestion is made onstage, other performers never challenge or reject the statement; instead, they agree to what was said (Yes!), and then add something new from their own perspectives (and . . .). In a learning experience, action-first learning says yes to the learner's need to participate first, and then adds more information, questions, or actions from the learning designer's perspective. It is learner centric in a way that is understandable. It's not abstract; it's a concrete, tangible approach.

A Far-Reaching Definition

In this book, I define *action-first learning* as, "A philosophical approach to designing meaningful instruction that highlights the need for learning experiences to require learners to take immediate or initial actions that gain their attention, activate their senses, and encourage them to think critically and carry that orientation toward action throughout an entire learning experience, culminating in active reflection."

Let's analyze each element of this complex definition and check yours to see how they compare. (I'll bet your definition was a lot shorter.)

A Philosophical Approach

From ancient Greek, the word *philosophy* means a "love of wisdom." In a practical sense, philosophy is the study of how we understand fundamental truths about the world we live in and our relationship with that world, gaining wisdom in the process. Action-first learning is a way of understanding learning and learners' relationship to what they are learning. It is not a step-by-step design methodology. Action-first learning allows us to view the process of crafting instructional design from a higher vantage point and to drive more practical, on-the-ground decisions from that philosophical point of view.

Designing Meaningful Instruction

Again, action-first learning is not action for action's sake. We should never make learners do silly things or just keep them busy, and we should always aim toward action as meaningful instruction. You will need to undertake a rigorous analysis process to determine what actions and activities are most valuable to individual learners and your organization.

Because designing and delivering instruction requires significant investments of time and money, you should focus on the desired outcomes. If learners and your organization don't see the benefits of the action-first learning designs you create, go back to analyze whether the instruction is needed and if you're using the right design to achieve the desired results. This is a critical aspect of moving toward action-first learning.

Make. It. Meaningful.

Learners Take Immediate or Initial Actions

Many learning designers have gotten into the habit of including an initial period of lecturing in their designs without allowing learners to engage in any action first—or at all. In part, we can blame learning objectives for this. In fact, a better name might be *learning objections*.

Take, for example, a sales training class that opens with the objective, "You will learn three ways to close a sale." The experienced salesperson in the classroom immediately thinks, "Well, I know five ways to close a sale. This is a waste of my time. I object to this whole course." You've now lost that learner for the duration of the class.

What if, instead, the class started with the facilitator saying, "Here are three ways to close a sale. Guess which one was the most successful in our organization last year and why." Now, the facilitator has the attention of the learners! Instead of rejecting the objective, they are genuinely curious to know the answer.

Other options to defeat learning objections include asking participants to:

- Make a decision.
- Choose a team.
- Solve a problem.
- Safely operate a piece of equipment (physically or virtually).
- Play a game.
- Place a bet.

These and other immediate actions pull learners into the flow of instruction, getting them involved, setting the tone for learning events that follow, and leading to better retention and application of the information to on-the-job tasks.

Actions That Gain Attention

Many educational models—from Robert Gagné's Nine Events of Instruction to John Keller's ARCS Model of Motivation (attention, relevance, confidence, and satisfaction)—start with gaining the learner's attention. You've likely heard that the contemporary world of smartphones, bite-sized news clips, and 30-second videos on TikTok and Instagram have led to attention deficits. Some people even claim that goldfish have longer attention spans than humans. (Spoiler alert: They don't.)

But modern distractions certainly make gaining and holding learners' attention more difficult, so the action-first approach begins with *immediately* asking learners to do something meaningful, setting the tone for the instruction to follow.

Actions That Activate the Senses

We have five primary senses. Delivering instruction focused only on one makes no sense. We don't necessarily learn better with one sense or another; however, the more senses we can use to encode knowledge, the easier it is to recall a learning experience. Mimicking the sights, sounds, smells, and tactile experiences of an actual work environment during a learning event means that learners will have more cues that they can use to recall the content.

Visceral or emotional events (in what academics call the *affective domain*) also aid our recall. As humans, we tend to remember particularly enjoyable and tragic events. As designers, if we focus on enjoyable events, we can leverage positive memories to help learners recall our instruction. In short, don't limit your imagination when designing action-first learning events—activate as many senses as possible to make the learning enjoyable and, therefore, memorable.

Actions That Encourage Critical Thinking

As AI handles more menial tasks, humans may be freed up to handle more of what we do best: critical thinking. We can think about thinking! We can connect dots that don't at first seem to be connected. We can determine the best strategy and direction for learning.

Action-first learning is all about thinking critically by forcing learners to evaluate information objectively and fairly, to consider multiple perspectives and solutions, and to analyze complex situations at a deep level. Taking action allows learners to focus on the situation they're in and asks them to critically evaluate what they need to do to be successful.

Carry the Action Orientation Throughout the Entire Learning Process

Keeping a learner's attention is a continuous struggle. Keeping your attention as a reader is a struggle, too. Novelists often try to end each chapter with a cliffhanger moment to encourage readers to immediately continue to the next chapter. Television shows do the same thing with each episode, and in the streaming era, the next episode often begins before the previous one's credits have finished rolling. Action-first learning follows a similar approach. You should work constantly to keep learners' attention by introducing new situations and methods throughout a course or program (not just at the start) and by including unexpected twists, Easter eggs (hidden, surprising features), and instructional cliffhangers.

End With Active Reflection

There is no learning without reflection, only an experience.

One danger of action-first learning designs is that learners will be so caught up in the action part that they forget about the learning outcomes. This is solved by requiring learners to reflect on their experiences and articulate in writing or verbally how they plan to apply the knowledge and behaviors they have learned on the job or in other situations. Reflection is a powerful learning tool and an integral part of action-first learning.

To sum up, all the elements of this definition of action-first learning are critical to preventing a superficial or haphazard approach. They are broad enough to encompass many kinds of learning designs but specific enough to offer parameters that can help ensure you produce a successful learning event.

The Action-First Learning Framework

The definition of action-first learning is just one part of the Action-First Learning Framework presented in this book. The framework shows how an instructional designer can best craft an action-first learning experience (Figure 1-1). The following sections describe each aspect of the framework in more detail.

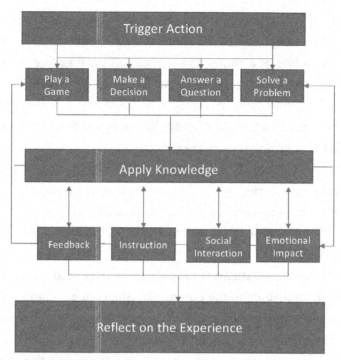

Figure 1-1. The action-first learning framework.

Triggering Action

The Action-First Learning Framework begins with a triggering action—an event or situation that starts the learning process. That trigger could be dealing a set of cards, arranging learners in front of a board game, sending them to an escape room, or asking them to don VR goggles. After the trigger action occurs, the learner then must act. Maybe they'll need to move a token or take a card. They might click on a decision point in a branching scenario, answer a question, solve a puzzle, or look for clues. The point is that the learner is doing something immediately when the instruction begins.

Applying Knowledge

The learner then applies knowledge to the action they are taking. As I mentioned before, this is not action for action's sake—it is part of reaching a desired instructional outcome. The application of knowledge should involve problem solving and nonlinear thinking.

During the process of applying their knowledge, the learner will receive more information and reactions in various formats. The feedback might be as subtle as a character's expression turning from neutral to a frown or as overt as a drawer opening after they enter a combination to unlock it. They may receive instructions, hints, or tips that guide them toward their learning goal, so they don't miss it, and then continue participating in the action-first learning event.

Often the learner will engage with others in an action-first learning activity through a variety of social interactions, cues, and feedback. But even if another person is not present during the activity, the learner in an action-first situation could interact with a character onscreen who is providing social cues.

These social cues, attempts to apply knowledge, and various forms of feedback all contribute to the emotional impact of a situation—an often overlooked but crucial aspect of learning. The process of responding to actions, applying knowledge, and processing feedback, instruction, social interactions, or emotional impact continues until the action-first learning experience ends. However, just because it ends, doesn't mean the experience is over.

Reflecting on the Experience

Action-first learning requires that time be set aside to reflect on the experience. The learner should think about how to:

- Leverage the action-first learning experience for future applications.
- Change their current behaviors.
- Act differently to achieve new results.

The reflection could include journaling, answering a series of questions, or discussing ideas with a fellow learner. This is a powerful tool for learning and an integral part of the action-first learning framework. Without reflection, learning can't take place.

Foundations of Action-First Learning

The Action-First Learning Framework is built upon a theoretical foundation, a rich body of research illustrating the benefits of actively engaging learners, and practical experience.

Theoretical Foundation

The theoretical foundation of action-first learning is primarily the work of pioneering psychologists Jean Piaget (1896–1980) and John Dewey (1859–1952). Jean Piaget, a Swiss psychologist known for studying the cognitive development of children, is considered the father of the theory of *constructivism*, an important component of the Action-First Learning Framework. Piaget's research had a profound influence on our understanding of how adults learn and process knowledge. He suggested that we actively construct our knowledge of the world as we reflect on our ideas and experiences. We all build representations of reality and continually incorporate new information into our pre-existing knowledge base.

Before Piaget put forth his theories, John Dewey—an American philosopher, psychologist, and education reformer—advocated for hands-on learning and experiential education. Dewey believed that instruction should foster deep, meaningful learning through active engagement, problem solving, and social interaction.

Finally, as I mentioned earlier, Reg Revans (with his 23 criteria for action learning) was another early inspiration for my ideas about action-first learning.

Modern Research

Hundreds of scientific studies have demonstrated the powerful benefits of actively engaging learners during the instructional process. In STEM (science, technology, engineering, and math) fields, a meta-analysis (study of studies) of 225 studies of undergraduate courses showed that active learning not only increased examination scores, but students in classes dominated by traditional lectures were more likely to fail than those in classes using active learning techniques (Freeman et al. 2014). A meta-analysis of 104 studies in the humanities came up with similar conclusions, finding "sound scientific evidence for the overall superiority of active instruction for learning achievements. . . . Institutions and policymakers should encourage their instructors to adopt active teaching methods" (Kozanitis and Nenciovici 2022).

One study examining both active learning and a constructivist approach to learning concluded that the "'constructivist learning approach' and 'active learning' have a large effect on environmental education compared to 'traditional learning.' Therefore, these methods and techniques should be frequently used in environmental education classes, projects, and activities" (Arik and Yilmaz 2020). Although the study was limited to the environmental education field, the data pattern is clear: Active learning experiences—in which learners build their own knowledge and actively participate in the instructional process—lead to gains far beyond those available with passive learning techniques.

Critiques of Active Learning

I'm not arguing for tossing out all lectures or other passive approaches to instruction. We don't need to create a false dichotomy between "bad" lectures and "good" active learning techniques. However, some scholars who advocate for traditional approaches also question the validity of studies looking at active learning techniques. For example, one group of educational psychologists declared they could not "determine the extent to which active learning interventions are effective and if there are any boundary conditions for when active learning interventions are or are not effective" (Martella et al. 2023).

Active learning initiatives work in many situations, but how and why is unknown. More research is needed to determine the optimal mix of passive and active learning techniques. However, we can't wait for the research to be completed and tied up in a nice, neat bow. Research isn't static; it evolves as new theories and research methods are discovered. Practitioners can't wait for the absolute truth; it may never be found.

What we know now from the research is that active learning techniques lead to positive learning results. And, in my experience, instructional designers lean too far in favor of passive strategies. The bottom line is that we need more action-first learning, and it must be applied correctly and wisely.

Experience-Based Evidence

From practical experience, organizations of all types are espousing the benefits of active learning. They have seen the results, energy, and motivation of learners exposed to an approach fully aligned with action-first learning design. According to one edX senior learning designer, "Active learning is a crucial component in developing skills and being able to do things rather than just know them or know about them" (França 2020).

The venerable business publication *Forbes* published an article in 2019 saying, "With active learning, outcomes are better, and the knowledge is retained so that a worker can access, adapt, and apply [it] repeatedly and build upon it" (Agarwal 2019). The article mentions three benefits of active learning that may be even more relevant today:

1. **Transferable learning.** Action-first learning with built-in time for reflection provides a clear path to transferability across contexts and situations.
2. **Tangible skill building.** Working on solving a problem or overcoming a challenge builds skills more effectively than passively absorbing content.
3. **Opportunities to practice.** Action-first learning provides plenty of opportunities to practice, and while practice doesn't make perfect, it makes learning permanent. Practice helps solidify what the learner is supposed to understand and allows them to test their abilities as they apply the new skill or knowledge. When successful, learners gain confidence to apply their new skills or knowledge in a variety of other situations.

Caution: Resistance Ahead

Note: Research has found that learners in active-learning classrooms believe they learn less, even when they are, in fact, learning more (Deslauriers et al. 2019). This problem can create resistance if learners think they are wasting their time. As L&D professionals, we have to work to overcome this mistaken understanding of action-first learning by preparing learners for the possibility that it feels like their learning is not paying off.

Slowing down the learning process and making it feel a little more difficult is known as adding *desirable difficulties*. This may seem counterintuitive, but by creating a difficulty or struggle during the learning process, you can improve learning outcomes. By making learning purposefully difficult in key areas, an instructional designer can improve long-term retention and use of the learning material (Allen 2024).

We don't want to create difficulties just to create difficulties, but when properly implemented, desirable difficulties can be an effective tool for long-term retention and application.

Meaningful Action-First Learning Experiences

Crafting a worthwhile learning experience requires infusing two levels of meaning and purpose into the action-first learning design. The first is that outcomes need to *result in behavior changes* that the organization values. Second, learning experiences need to be meaningful *to employees themselves*. Employees should want to undertake the experience and value the outcomes on both a personal and professional level.

In today's AI-driven, hyperconnected world, employee attention, priorities, and engagement can be fragmented. Combining learning with a bit of fun, interactivity, and memorable experiences can make all the difference for improving meaning and purpose. If we don't make an effort to capture learners' emotional or affective domain, our desired outcomes can be in danger.

Implications and Importance of the Action-First Learning Framework

To achieve success, action-first learning designs need to go beyond the gamification of the operational outcomes we desire. They need to target individual behaviors that lead to those desired outcomes while motivating employees to actively participate. Motivating and engaging employees still requires that an aspect of the design is devoted to those goals. Careful implementation of the learning designs discussed in this book can provide engagement, motivation, and desired organizational outcomes.

Action-First Learning Designs

One powerful way to add meaning at the organizational and individual levels is to deploy action-first learning designs. In the following chapters, we'll explore how to create these designs for behaviorally focused, authentic, action-based learning experiences that are also engaging and fun. The first method we'll explore is card games.

Key Takeaways

Now that you're ready to learn how to create an action-first learning experience, remember these tips:

- Action-first learning gets learners involved early in the learning process, activating their senses, and asking them to think critically about their learning experiences.
- Action-first learning is a philosophical foundation for designing learning experiences rather than a step-by-step methodology. It's based on a body of research demonstrating the value of active engagement instead of the passive consumption of content.
- Action-first learning builds tangible, transferable skills by providing practice opportunities and time for reflection—there is no learning without reflection. It's carried out throughout an instructional experience, not just at the beginning.
- Meaningful learning design requires that both learners and their organization benefit from the learning experience.
- Action-first learning improves long-term retention and application of knowledge, even though people often think they are learning less during an active learning process.
- There is no set action-first learning design. The philosophy allows for many methods that encourage action, engage learners, and require critical thinking and reflection.

EXPLANATION OF THE ACTION-FIRST ACTIVITY

Asking you to develop your own definition of a term before presenting a standard definition is an example of an effective action-first learning technique. The task taps into your prior knowledge and activates your existing mental framework related to the topic. This makes it easier for you to connect new information with what you may already know about the subject. The process not only enhances understanding, motivation, and engagement, but it also aids in the retention of new concepts like, in this case, action-first learning.

The process of comparing the definition you wrote with the definition I provided in the chapter offers an opportunity for critical thinking. When you check your definition against the mine, you make a connection that forces you to think through your own knowledge, speculate about a possible definition, and identify gaps in your understanding as you read the chapter.

2
It's in the Cards
Card Games for Learning

 Let's play a quick and simple card game. Grab a deck of cards and a friend or two. Shuffle the cards. Deal four cards to each player. Place the deck in the middle. Each player draws a card one at a time. After three cards are drawn, the player with the highest score wins. Face or court cards are worth 10 points, aces are low, numerical cards are face value, and red suits are worth an additional two points. *(Find the explanation at the end of the chapter.)*

At the end of this chapter, you should be able to answer these questions:
- What elements make card games effective for learning?
- What type of learning outcomes are best suited for card games?
- What design principles should you focus on when developing a card game for learning?
- What are some examples of effective card games for learning?

B rittany had been sitting through a new-employee online orientation for a day and a half, and her boredom level was high and painful. She and her fellow new recruits watched half a dozen standard lectures and slide presentations about company history, products in the company's online store, and IT rules and regulations. She was starting to regret joining the organization. But after lunch on day 2, the HR rep announced that they were going to play a card game. "Well, this could be interesting," she thought, her mood brightening.

The card game, called "Benefits Quest," was designed to help new hires understand and think critically about all their options for health

insurance, life insurance, wellness programs, and retirement plans. It was developed cooperatively by the company's HR staff and training team to make the complex and sometimes overwhelming pile of information about employee benefits more understandable so each employee could make the right choices for their unique situation.

Brittany understood the rules almost instantly because Benefits Quest worked like other card games. Each player took turns drawing a card and responding to the card's scenario. They all engaged in lively discussions about the pros and cons of benefits and options as the game continued. A player could challenge another player's response by playing a card that required an opponent to add something to their answer or consider another benefit they might need. Brittany not only began to understand the company's benefits but also got to know her fellow players while laughing, sharing stories, and building a sense of camaraderie. By the end of the game, she was confident she could make informed choices about her benefits selections. She had forgotten she'd been bored a few hours earlier and was no longer second-guessing her decision to join the company.

※ ※ ※

Most of us are familiar with card games by the time we're in kindergarten. We start out playing Go Fish and Slapjack, and then graduate to hearts, gin rummy, or poker. We discover along the way that cards can be drawn, sorted, matched, stolen, discarded, aligned, hidden, visible, flipped, shuffled, collected, and handled in dozens of other ways. Playing cards come in a variety of sizes and shapes beyond the traditional rectangular cards with red or blue designs on the back; they can be circular or triangular, oversized, or tiny. Their faces can include abstract shapes, images, words, faces, or even paragraphs of content. The variations are staggering, and this is part of what makes cards such effective learning tools. According to the International Playing-Card Society, there may be more than 10,000 different card games worldwide (IPCS n.d.).

Many card games seem simple at first glance, but appearances can be deceiving. Take a game like solitaire—it can teach you how to count and remember cards quickly, the value of thinking ahead, and the importance of analyzing your current situation and considering all the alternatives. It can also teach a deeper lesson: No matter how careful or calculating you are, sometimes you just can't win.

When we design card games specifically for learning outcomes, they can have a powerful impact. Professor Mohd Nor Akmal Khalid from the School of Information Science at the Japan Advanced Institute of Science and Technology (JAIST) has spent years researching card games. "Card games are typical incomplete information games," he says. "Short, repeatable rounds, chances, and strategizing make them among the most entertaining, even addictive, games" (JAIST 2023).

Why Are Card Games Effective for Learning?

A card game is a low-barrier, low-friction way to ask learners to take action. Card games encourage us to think deeply about subjects, explore ideas, plan, analyze strategies, and communicate effectively. They also require a commitment: Pick a card! Make a wager! Pursue a strategy! Many require a player to guess what an opponent might do next. Let's look at four characteristics of card games that make them great tools for action-first learning.

Familiarity

Card games are played in just about every society and social group in the world. Therefore, a "serious" card game designed for learning is unlikely to make someone feel intimidated. Anyone familiar with card games will understand a few basic rules or norms (as illustrated in this chapter's opening action-first activity):

- Each player usually receives their own hand or collection of cards.
- The deck or decks of cards is usually shuffled and dealt.
- Cards are played when they are valuable and discarded when they're not.
- Cards can be collected or traded.

When learners are familiar with a construct, such as a card game, they'll be less anxious and more open to embracing new rules and strategies because of that built in framework to guide them.

Simple Rules

Contrast the simplicity of a card game with universally understood elements to the complexity of a sophisticated first-person online learning game involving experience points, inventory control systems, or health meters. They may use the keyboard's *W*, *A*, *S*, and *D* keys—which are often used in place of arrow keys in gaming—for character navigation. Or, consider the complexity of multicharacter digital role-play games like *Pokémon Yellow* or *World of Warcraft*.

Most card games can be rapidly and easily learned because there are a limited number of rules and options for play. In a training situation, players can quickly understand and begin to play a digital or physical card game without having to do a long, complicated tutorial. Yet card games can have powerful learning impacts equal to or beyond those of more complex games.

Real-Time Application of Knowledge

When playing a card game in which you need to sort concepts into distinct categories, respond to a prompt, or collect cards of a certain type, you are applying knowledge immediately. You are making decisions based on classifications, a model, or methods you've just learned or should already know. Also, the need for quick action can make the game exciting.

A well-designed, learning-focused card game forces players to use certain ways of thinking to classify information and can reinforce knowledge and provide immediate feedback on whether they have applied knowledge correctly.

Sophistication and Seriousness

Playing cards have a rich, long history. Historians believe the first card games may have been played in the ninth century in China. In those ancient games, the cards contained written scenarios, rather than the traditional suits and numbers we know today. The centuries-old tradition of playing card games carries a sense of sophistication similar to other games with storied histories like chess and backgammon.

High-stakes popular adult games like poker and blackjack double down on the need for concentration and seriousness of purpose, which allows us to play card games in more earnest settings like university courses and workplaces. In other words, in learning situations, card games are often seen as more legitimate and "mature" than other types of games that may seem silly or frivolous to adult learners.

What Can Card Games Teach?

Card games can teach an almost limitless array of topics and skills from medical procedures to world history, and from mathematics to languages and literature. The US CIA has used card games to train analysts, and during World War II, civilians and soldiers used "spotter decks," which featured cards with a silhouetted image to identify enemy aircraft.

Card games are ideal for helping learners grasp and practice specific skills, especially memorization, observation, communication, critical thinking, strategic thinking, and leadership.

Memorization

Think of all the flashcards you used in high school or college, whether you were learning Spanish, human anatomy, or how a bill becomes a law. Each card had a term on one side and a definition on the other. Flashcards are a great way to memorize important, must-know information because each new encounter with a word or phrase helps to reinforce our memory. But flashcards don't have to be limited to text. Cards can contain images, mathematical formulas, or—in digital format—they can include animations or videos like the example in Figure 2-1.

A card game designed for memorization doesn't need to be as straightforward as "flip a card and see an answer." When players are reviewing terms, exchanging knowledge, and correcting one another during any card game designed for learning, they're also discussing and often defining concepts, vocabulary, and specialized jargon, which are then reinforced naturally during gameplay.

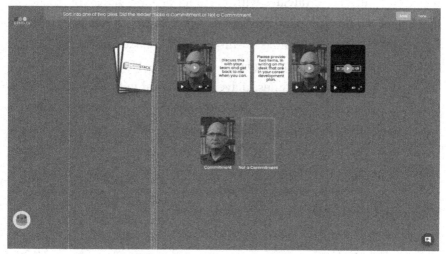

Figure 2-1. A digital card game. Digital card games allow you to include video, audio, and even QR codes on your cards. *Source: Image courtesy of Enterprise Game Stack: Digital Card Game Company.*

Observation and Discernment

The ability to observe and make informed judgments about two or more items is a critical business skill and one that card games can teach effectively. When playing a card game, we are often required to discern subtle differences among the cards themselves, situations in which we are playing or trading cards, or overall strategies. We identify patterns, sequences, or sets in a series of cards. These cognitive operations demand keen observation, attention to detail, and the ability to quickly spot similarities and differences.

The high-level skill of judgment extends observation beyond just recognizing different characteristics. We may need to evaluate the relative value or potential impact of drawing or discarding different cards or making specific moves. In strategic games, players often must distinguish between a good hand and a bad one, or decide when to fold or keep playing, based on the strength of their hand compared with their perception of other players' hands.

Communication

Most card games require players to speak to one another or communicate in another way, such as through nonverbal cues or signaling. Players often need to discuss strategies with partners or teammates, negotiate, or make declarations. In many card games—including the HR-focused game I mentioned at the beginning of this chapter—relaxed conversation and collegiality are also important goals.

In team-based card games, players often deal with the further challenge of communicating their intentions and strategies to teammates without revealing too much to their opponents. These kinds of games enhance everyone's verbal and nonverbal communication skills, including active listening.

Critical Thinking

When we play almost any card game, we are constantly evaluating our situation, considering consequences and outcomes, and making decisions based on incomplete information. Don't we also do these things daily in our roles at work? While playing a card game, participants assess probabilities, try to understand the significance of different card combinations, and anticipate their opponents' moves. These processes are versions of analytical thinking, problem solving, and decision making—under the big cognitive umbrella of critical thinking.

In the workplace, critical thinking is among the most valuable skills, and card games can be used to reinforce and practice it. For example, while it's not specifically a learning-focused game, *Magic: The Gathering* or an adaptation can be used to help reinforce critical thinking. In the game, players strategically build decks with a variety of cards representing magical spells, creatures, and artifacts—it requires resource management and adaptability to different opponents and situations. Now, instead of spells, creatures, or artifacts, imagine working with budgets, performance levels, and employees. Adaptations of entertainment-focused card games can serve as jumping-off points for creating action-first learning–oriented card games.

Strategic Thinking

One obvious learning outcome of most card games is strategic thinking. During gameplay, we develop both short-term tactics and long-term strategies to help us win. These tactics and strategies require us to understand the rules and mechanics of the game and to predict our opponents' actions, plan our own actions several moves ahead, and adapt to changing circumstances with new tactics and strategies as the game progresses and evolves.

Card games such as bridge, poker, and blackjack require an abundance of strategic thinking, as players balance immediate benefits against potential future consequences.

Leadership

Leadership skills can be honed and practiced in multiplayer and team-based card games, such as a card game I developed called "Business Conquest." The goal is to solve a business problem by effectively leading your team through various leadership challenges. A player draws a business problem card from the deck, and then each player must look at their hand and decide how they would address the business problem. Players take turns as the leader and determine which combination of influence, power, and strategy cards to play. They must balance the use of their cards to maximize their impact on each challenge. Within the game, just like within organizations, collaboration and competition coexist, as players work together to solve challenges while also vying for leadership points and promotions. At various points in the game, each player may need to take charge, act as a mediator for the other players, make strategic decisions, or motivate others toward a common goal.

Card games provide safe spaces in which emerging leaders can experiment with different leadership styles, including sharing decision-making power with others or making unilateral decisions. They can learn to adapt their approaches based on different situations and team dynamics. Some learning card games specifically require a designated leader, but others, including Business Conquest, require a rotating leadership role. These variations offer valuable opportunities for many players to practice leadership and team management skills.

Card Game Mechanics

If you're considering using a card game as an action-first learning experience, you'll want to apply several essential principles of good design and game mechanics. As we've already discussed, card games are incredibly versatile, and almost any recreational card game can be converted into a learning-focused game. Let's dive into four specific game designs you should consider.

Sorting

In sorting games, the player moves cards into one or more piles based on commonalities. The piles can be predesignated; for example, you might say, "Sort all the functions and features of our new product into this pile." Alternatively, learners can sort cards of desired managerial traits into piles themselves and then label those piles as they see fit. They can then discuss what they sorted into which pile and why.

Consider using a sorting game when you want the learners to apply their knowledge and understanding to make informed decisions. For example, in a game centered around startup management, players might sort different business activities into categories like *essential for launch* or *long-term goals*. This type of sorting game can help with comprehension of business planning, strategy, and prioritization. Another option would be to sort statements about a product into *features* versus *benefits*. Engaging a learner in actively categorizing, prioritizing, and organizing information helps facilitate a deeper understanding of complex concepts and encourages the development of essential analytical skills.

Sequencing

As a game mechanic, sequencing is particularly effective because it demands players apply their knowledge and insight to arrange cards in a specific order. This, of course, may require critical thinking (such as considering the actions one might take when responding to an upset customer), or it could involve basic recall of the specific order of a predetermined set of steps within a standard process.

Try a sequencing game when learners are required to know the proper steps in a standard operating procedure or the correct order in which operations need to be performed to fill out a form, build a product, or troubleshoot a problem. You might ask players to arrange the steps in a manufacturing process correctly, for example, to help them better understand how products are built. In a game focusing on project management, players might sequence tasks based on priority and dependency, thereby learning about effective project planning and execution. Or, if you're teaching complex sales scenarios and how to adapt to new situations, you might ask players to sequence their approaches based on customers' personality types, product features, or a variety of sales techniques.

Matching

In matching games, players identify and pair related concepts or steps. Learners must make connections between and among all the items they are attempting to match. This process helps to deepen the participants' understanding of a process, procedure, or concept.

Consider using a matching game when you want to reinforce key skills, including attention to detail, observation, quick thinking, and the ability to compare items or scenarios to determine commonalities and differences. If you want to use a matching game to train a sales team, for example, the cards could feature elements such as customer needs, product benefits, customer objections, and effective closing techniques. Players would be challenged to match cards that connect logically, such as pairing a customer need with the appropriate product benefit.

Role-Playing

Most people don't associate card games with role-play exercises, but card games can be an effective method of introducing role plays into a learning situation while avoiding the typical moans and groans from participants.

You may want to try a role-playing game when you want learners to practice conversational and listening skills, as well as the ability to think on their feet. Consider this example: A player who is a sales professional turns over a card. On the card is a sales scenario typical for their company.

The player reads it aloud and then responds as if addressing the customer in the scenario. The other players vote to indicate whether the answer is inadequate, acceptable, or excellent. The other players could also challenge the first player to provide more information or a better answer. The scenarios could be developed for any area of the organization from accounting to marketing to operations. Figure 2-2 shows a digital version of a multiplayer role-play card game.

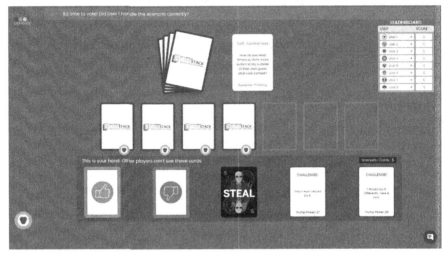

Figure 2-2. Digital multiplayer role-play card game. Card games can be used to disguise role-play exercises and keep all learners active during the role-play process. *Source: Image courtesy of Enterprise Game Stack: Digital Card Game Company.*

Let's Design a Card Game for Learning

Now that you understand some basics of card game design for learning, the next step is to begin developing a game. Fortunately, you can do so inexpensively. To create a prototype, you can simply write or draw on a set of index cards—this allows you to try out your game before committing to an expensive printing of card decks. Tools are also now available to create digital card games that allow people to play with each other over a distance. As I mentioned earlier in the chapter, a digital card game can be a welcome break from traditional virtual, online training presentations.

Whether you're designing for digital or good old-fashioned physical cards, the steps are the same. I present them here in sequential format, but more often than not, you'll probably combine some steps, go back to a previous step several times, or think about one while working on another. Card game design is an iterative process, and it can get messy!

However, by following these steps, you should be able to create a design that works for your learning objectives.

Step 1. Define Your Desired Outcome

This step is necessary for any action-first project design. Your focus should be on learning and behavior change, so the first task is to determine what learning behavior change you want to see as a result of the game. Your design should support this outcome.

Step 2. Review the Available Content

One technique that is useful to employ early in the card game development process is reviewing the content supporting your desired learning outcome. By examining the content, you can often determine which mechanism (sorting, sequencing, matching, or role-playing) is most appropriate for your needs. Create a spreadsheet containing the behaviors you want to teach and the corresponding content, and then determine the best mechanism to use (as detailed in step 3). Steps 2 and 3 are often done simultaneously.

Step 3. Determine the Right Mechanics

While you are reviewing content, keep the different types of game mechanics in mind. Ask yourself, "Does my desired learning outcome lend itself to a sorting game, sequencing game, matching game, or role-playing game?" Then, examine your learning outcome and think about how you want players to achieve it. Are they matching the delivery of a sales presentation with the needs of a customer? Are they categorizing a situation on the shop floor as dangerous or safe?

Take plenty of time to think through the various aspects of the behavior you want to change and the results of your content review. Break both the behavior and content into the most basic elements you want to teach. This will provide insights into which card game mechanic is the best option.

Step 4. Create Rules and Gameplay

The mechanic you've chosen will provide the general rules for your card game, but you also need specifics: How do you determine who goes first? How are points scored? What do players do when it's not their turn? What determines the winner? You can think through some of these questions by playing commercial, entertainment-focused card games that use the same or a similar mechanic as the one you have chosen. As you play, take note of the game's rules and flow. Chances are you won't want to exactly copy commercial game, but you'll gather valuable information to inspire your own choices.

Step 5. Playtest the Game

Now that you have determined the rules and gameplay, open a pack of blank index cards; write down whatever words, images, or numbers need to appear on the cards; and then play the game. Your first rounds will be informal playtests to help determine if the game works, if players can understand the rules, and what changes you will need to make. Playtest first with your design group or training team and then broaden the group of players to people unfamiliar with the game's design process—especially people who will be honest and forthright in their assessment. Use their feedback to make any necessary modifications.

Step 6. Create a Theme and Aesthetics

At this point, you've playtested your card game and have a good understanding of how it works. Now it's time to develop a theme and associated aesthetics. The game's theme is your hook to capture players' attention. It should relate to your content, explain or reveal something about the game, and arouse curiosity. Once you have a theme, create artwork, choose typefaces, and find a tone for the instructions that will unify the content, theme, and aesthetics—everything should align.

For example, when I created a role-playing game to teach instructional design concepts, my hook was zombies. I know that above all, instructional designers don't want learners to become zombies who mindlessly progress through an uninspired wasteland of instruction. I called the game "Zombie Instructional Design Apocalypse." The aesthetic I needed quickly became clear. The letters on the cards were written in a font reminiscent of old horror movies, and each one had an image of a zombie.

A more corporate-appropriate example would be a card game I helped develop to teach sales professionals to be savvier and apply practical knowledge to a variety of sales situations to make good judgments. The game was called "The Savvy Sales Associate" and had a James Bond espionage theme. The artwork included debonair characters who knew exactly what to say at exactly the right time to win sales and achieve the savvy sales associate title.

Step 7. Ensure the Game Is as Accessible as Possible

Whether you are producing a digital or physical card game, keep accessibility in mind at every stage of development. It's essential to use highly contrasting colors so the game is accessible to learners with visual impairments. For instance, using a light background with dark text or imagery will make the content on each card more discernible. High-contrast images and a simple color palette also help reduce cognitive load, making it easier for all learners to focus on content rather than deciphering visuals. A plain, evenly spaced font (such as Comic Sans, Sassoon, Verdana, or Open Dyslexic) is easiest for learners with dyslexia. If you are using physical cards, try adding different textures to each card to provide tactile feedback, which is also helpful for learners with visual impairments. Textured cards could also denote different categories or actions within the game, allowing all learners to distinguish between different elements through touch.

Step 8. Produce and Distribute the Game

At this point, you've nailed down the rules, gameplay, theme, aesthetics, and accessibility elements. Now you can produce the artwork and create the cards and a formal rule book. A printer can create not only the physical cards but also a tuck box and rule book. One nice thing about providing each learner with a card deck is that people are much less likely to throw them away. After a training class, I've often seen participants playing with the decks at after-hours events. I can't guarantee the game they're playing is *exactly the same* as the one from training, but at least they are interacting with the content again.

When producing digital card games, you will be able to include audio, video, and animations, which creates a dynamic and engaging learning experience. Digital games also allow for fast updates if needed and distribution over wide geographic areas.

When deciding between producing a virtual card game or a physical one, consider the environment in which you want to deploy the action-first learning experience.

AI Assist

The following prompt can assist you in generating concepts, gameplay mechanics, rules, and other essential details to create a card game. Adjust the content within the square brackets to include relevant information for your particular game.

> You are a card game developer. Your job is to create
> an instructional card game. The game is for [*two
> to four*] players. The game should include the need
> for [*deduction, collaboration, and strategy*]. The
> card game's objective is to [*identify and prevent
> different types of insurance fraud*]. Targeted at [*new
> claims investigators*], especially those in [*finance
> or insurance sectors*], the card game should last
> approximately [*20-30*] minutes. Include components
> like [*dealing random fraud case cards to players and
> drawing cards that represent levels of investigation
> and cards that represent constraints, such as
> time and resources for the investigation*]. Also,
> include an element of chance with cards containing
> instructions such as [*skip a turn or draw two
> fraud case cards*]. Players should interact through
> [*discussion, discarding cards, drawing cards, and
> strategizing to uncover fraud schemes*]. The card game
> should include challenges like [*deceptive tactics and
> resource constraints*]. The victory condition is to
> [*successfully identify and prevent the most insurance
> fraud cases*]. Describe the rules, game setup, player
> progression, and how the theme of [*combating insurance
> fraud*] is visually and strategically represented
> within the cards.

Case Study: Deal Me in for Increased Sales

Note: The name of the firm and other details in this case study have been changed to ensure confidentiality.

Interpryze—a large multinational company that develops software to manage business operations and customer relations—wants to provide a new training program for its sales force, which is dispersed throughout the world. Most of the sales team lives and works in Europe, but significant numbers reside in North and South America, Africa, Asia, and Australia. The company's cloud division is especially keen on training sales reps to have more effective conversations with clients during new product rollouts.

The Interpryze management team is dedicated to consultative sales, an approach in which sales representatives provide detailed information and guidance in the mode of advisors rather than dedicated salespeople. This means that the sales team, in addition to understanding their products, has to know how to ask probing questions, determine the real needs of customers, and analyze the forces driving each customer's business. The sales reps must frequently practice asking questions, responding to inquiries, and thinking on their feet.

The Challenge

Ensuring that Interpryze sales representatives are up to the challenge of consultative sales means preparing them for a variety of realistic, sometimes complex discussions with clients and potential clients. The training team often uses role plays to prepare reps for situations they will regularly encounter. In these situations, a training team member acts as the customer, and the salesperson asks probing questions and attempts to create meaningful recommendations. Unfortunately, the sales team members don't enjoy the role-play activities and often give those experiences the lowest scores in feedback forms.

On the other hand, the training team believes that role-playing is the best way to provide authentic dialogue practice and measure how well the sales reps can think on their feet when confronted with a barrage of industry-specific questions and situations similar to those they'll face in the field.

Making the Case

Maria, Interpryze's training manager, needs a solution to her dilemma. She wants the sales professionals to have an experience that is engaging and fun but also retains all the benefits of a role-play exercise in terms of equipping the sales professionals with enough practice and experience to be effective at consultative selling. Maria began working with a consultant who suggested creating several different scenario-based role-play card games.

Maria had used games in training programs at her previous company and was curious about the idea of "disguising" role-play exercises as card games. She was open to trying a pilot program. The results would provide information on how salespeople reacted to the game and whether to move forward and roll out the game to the entire sales group.

The Solution—and a Twist

Together, Maria and the consultant created a game in which each learner would draw and then respond to prompts on a card. The game included 25 cards, each of which explained specific situations, client questions, or common client concerns. During the game, learners alternated between responding to a situation and challenging others' responses. If someone challenged a response, the other players voted on the effectiveness of the challenge.

The game was designed to be played several times. First, sales reps would play the game "cold," without coaching or instruction on the consultative sales process. Then, after going through coaching and instruction on the consultative sales process, they played the game again.

Maria hoped the players' responses would be better and the challenge would be more effective the second time they played the game. She piloted the game live, with a small group of sales reps. It was a success. Some participants were even seen using the card deck in the hotel bar at the end of the first day of training. Interpryze decided to roll out the game internationally at regional sales meetings when employees gathered to discuss new projects and strategies.

Unfortunately, right after the pilot program, the COVID-19 pandemic began. Company travel was canceled worldwide, and everyone began working remotely, putting an end to plans for in-person physical card games. The company pivoted and began hosting some live, online role plays using virtual classroom software, but the sales representatives were not focused on the activity, which meant high dropout rates and low overall participation.

Maria challenged the consultant to develop an online card game with similar gameplay and learning goals as the physical deck experience. Within a few weeks, Enterprise Game Stack (EGS) was born. EGS is a digital card creation platform that supports not only multiplayer role-play games but also sorting and matching games. The digital card games can be played by learners scattered across vast distances. Each breakout room in the virtual classroom can be thought of as a virtual table on which the card game is being played.

Benefits and Results

The Interpryze card game—both the virtual and physical versions—became a robust opportunity for sales reps to practice applying sales skills without having to resort to the dreaded role-play exercise. The card game's outcomes and learning opportunities are similar to, and in some cases better than, a traditional role-play exercise. Maria's feedback to the consultant indicated that the participants were much more engaged than they had been in earlier role-play training exercises.

Additionally, the second time salespeople played the game (after the coaching session), the conversations were richer and more insightful. Several members of the sales team commented that they felt well prepared and comfortable addressing client questions and concerns because they had practiced responses and been challenged on their answers during the game.

Lessons Learned

Maria told Interpryze upper management that the card game encouraged robust conversations, helped participants make strong connections, and created a deeper understanding of the nuances involved in a sales interaction. She said the game environment provided a powerful experience for learning, reinforcement, and retention. Her final evaluation included a few key lessons that she wanted to pass on to other managers considering using card games for training:

- **Focus first on good game design and worry about how to deliver it later.** The design of the game is critical. Maria and her team were able to pivot from a face-to-face format to a digital one quite easily because their game design was solid and could be played in a variety of settings, both in-person and online.

- **Strive to create a game that gets people talking and challenging themselves and other players.** Conversation is key to a good card game. The role-play card game fostered conversations especially well. When good conversations were occurring, it became easier to determine whether each sales representative was providing the desired response.

- **Take time to onboard players to your specific game, even though card games are universal and the rules are usually easy to grasp.** Maria conducted the pilot program in the US, but the digital version went out to an international audience. People in each country were familiar with different types of card games, so Maria insisted that learners should play a practice or tutorial game first to make sure everyone understood how it worked and how it should be scored.

Key Takeaways

Now that you're ready to create an action-first learning experience using a card game, remember these tips:

- Card games offer learners low barriers to entry and a high degree of familiarity and comfort.
- Card games for learning are highly versatile and can teach many types of content and topics.
- Card games are excellent tools for teaching skills that require sorting, sequencing, matching, and role-playing. They are especially valuable for disguising role-play exercises and gaining buy-in from learners who traditionally resist that type of activity.
- Card games foster conversation and team building among players.

EXPLANATION OF THE ACTION-FIRST ACTIVITY

Why the card game? Notice the terms used in the instructions: *shuffle, deal, deck, draw, face or court cards, aces low,* and *suits*. Chances are you knew exactly what each one meant. As an instructional designer or facilitator, you don't need to explain these terms or actions to the learners. Familiarity is one of the advantages of card games for learning. They have little cognitive overload because most learners know the basics and don't need to have play-related terms explained to them. This means the focus can be on the learning rather than on the rules of the game.

Tool 2-1. Tips for Effective Card Games

✓ Make your game accessible. Use high-contrast colors, add textures, or augment digital cards with assistive technologies.

✓ Align your learning objectives with the appropriate card game mechanics.

✓ Decide whether your objectives are best served by delivering the game physically, digitally, or both. If using physical cards, try to provide a deck for each player to take home so they can continue to interact with the content over time to gain more value.

✓ Enliven the game and capture players' attention with a variety of words and images—or even more information via QR codes—on physical cards. If your game is digital, add audio, video, and animation that serves your learning objectives.

✓ Is your budget tight? Remember that card games are among the least expensive options to refresh your training program. In a pinch, use index cards and add words or images by hand or with stickers. You can also create a playable prototype game for learning. Don't get caught up in developing an elaborate visual design with high production costs.

✓ Playtest. Playtest. Playtest. Before releasing your game to trainers and players, ensure that you've learned its strengths, weaknesses, and quirks by testing the game as many times as possible and then applying any lessons learned.

3
Pass Go, Collect $200
Board Games for Learning

Let's start with a riddle. What classic board game is being described? I am a game of battle. Blue and red armies clash hidden in plain sight, their ranks and numbers masked. Capturing the flag is the ultimate quest. Move with caution and outsmart your rival. Avoiding bombs is the key to survival. *(Find the explanation at the end of the chapter.)*

At the end of this chapter, you should be able to answer these questions:

- What elements make board games effective for learning?
- What type of learning outcomes are board games best suited for?
- What design principles should you focus on when developing a board game for learning?
- What are some examples of effective board games for learning?

When June walked into the conference room, she was excited to see a board game on the table with space for her and seven of her fellow sales professionals to play. She had heard rumors that they would have a chance to hone their skills at this year's annual sales meeting by challenging their co-workers in Sales Showdown, a game designed to simulate the challenges and strategies of the highly competitive sales environment.

The gameboard was a colorful map of a fictional sales territory that coincidentally looked a lot like some of the company's real territories. The map was divided into districts representing different market segments, and the players had to move their tokens around the board to encounter a variety of challenges and opportunities. They drew cards representing

potential clients, each with unique needs and preferences. Some clients were more receptive to certain standard sales strategies, while others required unique, tailored methods. Each sales representative had to figure out how to play the right strategy, and they lost the sale if their strategy didn't match the client's needs.

The sales reps also had to manage their resources wisely, deciding whether to invest in a face-to-face visit, bring in an industry expert to help make their case, or demonstrate their product using virtual meeting software. Each resource had a cost, and June soon realized she had to monitor everyone else's play to keep track of how much they had invested in each resource.

Throughout the game, June and her colleagues had a great time debating each other in lively discussions and sharing strategies and insights. Before they knew it, the two hours allotted for the game were over, and it was time to head back to the ballroom for closing remarks. But June and the other sales reps continued to think about the game; it was the hottest topic at dinner that evening. They discussed lessons learned, who had the most effective and least effective strategies, and how the game had revealed new, better selling strategies.

✺ ✺ ✺

Board games, tabletop games, and simulations have served as teaching and learning tools for thousands of years for everything from predicting battle outcomes to plotting corporate strategies. The basic concept of moving or placing objects on a premarked surface or board following an agreed-upon set of rules remains the same, and the games often include cards, tokens, meeples, spinners, dice, timers, currency, and even health meters.

Board games such as chess and Stratego focus on one player strategizing against another while games like Catan feature multiple players or teams vying for resources and advantages over one another. Monopoly combines clever strategies with chance elements, including dice rolls and card drawing. Some board games, such as Trivial Pursuit, demand broad knowledge, while others, such as Pictionary, demand a skill like the ability to draw. Additionally, some games are cooperative. In the game

Pandemic for example, a team plays against the board game itself to accomplish a common goal. The complexity of board games also varies widely, from simple children's games like Candy Land to those focused on complex, creative tasks. In Ticket to Ride, for instance, players try to build a railroad empire.

What all board games have in common is a shared space in which players interact. The gameplay creates a community operating in a unique environment with specific rules, transactions, and communication. In the parlance of game designers and developers, the board game community is a "magic circle." When this circle is based on realistic behavior models and consequences, the insights, knowledge, and skills participants acquire while playing it can be applied in the workplace to enhance decision making, manage trade-offs, optimize investments, and improve other critical skills for an organization's success.

Most of us associate board games with good old-fashioned cardboard, paper, and little plastic tokens, but most games now have digital versions you can play online. Digital play expands board games beyond their traditional face-to-face boundaries so they can reach people who aren't in the same room or even the same country.

Why Are Board Games Effective for Learning?

Board games actively involve participants in the learning process. They provide a hands-on experience, allowing learners to explore complex concepts and develop new skills. The tactile and visual elements of board games, along with their often intricate rules, challenge players to understand and adapt to diverse situations. Learners must apply previous knowledge to solve the scenario that the board game and fellow players present.

It's easy to see how board games foster communication and teamwork, but let's consider some other equally effective—but often overlooked—reasons board games are great action-first approaches to learning.

Seeing the Big Picture

The board itself often presents a big-picture view of the situation, landscape, or ecosystem being studied in an instructional situation. The board and other elements—including cards and how scores are calculated—provide a tangible context in which learning will unfold. Sometimes, simply seeing all the elements together during gameplay is an eye-opener for the learners. For example, in the Total (re)Call game board shown in Figure 3-1, the sales representatives learn how a physician's office functions. They need to know the flow of patients through the various parts of the office and how vital it is for them to understand the workings of the entire office. The game board becomes the perfect visual reference.

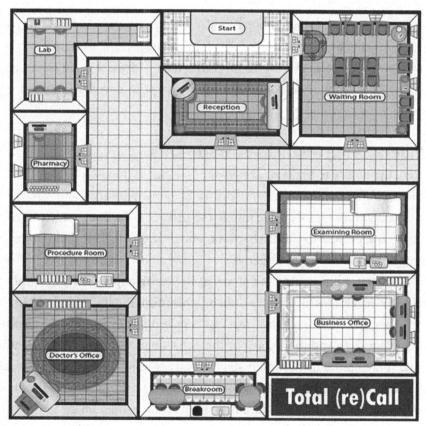

Figure 3-1. The Total (re)Call game board. This board game was designed to teach a total office. *Source: Created by Beth Myers and Karl M. Kapp.*

Highlighting Relationships

Board games can highlight relationships and dependencies in a much shorter period than real life can. Let's consider how Monopoly illustrates the point. In the game, after you buy a hotel, rather than waiting months for a return on your investment like you would in a real-world business transaction, you collect rent as soon as the next person lands on the space containing your hotel. In a game about project management, a player may land on spaces such as "task assignment" and "skill level" and then collect tokens or cards representing the various skills they need to build and tasks to be assigned. This type of gameplay may be used to highlight the relationship between balancing the right task assignment for each team member with the right skill level.

Knowing how to match a person's skill level with assigned tasks is an important element in effectively running projects. Misalignment can cause serious problems, so highlighting and addressing the issue in a game environment is better than waiting for it to develop in an actual on-the-job situation.

Underscoring Nuances of Trade-Offs

Often, the ability to make reasoned and intelligent trade-offs is a defining skill of effective leaders, supervisors, sales representatives, and others in an organization. Board games mimic the process of making trade-offs, often forcing players to choose between one or more options that require a compromise to achieve a larger goal.

One such game could ask a player to choose an appropriate investment based on several factors affecting an organization. But if the player doesn't have adequate resources to invest in everything, they will need to make tough decisions and then play out the consequences. Each team or individual playing the game would start with a set amount of chips to spend on various investments. The teams must decide how many chips they are willing to invest in various corporate items represented on 25 cards. The need to make trade-offs forces players to reassess and adapt their strategies constantly, highlighting the balance between short-term necessities and long-term planning. Furthermore, the presence of competitors requires players to anticipate rival strategies, adding a layer of complexity to their decision making and trade-offs.

Sharing an Experience

As we've discussed, board games can require players to work together, communicate effectively, and negotiate or make collective decisions. This shared experience mirrors many workplace scenarios. By engaging in these activities in a low-stakes environment, employees can practice and improve. This experience translates into better collaboration and efficiency in professional tasks, because team members learn to coordinate their efforts, resolve conflicts, and leverage one another's strengths.

The board game experience also provides a common reference point that employees can use to explain real-world situations and perspectives to one another. For instance, an employee might say, "Remember when we allocated too many resources too early in the game? I'm worried we're doing that in this situation."

What Can Board Games Teach?

As interactive abstract versions of real-life situations, board games are ideal for teaching technical skills, higher-level thinking, and soft skills such as communication, negotiation, and decision making. Try playing entertainment-based games with an eye toward how you could use their elements when developing your own learning games. Some of the diverse, valuable lessons that board games can teach are discussed in more detail in the following sections.

Systems Thinking and Connections

Organizations are complex systems in which a variety of forces interact and affect success. Systems interact with market forces and may be influenced by government decisions or competitor actions. It can be difficult to understand how these forces interact in real time when employees participate in day-to-day operations. Board games can put players in complex scenarios where they must consider multiple variables and interrelations to be successful. They can learn to recognize how different components of a system are likely to interact, foresee the consequences of their actions, and understand the importance of adaptability and strategic planning.

Recognizing and understanding the interconnectedness of different departments and roles can help players think beyond their immediate roles and consider the bigger picture—an essential skill for effective decision making and strategic leadership. For example, a game called Power Grid requires players to think at a systems level and consider the interconnection of many actions. Players have to bid for power plants, expand their power grids, and manage resources like coal, oil, and renewables. The interconnection of all their actions is evident when a decision in one city affects resources and opportunities elsewhere.

Making Decisions With Incomplete Data

In board games, players often must make decisions without all the data or information they need. In the military, this circumstance is known as "the fog of war." In business, that fog is often the status quo; therefore, the ability to make decisions quickly, without all the key information, is critical to success.

When playing a board game, elements of chance—such as dice rolls, card draws, or other players' actions—introduce unpredictability, forcing players to make decisions without a complete picture of the outcome, simulating the uncertainty they will encounter in everyday business situations. For example, in the classic board game Risk, players conquer territories through a combination of strategy and chance (dice rolls). In a learning-focused board game designed to teach business concepts, players may learn about risk assessment and decision making in situations where outcomes are influenced by factors beyond their control, such as market fluctuations or consumer trends.

Potential Consequences of Actions

During World War II, battles were often war-gamed before any shots were fired. Just as war gaming helped military leaders anticipate and adapt to dynamic battlefield conditions, organizations can use board games to help forecast changes in the business environment and determine appropriate reactions to changes in market conditions, competitor actions, regulatory shifts, and technological advancements. Companies can run what-if scenarios to predict and help prepare for reactions to their actions and changes in the competitive climate. Such scenarios can help companies anticipate for what might otherwise be unthinkable.

A good example of this kind of what-if scenario is the 1970s entertainment board game, BP Offshore Oil Strike, which predicted aspects of the Deepwater Horizon oil rig explosion in 2010 with surprising accuracy relating to the environmental crisis, clean-up effort, and public relations nightmare. Although the game was created for entertainment, it focused on real-world scenarios related to oil exploration and included hazard cards that warned players about the inherent dangers, including oil spills and cleanup costs. If the company executives and engineers had played that game, would they have been better prepared for what unfolded leading up to and following the spill? Perhaps.

Often, gameplay can help organizations prepare for the future, including surprising and dangerous situations. In the process of designing a game, you may uncover an idea that seems unthinkable, but you can make it real and actionable within the board game, allowing players to explore solutions in a safe environment.

Resource Management

Resource management involves careful and thoughtful allocation, deployment, and manipulation of resources (human, financial, material, and informational) to achieve an organization's objectives. It requires balancing competing needs and priorities, ensuring that each person in the department, group, or team has the necessary resources to function optimally.

Board games can simulate situations during which essential thought processes occur and decisions must be made to manage resources. For example, in the entertainment board game Catan, players build settlements, roads, and cities on a fictional island by acquiring and trading resources including wood, brick, wheat, sheep, and ore. These resources are gathered based on the layout of the game board and dice rolls. Players make decisions about resource allocation, balancing the need to expand against the risks of overextension and strategically trading resources with other players. These actions require negotiation skills and foresight. Players must anticipate future resource needs while adapting to the availability of current resources, which change constantly because of other players' actions and random dice rolls. In many ways, Catan's challenges mirror those in departments, groups, and teams for which resource allocation and strategic planning are vital. Games focused on actual corporate resources can be even more effective in allowing players to hone resource allocation skills.

Suboptimization Avoidance

Suboptimization occurs when one part of an organization or system does well at the expense of others. For example, a sales team could aggressively increase sales without aligning those sales with the production department's capacity. This misalignment could lead to the inability to fulfill orders on time, unhappy customers, and cancelled orders. Instead, they need to optimize collective output, ensuring that all parts of the organization work together harmoniously toward a common goal. In the situation I described here, the sales department should have carefully coordinated with production before a huge sales campaign.

While games can't eliminate suboptimization, they can highlight dangerous situations that it might cause. This knowledge can be used to help an organization avoid these potential problems. By helping players understand the interdependencies of departments and functions, games can also reveal how decisions that help the entire organization at the expense of one of its subgroups can be beneficial.

Board Game Mechanics

Board games use a lot of different mechanics during gameplay, including moving forward based on the spin of a wheel or roll of the dice, collecting or discarding tokens or cards, and acquiring currency to purchase items players need. The elements you add to your action-first board game for learning help make it engaging and instructional.

You can find inspiration in a game style that's popular in Europe, which is known as a Eurogame, designer board game, or German-style board game. The board games in this category have some of these characteristics:

- Conflict within the game is often indirect and typically involves competition over resources, points, or something else of value.
- Direct player-to-player competition or conflict (like that in Stratego or Battleship) is rare.
- Luck has a limited influence on gameplay, emphasizing strategy and player decision-making instead.
- There are many different ways to score points or secure a winning condition.

Catan, Pandemic, Ticket to Ride, and Forbidden Island are popular games that feature many Eurogame characteristics. Let's now consider how you can deploy these mechanics to make your action-first learning game as effective as possible.

Create a Randomized Board Layout

Board games don't have to be played on what we traditionally think of as a board. Several popular games, including Forbidden Island and Catan, use many individual tiles instead of one solid board. The tiles are rearranged at the start of each game, which means players face a different configuration each time. Every game is consequently more varied, because even though the rules are the same, the space in which the players move and interact is different. Tiles can be especially helpful for learning-focused games when you want learners to play multiple times without having an overly repetitive experience.

Allow Multiple Actions or Activities Per Turn

Rather than having a player perform one move, design your game to allow multiple actions per turn. For example, players might be able to trade cards with other players, trade in cards to the house, move from one space to another, team up with another player, or remove pieces from the board or game space.

When a player can choose from multiple actions during a turn, it forces them to prioritize their options and carefully weigh the pros and cons to maximize impact. Because they're always thinking about what they might want to do on their next turn, this mechanic keeps players fully involved throughout the entire game.

Create a Cooperative Playing Experience

In a cooperative game, gameplay focuses on players working together to solve problems or dilemmas posed by the game instead of trying to crush or beat an opponent. The goal is often to get out of a dire situation. In the game Pandemic, for example, players cooperate to cure an epidemic before it infects everyone. Creating a cooperative experience in board games fosters teamwork and social interaction as players work together toward a common goal.

In cooperative games, each player's contribution is vital to the group's success, which fosters a sense of unity and shared purpose. This mirrors the situation in many organizations and contrasts with competitive games, in which individual achievement is often the primary goal. Cooperative games encourage players to think collectively, share ideas, and make decisions that benefit the group.

Encourage Creation

In a game like Ticket to Ride, the goal is to create a railroad empire, but the game entails much more than just building this empire. Gameplay provides lessons in strategic planning and network optimization. Players must decide where to build routes, how to connect cities, and when to compete for certain paths. In a business context, decisions about where to expand operations or how to optimize logistics networks are crucial. Playing such a game can sharpen strategic thinking and decision-making skills, which are applicable in managing real-world business operations.

In Catan, the goal is to build a community, and in the game Agricola, the idea is to build a farm. In an organization, goals might include building a client base, a support operation, or a product. The parallels between building within a board game and building within an organization quickly become obvious during gameplay, and a well-crafted board game can serve as an effective metaphor or simulation of your organization's building and growing process.

Design Participation Into the Entire Game

Many Eurogames include a turn or time limit as well as opportunities for every player to be involved until the end. In a game like Monopoly, on the other hand, if your opponent has a bunch of hotels and you own one railroad property, you're doomed. When creating your learning board game, allowing equal participation and keeping all players involved until the end ensures the learning process extends for the entire gameplay experience.

Let's Design a Board Game for Learning

One common mistake that learning game developers make is turning a board game for learning into a knowledge-only activity like Trivial Pursuit. When this happens, the opportunity to help learners understand systems thinking, suboptimization, resource management, and how to make decisions with incomplete data is lost. Board games or tabletop simulations allow you to engage learners at a deeper level, so take advantage of the chance to design an action-first board game that leverages maximum learning potential. In the following sections, you'll find steps you can take to help make that happen. Although they are listed in a particular order here, you don't need to follow that order, and sometimes steps will overlap.

Step 1. Define the Desired Learning Outcome

Ensure your learning outcome is sufficiently ambitious to warrant a board game. For example, you might want to help learners understand the interconnectedness of departments within an organization or focus on the trade-offs among costs, innovation, and employee satisfaction. Or you might want learners to see how market forces can influence competitor actions. As you create your game, break the larger goal into smaller, measurable learning objectives. If the board game or tabletop simulation is a culminating activity, create one in which players apply knowledge, make connections, and gain insights related to concepts and ideas they've already learned.

Step 2. Create the System and Interconnected Elements

If you are leveraging a board game to teach systems thinking and interconnections, you must first map the system you want to teach. For example, if you'll demonstrate your industry's competitive landscape in the board game, you'll need to identify the attributes of the key competitors. What are their general strengths, weaknesses, market share, and strategies? You should also spend time understanding your customer base and how competitors meet their needs. Consider how industry trends and external factors affect competition. After you have mapped out the competitive landscape, begin developing game situations and incorporating roles for players that represent different business functions, including finance, marketing, and operations.

Step 3. Add the Appropriate Mechanics

There are several different game mechanics for board games that can make them interesting and challenging. Determine which ones make the most sense given your model and desired learning outcome. You may want to incorporate a random board with tiles (instead of a single traditional board) if you want to introduce variability and replayability. If you want players to think strategically and weigh multiple options, you may want to allow multiple actions per card. Encouraging creation and strategic planning, akin to the game Ticket to Ride, parallels real-world business strategy and decision making. You should also try to keep all players engaged throughout the game.

Step 4. Create Scenarios and Situations

Develop a variety of engaging scenarios that align with the board game's learning goals, such as market expansion, product innovation, or customer acquisition. A series of short scenarios contributing to overall gameplay is usually easier to manage both from a development perspective and from the player's perspective. You want a series of game experiences that vary in complexity, from simple operational tasks to complex strategic initiatives. You can also design the scenarios to offer multiple approaches to success, just like in actual business situations.

Step 5. Create Roles and Parameters Around Roles

Determine all the roles the players will take on during gameplay. You might have teams representing operations, marketing, human resources, and leadership. The roles you create will be based on the learning outcomes you want to achieve. You need to ensure that each one contributes to the overall goals and works within the game's scenarios. Establish each role's scope and limitations, such as budget control, team size, or market influence.

Step 6. Write Up the Gameplay Flow and Rules

Before playtesting can begin, you should have a *sequence of play*—which outlines the rules that each group needs to follow—and a sense of how the entire experience will unfold. This involves writing up rules that will dictate the flow of the game. At this point, don't worry about getting the rules 100 percent correct because you won't! As you begin to playtest, you'll discover what went wrong in the planning stage, key elements the rules are missing, and how you have inadvertently allowed cheating. Don't underestimate the importance of honing and polishing the rules to make the game as cheat-proof as possible. But you need to start somewhere, so create an initial set of rules to use during playtesting.

Step 7. Review the Game for Accessibility

When creating a board game for learning, don't rely solely on any one sense for playability. Ensure that all players can engage fully with the game experience. Making your board game accessible for visually impaired players involves thoughtful design adjustments. To assist those with limited vision, all board games should use high-contrast colors and large, legible sans-serif fonts to make textual and graphical elements more discernible. Tactile components, such as pieces with unique shapes or textures, allow players to identify and differentiate game elements by touch. Braille can be used on cards and game boards. 3D printing technology can create distinct, touch-friendly models that represent a variety of game functions and statuses. For crucial information, audio descriptions can be made available via QR codes and played on smartphones. You can design a board game that's accessible to individuals with hearing impairments by visually conveying necessary information. You'll find more tips to improve accessibility in chapter 11.

Step 8. Playtest

At this point, take out a flipchart, pennies or other tokens, plastic game pieces, blank index cards, pens, markers, or pencils. Sketch the game on paper and begin to play. Start with your design group. No matter how careful you are in conceptualizing the experience, you'll find holes once you begin playing. Fill them in! Make changes and rearrange mechanics. The iterative process results in the best outcomes.

When you and your team think you have a solid board game, go beyond the design group and playtest with people who have not been involved yet. You will be surprised to see what questions and problems the design team didn't notice. After making more adjustments, create a passable, more aesthetically pleasing version of the game and test it using a small pilot group. This final playtest will help make the game as effective and airtight as possible and allow you to make the final necessary revisions.

It's hard to create a perfect game, of course. You'll still need a game master to run gameplay and address any arbitrary circumstance encountered along the way. However, the testing process will make it more effective and enjoyable so players can focus on the learning outcomes rather than questions about the game itself.

Step 9. Design Final Artwork, Paying Attention to the Look and Feel

Whether online or physical, the board is an integral part of the game. This is not the place to skimp. The artwork should be visually appealing and instructional, incorporating elements like labeled maps, appropriate illustrations, and a cohesive look and feel. Balancing complexity and simplicity is the key to ensuring that the visuals enhance gameplay without overwhelming learners.

Step 10. Produce and Distribute the Game

Now is the time to create the game's physical components. This includes producing the artwork, manufacturing game pieces, and printing the game board. Quality production enhances the player experience and ensures longevity. This is important because board games can become staples in training sessions, used repeatedly in multiple sessions. Fortunately, it's now easier than ever to send artwork to board game companies that can manufacture your game for a relatively low cost.

Don't forget to consider digital board games for multiplayer experiences across distances. An advantage of digital board games is that they can incorporate multimedia elements like audio and animations to create a dynamic and engaging experience. They are also easy to distribute and update. The choice between physical and digital formats depends on the intended use and player environment.

AI Assist

The following prompt can assist you in generating concepts, gameplay mechanics, rules, and other essential details needed to create a board game. Adjust the content within the square brackets to include relevant information for your game.

> You are a board game developer tasked with creating a [business-themed or education-themed] board game for [six to eight] players, focusing on the mechanics of [territory acquisition, trade-offs, and collection]. The game's objective is to [dominate new market territories]. Targeted at [experienced sales professionals], the game should last approximately [90-120] minutes. Include components like [market cards, resource tokens, and a modular board representing different market regions]. Players should interact through [negotiation and trade], facing challenges like [market fluctuations and competitive bids]. The victory condition is to [control the most diversified portfolio of markets]. Describe the rules, game setup, player progression, and how the theme of [acquiring new markets] is visually and strategically represented.

Case Study: All for One: The Strategic Alignment Game

Note: The name of the firm and other details in this case study have been changed to ensure confidentiality.

Vapor Innovations, a company that creates cloud-based applications, implemented an action-first board game to train its division managers. The US–based company caters to large and midsize enterprises and streamlines processes (including payroll, talent acquisition, and expense management), combining finance and HR functions in one system.

The Challenge

The primary challenge for Vapor Innovations was to shift managers' mindsets from a narrow focus on their individual divisions to a broader, enterprise-level perspective. This transition was essential to addressing the prevailing problem of suboptimization, manifested by managers making decisions that benefitted only their own divisions at the expense of the organization's overall strategy and performance.

The company wanted to encourage a more holistic approach to decision making, directly aligning divisional goals with its overarching objectives. The ultimate objective was to enhance strategic alignment within the organization by fostering better collaboration and communication among division managers.

Why a Board Game?

Management chose a board game for this training opportunity for two reasons. First, the training experience was designed for a face-to-face environment. The training team wanted an experience that would leverage the opportunity to bring managers together in person. A board game seemed likely to foster collaboration and teamwork because it would require players to work together, communicate effectively, and make collective decisions. It would also help the managers become better acquainted with one another, which might be helpful in future discussions and strategy sessions about business needs.

Second, management and the training team viewed board games as especially helpful in highlighting the dangers of suboptimization. Often, decisions that lead to suboptimal results take weeks or months to unfold, and the causes and effects aren't immediately visible. A board game could demonstrate a decision's impact during a brief period of gameplay.

Everyone involved in planning the board game believed the hands-on activity would reveal the negative impact of decisions that only consider one division's perspective rather than the good of the entire organization. Through gameplay with other managers, that negative impact could be cemented firmly in players' minds and they would avoid suboptimization in the future.

Making the Case

The trainers who developed the board game made the case for using it as a teaching tool in this situation by highlighting its direct relevance to the real-world business problems Vapor Innovations was facing. Their key argument to executives was that the design of this board game would force managers to consider the broad impact of their individual decisions on the overall system during each turn in gameplay. This aligned with the learning need to avoid suboptimization and shift from maximizing the performance of individual departments to enhancing the organization's efficiency. The game would mimic the interdependence of various divisions and the need to collaborate in a practical, hands-on learning experience. The executives were convinced by the trainers' logic and signed off, allowing the game to be deployed in the live meeting.

The Solution

The designers decided to name the game "All for One: The Strategic Alignment Game." Managers played it over three days during a face-to-face retreat, completing one round each day. Between each round the retreat focused on educating attendees on how to work together to achieve organizational success.

On the first day, the trainers planned for the game to have the worst results and the most suboptimization. Over the next two days, the players learned more about the value of working together and considering the impact of their decisions on other groups within the company. This meant that each day the player worked better and more and more effectively.

Scoring was based on accumulating chips in the right areas on a dashboard. Chip counts were converted into organizational revenue to make the score as relevant to the business environment as possible.

A total of 45 managers attended the retreat, with nine players at five boards playing All for One. The nine players on each board were divided into three subteams of three, each representing a large division or role within the company. These subteams, while competing on the same larger team, had to navigate the complexity of working toward a common goal with the other two teams on their game board. In other words, the subteams had to figure out how to work together before they could effectively compete against the other eight larger teams.

The subteams, which represented operations, marketing, and human resources, each had a corresponding area on the board containing spaces for scenario, option, and consequence cards. The game had three rounds with three unique scenarios. Each subteam pulled a scenario card with information about an actual situation that had happened at the company. After they read their scenario, they pulled an option card, which provided several responses or options to address the scenario.

Each option had consequences, of course. Depending on which one the players chose, the consequence card would reward or punish them for their choice. Some options were excellent for the division but not good for the overall company, while others were good for the company but not the division.

In the middle of the game board was a dashboard containing a space for chips (Figure 3-2). It was divided into five areas for costs, innovation, employee satisfaction, customer satisfaction, and cybersecurity.

Each option's consequences affected the number of chips in the various areas of the dashboard. For example, if a player chose to invest money in cybersecurity, the costs in the current round might increase by three chips, but in subsequent rounds, the customer satisfaction score might increase by five chips. Or a player might choose to cut costs in one round by four chips but in the next two rounds, the employee satisfaction would be reduced by six chips and innovation scores might decrease by three chips. The teams' scores were calculated based on the number of chips and converted into revenue generated, directly tying the teams' choices to measurable financial outcomes.

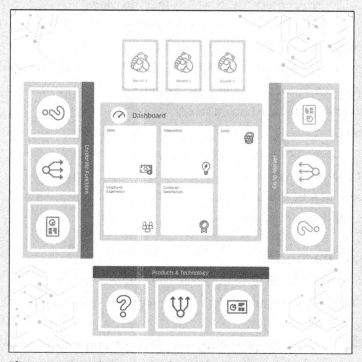

Figure 3-2. Board game setup for "All for One: The Strategic Alignment Game." This game was designed to teach mangers to think at the enterprise level. *Source: Created by Beth Myers and Karl M. Kapp.*

Three rounds were played each day, and on the third day, one overall winner was declared. The teams learned they had to work together for the good of the company even if it meant short-term losses for their subgroup or division. They also learned that some of the scenario cards at their table were the same as those held by other subteams, and if they communicated with each other about what they were experiencing, they could better optimize the outputs of their organization and increase revenue.

Benefits and Results

The implementation of the board game was successful, as evidenced by positive feedback from participants and measurable improvement in their decision-making processes and ability to consider the needs of the overall enterprise as well as their divisions.

Postgame assessments and discussions revealed a significant increase in participants' understanding of the systemic implications of their decisions. Managers began to demonstrate a more holistic approach in their strategic planning, considering the organization as an interconnected system rather than isolated divisions. This shift in mindset was a critical step in mitigating suboptimization, leading to more cohesive and efficient organizational operations. The next quarter's overall numbers improved, and the organization attributed much of the improvement to the three-day retreat and the work—and play—the managers did there.

Lessons Learned

Vapor Innovations learned a number of valuable lessons during this process. These lessons can also help guide your own development of a board game for learning.

- **Test your game for playability, engagement, and educational outcome but also for resources.** The first time Vapor Innovations tested the game, one of the teams made several bad decisions and didn't have enough chips to make it to the next round. Playtest with the game resources to ensure that you have enough pieces, cards, and other game elements to last throughout the entire game regardless of the circumstances—including the possibility that a team gets everything wrong or everything right.

- **Allocate enough game masters or facilitators to ensure a smooth launch and running of the game.** When you run a game like this, especially in the first round, you'll encounter questions and player uncertainty about what is allowed, what is not allowed, and the general rules no matter how carefully you plan or explain the instructions. Having enough facilitators during the gameplay to ensure everyone's questions are answered in a timely fashion is important for a smooth experience for all learners. Vapor Innovations decided on three facilitators for the first day of play but only needed one on the subsequent two days.

- **Double-check all materials when they come back from the printing company.** Vapor Innovations had many cards printed to go along with the game, but the printer originally sent two batches of one type of card and no batches of another. This is why it's important to complete your game creation and testing early so you have plenty of time to correct printing errors. Make sure you review game pieces, cards, chips, and any other items so everyone has a complete set when players interact with the game. Vapor Innovations also ordered boxes for each game, which helped players keep all the items together and made it feel even more like a professional game.

Key Takeaways

Now that you're ready to create an action-first learning experience using a board game, remember these tips:

- Board games help learners see the big picture in a learning situation through its visual aspects and by highlighting relationships and interconnection among elements in an organization or situation.

- Board games can be delivered to learners physically in-person or online via virtual boards. If you choose to create a physical game, use print-on-demand services to create a highly polished, professional-looking game that will impress learners.
- Opportunities to gather in face-to-face learning situations are becoming more limited. Don't waste them with traditional lectures or other experiences that fail to engage learners. Leveraging action-first learning designs like board games will maximize this face-to-face time.

EXPLANATION OF THE ACTION-FIRST ACTIVITY

The board game being described in the riddle is Stratego, a classic board game that combines elements of strategy, memory, and deception. The game is played on a 10x10 grid by two players who each control an army of pieces. One side is red and the other is blue. The goal is to capture the opponent's flag while protecting your own. The armies face each other but the value of each piece is hidden from the opponent until an "attack" where each player reveals the value of their piece. Each piece in the game has a rank, and higher-ranked pieces capture the lower-ranked ones, with a few special rules that add complexity and balance to the game.

Players must develop and adapt offensive and defensive strategies, remember the identities of hidden opposing pieces, and solve problems in real time. Deception plays an important role as players bluff to protect their flag or trap opponents. This seemingly simple game forces players to think through the consequences of moves and guess the strategies and tactics of their opponent as the game unfolds.

Tool 3-1. Tips for Effective Board Games

✓ Play lots of entertainment-focused board games to understand the variety of available mechanics and elements before you design a board game for learning.

✓ Ensure your game's mechanics and scenarios align with the learning outcomes you want to achieve.

✓ Try to go beyond Monopoly-style games by studying Eurogames for mechanics that lend themselves to learning games.

✓ Before you develop a learning game to teach a complex system, make sure you fully map and understand its elements. Investing this time at the start will help you create a better and more accurate experience.

✓ Design continuous participation into your game. Learners should be involved the entire time. Challenge them by requiring action and thinking ahead to anticipate opponents' moves.

✓ Ensure that there are enough facilitators or game masters to answer questions and keep the game running smoothly. This is especially important for initial onboarding into the game.

✓ Invest in a well-designed board and a box for the most professional-looking game.

4
The Great Escape
Escape Rooms for Learning

You need to have an escape room experience. There are escape room books such as *Journal 29* or *S.* by J.J. Abrams and Doug Dorst or *Escape Room: Getaway from the Dungeons* by EnigmAction Ed. There are escape room card games such as Space Cowboys Unlock! Short Adventures: The Secrets of The Octopus and even escape room board games such as Mattel's Escape Room in a Box Game: The Werewolf Experiment and EXIT: The Professor's Last Riddle. Not to mention actual, physical escape rooms in most cities that you can visit and try with friends. For this action-first activity, obtain and play an escape room card game, board game, or book. Better yet, get your friends or colleagues together and go to an escape room to test your skills!

At the end of this chapter, you should be able to answer these questions:

- What elements can be added to a traditional escape room to make it effective for learning?
- What types of learning outcomes are best for leveraging escape rooms?
- What basic design principles should you consider when designing an escape room experience?
- What are some examples of escape rooms used for training and improving employee performance?

Groups of consultants walked into a massive hotel ballroom where the lights mimicked the intense, annoying, fluorescent glow of an airport at 7 a.m. The whole room looked, felt, and sounded like an airport. There were gates, monitors displaying arrival and departure times, travel

posters, airport lockers, and check-in areas buzzing with background conversations. Each of the 18 check-in areas was an escape room (Figure 4-1).

The teams of newly hired consultants for a large globally dispersed organization were participating in a complex event, competing against time and one another. Each of the more than 140 participants had been assigned to an escape room with seven or eight teammates. The puzzles, riddles, and clues in each escape room were identical.

Figure 4-1. An airport-themed escape room used by a large consultancy firm to practice teamwork and communication skills. *Source: Created by The Escape Game. Photo by Karl M. Kapp.*

When a timer pinged, the experience started and teams ran to their assigned areas where they found luggage, a terminal, a monitor with flight information, and a check-in counter with multiple drawers and a locked door.

"All right, team, let's focus," said Rachel, a newly hired consultant from England. Her voice was steady, disguising the fact that she felt nervous and eager to begin. "Communication is key here. Let's start by sharing what we see." She was determined to finish in the top five.

Amidst chaotic shuffling, Marco, a new hire from Mexico, opened a drawer filled with keys. "I've found something!" he exclaimed. "I see like a hundred different keys. At least one of these must be important. If somebody else finds a lock, I'll look for the right key."

Meanwhile, Julia, from Spain, noticed a series of travel posters with numbers. "Perhaps these numbers correspond to the keypad lock on the door behind the counter," she suggested, her mind quickly adding and subtracting numbers to decipher the right code to enter into the keypad.

As the minutes ticked away, the team encountered additional obstacles and clues that tested their problem-solving skills and ability to collaborate under pressure. Each member contributed unique insights, leveraging their knowledge and experiences to decipher riddles and unlock more compartments. They eventually unlocked a door labeled "airport operations" and found a console that had to be manipulated to find the final clues (Figure 4-2).

Figure 4-2. Console from an airport-themed escape room reinforcing problem-solving skills among associates. *Source: Created by The Escape Game. Photo by Karl M. Kapp.*

With a few moments to spare, they discovered what was clearly the last clue, and several team members gasped with relief. Time was running out, but they completed their mission and finished in fourth place.

As the training leaders debriefed everyone, each team listed key lessons they had learned, including how critical continuous communication is to success, how valuable collaboration is in solving challenges, and how important it is to remain calm under pressure and adapt quickly to new information. Everyone agreed the experience had helped them bond with their teammates.

In the after-action review, the participants created a plan to apply the lessons learned in their work environments back home. The escape room turned out to be an eye-opening and effective action-first learning experience that helped build the organization's culture and underscore its core values.

● ● ●

Often, we think of an escape room as a physical location, such as the one described in this example, but that's not always the case. You don't have to create a physical room learners must escape from. Instead, think of an *escape room* as a series of puzzles, problems, or challenges delivered physically, virtually, in a book, or through card or board games that must be solved to reach a desired outcome. All types of escape room experiences can provide the same lessons in teamwork, collaboration, adaptation, and problem solving.

When you use an escape room design to teach technical or soft skills, you create an engaging and memorable activity that reinforces knowledge and helps learners practice, retain, and apply those skills with an action-first approach.

Why Is an Escape Room Experience Effective for Learning?

Escape rooms are an effective, fun way to implement action-first learning. Compared with other training formats, they provide a quick and intense instructional experience that can be completed within a short, approximately one-hour time period. They also provide a safe space for learners to make mistakes and test themselves under pressure, as well as a place to foster teamwork and collaboration.

A Quick, Intense Experience

While it does take a designer significant time to design, develop, and set up an escape room, the actual time learners need to work through the learning experience is often only an hour, which is the standard time limit for most virtual and physical escape rooms. Even if you add 30 minutes for a debriefing session, the total required time is only about an hour and a half. This relatively short period is particularly beneficial because it provides a concentrated period of engagement and focus, ensuring that learners remain fully immersed in the experience without losing interest or attention. This further enhances the learning experience and outcomes because participants are more likely to retain the information and skills acquired during this high-pressure, highly focused event. From an organizational perspective, the short duration can be more cost-effective, requiring less time for employees to be away from their jobs compared with longer training sessions.

A Safe Environment

An escape room creates a sense of uncertainty for participants. They don't know if they will be able to escape in time, they don't know the clues, and they don't know exactly what they'll need to do to be successful. However, the escape room's designer knows all the clues, which information goes with which puzzle, and the sequence participants need to follow to apply their knowledge to escape. This pre-established knowledge creates a safe environment for the learners. Unlike real-world situations where mistakes can have significant consequences, the stakes in an escape room are controlled and contained within the game. This safe environment encourages learners to explore different problem-solving approaches without fear of failure or judgment. They can test hypotheses, try unconventional methods, and learn from their mistakes in real time. This freedom to experiment fosters creativity and innovation, because participants are more likely to think outside the box when they know that errors are part of the learning process and that they will not be penalized for mistakes (other than maybe not escaping!).

Pressure!

Although an escape room is usually a quick experience, it is also stressful. Many people work in high-pressure environments. The sense of urgency imposed by the time limit mirrors real-world scenarios in which deadlines and quick decisions are crucial. But again, the stress participants feel in an escape room is safe because it is contained within a game setting and the consequences of failure are minimal. One way of creating this pressure is to hide items in the escape room. The learners might uncover a hidden safe (like in Figure 4-3), but then the pressure builds because they need to find the right combination to open the safe, which then contains a clue to another puzzle they need to solve before time runs out.

Figure 4-3. A virtual escape room where the learner must enter a code to find the next clue. *Source: Created by Karl M. Kapp and Paola Terreforte.*

This controlled pressure allows participants to practice and improve their stress management skills without the fear of real-world repercussions. They can practice staying focused, prioritizing tasks, and maintaining composure as the clock ticks down—all valuable skills in their professional lives. They can also practice quickly delegating tasks, sharing information, and supporting teammates while under stress. In this environment, learners will understand the importance of relying on others and leveraging collective strengths when faced with challenging situations.

Finally, the pressure of a physical or virtual escape room offers a unique opportunity for self-reflection. After the experience, learners can consider their own reactions and behaviors under stress, gaining insights into their personal triggers and coping mechanisms. This self-awareness is highly valuable for personal and professional growth because it allows employees to identify their own areas for improvement and develop strategies for managing pressure more effectively in the future.

Teamwork and Collaboration

An action-first escape room design can present challenges that are too complex for one individual to solve alone. The diverse array of puzzles and tasks require different skill sets, perspectives, and abilities, making collaboration essential for success. The teamwork that happens in an escape room fosters a sense of camaraderie and shared purpose among learners. As team members work together toward a common goal, they develop stronger interpersonal relationships and a deeper understanding of each other's strengths and weaknesses, leading to better collaboration and communication in the workplace and other group settings.

The teamwork requirement in an escape room mirrors the collaborative nature of real-world work environments. By practicing teamwork in a fun and engaging context, participants are better prepared to work effectively with others in their personal and professional lives. They learn the value of cooperation, active listening, and mutual respect, all of which are crucial components of a successful team.

What Can an Escape Room Learning Experience Teach?

As I previously mentioned, by immersing participants in a challenging, interactive environment, either online or in a physical space, escape rooms require teams to work together to decipher clues, solve puzzles, and complete tasks within a time limit. They offer an engaging learning experience for teams, fostering communication, social connection, non-linear thinking, observation, and adaptation to unexpected events.

Communication

Many organizations suffer from poor communication. Escape rooms can't fix all communication problems, but they can provide instruction and practice in this critical area for both individuals and teams. Escape room experiences can foster direct interaction among team members and provide an environment in which to practice and refine communication skills while looking for clues, declaring what appear to be random finds, and working together to accomplish the shared goal of a final escape.

Players must actively listen to one another, understand relationships, and work in concert. Often, the escape can only happen through collaboration and cooperation.

Social Connection

In the modern workforce, employees often feel isolated from their co-workers due to the geographical distance in a nationally or globally distributed team or because of the prevalence of remote work. Isolation can manifest as low morale, employee disengagement, reduced productivity, and increased turnover. Bringing employees together, either virtually or physically, in an escape room environment fights isolation by creating camaraderie, which can have a strong positive impact on interpersonal relationships. When people meet face-to-face or engage in collaborative activities, they form stronger bonds and a sense of unity. Social connections can even help reduce burnout, contribute to better mental and emotional well-being, and build a positive organizational culture characterized by trust and understanding. This positive culture can, in turn, enhance an organization's reputation and enable it to attract and retain top talent.

Nonlinear Thinking

Nonlinear thinking is a powerful tool that involves exploring multiple possibilities and making connections between disparate ideas. In an escape room, participants are usually faced with puzzles and challenges that cannot be solved through straightforward, linear reasoning. Instead, they must use their imagination, intuition, and lateral thinking to find innovative solutions. For example, in an escape room where a team is trying to solve a mystery in a scientist's laboratory, the room could be filled with scientific equipment, books, and notes. One of the puzzles might involve a locked cabinet with no visible keyhole. Instead of looking for a physical key, participants must realize that the solution requires a series of chemical reactions. By using clues hidden in the scientist's notes, they could combine different chemicals found in the lab to create a reaction that generates a gas that triggers a sensor that unlocks the cabinet, revealing the next clue. In this situation, participants are encouraged to think nonlinearly by considering the relationships among different elements in the room and applying their knowledge in unexpected ways. The solution is not a simple, linear progression from finding a key to opening a lock. It requires a logical leap and an understanding of the broader context.

Observation

In an escape room, learners must meticulously observe their surroundings (either physically or virtually) to uncover clues integral to their progress. Clues can be discreetly embedded in decor, written materials, and what appear to be insignificant objects in a room or virtual image. Participants need a keen eye for detail to identify these crucial pieces of information, which are usually designed to be subtle and difficult to find. Puzzles in an escape room typically demand precision and scrutiny. In short, participants face challenges in every escape room that require careful analysis and interpretation. Imagine a set of numbers on a piece of paper. These numbers might represent a code that needs to be deciphered or a collection of objects that need to be arranged in a specific sequence to reveal a solution. Solving these kinds of puzzles demands keen observations and a thorough examination of every detail because overlooking even the smallest element can hinder a team's progress. This is why escape rooms provide such good practice for learners honing their observational skills and attention to detail.

Adaptation

Adaptability is a critical skill in the workplace and academia, where we must all adapt to competitors' actions, new government regulations, and changing customer preferences. Escape rooms require learners to quickly adapt to their thinking as they confront clues, puzzles, and each newly revealed piece of information. Individuals and teams in an escape room must think on their feet, shift strategies, embrace uncertainty, remain open to new ideas, and be flexible when choosing problem-solving methods. The time constraint adds an additional layer of pressure. After the exercise is complete, participants can reflect on their performance and gain insights into their ability to adapt, identifying areas for improvement.

Escape Room Mechanics

When designing escape rooms for learning, you'll need to incorporate a few essential mechanics to enhance the experience, including an engaging, relevant setting and theme, a variety of clues, a diverse mix of activities, and a well-planned debrief. Let's consider how to handle each of these effectively.

Create a Relevant Setting and Theme

Your escape room will be boring if all learners do is solve a series of seemingly unrelated puzzles and open a bunch of locks. Instead, you need to create a unifying theme that provides a reason for doing the activities, such as finding a hidden treasure, successfully escaping jail, or recovering a stolen painting. A theme adds a sense of adventure, fun, and context.

Your action-first learning experience in an escape room could have a fanciful theme, such as traveling on a spaceship or back in time to a mythical steampunk era. The experience could also be more practical, with participants locked in a competitor's office, dealing with a crisis threatening the company's reputation, or resolving a series of financial problems to ultimately escape from bankruptcy. The theme needs to be reflected in the backstory, messaging, fonts, graphics, and props you incorporate into the escape room, as well as the types of clues you provide.

Vary the Difficulty and How You Deliver Clues

If all the clues in your escape room are very easy, you risk boring the participants. However, if they're too difficult, you risk frustrating them. Always provide a range of clues to cater to the learners' varied knowledge and experience levels. The variety allows some participants to work on the tougher ones while others solve the easy ones.

Mapping out the flow of the difficulty for your clues can help ensure you have the appropriate variety. Sometimes you'll force learners to search for clues, and other times you'll just provide the clues in a drawer or hide them in a book. Sometimes you'll want learners to gradually decipher a clue by putting together puzzle pieces or analyzing an image hanging on the wall. *The clues are the backbone of the escape room experience,* which is why you'll need to balance their difficulty and diversity carefully so the learning experience you are creating is both instructionally sound and compelling for everyone.

Mix Up the Types of Activities

In addition to varying the difficulty levels of clues and puzzles in your escape room, you also need to mix up the types of clues you provide. The basic sequence for any escape room is *search*, *solve*, and *reward*. To add variety to this sequence, you should intermix different types of activities. For example, you could include audio clues to force learners to focus on listening skills or numeric clues and puzzles to hone their analytical skills. Consider writing secret messages for an element of mystery and including riddles and math problems to encourage creative and logical thinking. Mirrors can add physical problem-solving reflections and new angles, and you can write messages on paintings or walls that are only revealed with blacklights. Maps can tap into a learner's geographical knowledge. Of course, traditional padlocks, locked drawers, and secret compartments can always be included in an experience, whether it's physical or virtual. But adding variety keeps the escape room dynamic. Finally, don't be afraid to mix physical and virtual clues. There is no reason you can't place a QR code into a physical escape room to reveal an augmented reality clue or that a virtual escape room can't send you to find a page in the physical employee handbook.

Create a Plan to Debrief the Experience

You'll need a plan for the debrief before you create the escape room. Debriefing focuses everyone on learning outcomes and provides a structured opportunity for learners to reflect, articulate their thoughts, and make connections between the activity and real-world applications. Debriefing helps consolidate the learning by encouraging participants to discuss the strategies they employed, the challenges they faced, and the solutions they devised. This reflective process fosters critical thinking, problem-solving skills, and team dynamics.

An effective debriefing will also allow facilitators to highlight key learning points and reinforce the intended instructional objectives of the escape room. You want to ensure that the experience is not just an isolated event, but a meaningful learning opportunity that contributes to the person's overall development. A debriefing session should be part of every escape room learning design.

Let's Design an Escape Room Learning Experience

An escape room is a fantastic action-first learning experience. When you can build one from the ground up, it gives you the chance to create a unique and memorable event for all the participants.

Some organizations shy away from escape rooms because they are considered too expensive or time consuming to create. A customized escape room can indeed be a great learning tool, but if cost and time are an issue, you can consider leveraging existing commercial escape rooms to meet your team's goals. Find a local escape room and study it with an eye toward turning the entertaining experience into a learning experience. As another option, consider using an off-the-shelf education-focused virtual escape room or convert a card game, board game, or even a worksheet into an escape room.

If you decide to create your own escape room, here are the steps to follow for a successful learning experience.

Step 1. Define Learning Objectives and Outcomes

Clear learning objectives are critical for developing an effective action-first escape room experience. The more defined, measurable, and trackable the outcomes, the easier it is to design and evaluate the effectiveness of the escape room experience for the learners.

Step 2. Think About Accessibility

When designing accessible escape rooms, the goal is to create an inclusive experience without sacrificing the fun and immersive aspects of the game. Understanding the potential challenges faced by individuals who will be participating is key. Some solutions—like adding closed captions to videos or ensuring wheelchair access to all areas of the room—make a significant difference. Consider creating variations of puzzles, clues, or challenges that can be readily accessed by anyone. For example, if one challenge in the escape room requires a person to hold a magnet in their hand to manipulate a metal weight to unlock a secret drawer, consider an alternative solution, such as using a vocal command to unlock the drawer. Including more than one way of solving a puzzle or challenge will help make the experience more accessible. Keep the Web Content Accessibility Guidelines (WCAG) in mind if you're designing online, virtual escape rooms.

Step 3. Choose a Theme and Story

Select a theme that aligns with your learning objectives and will engage your target audience. Then, create a compelling story to serve as the backdrop for the escape room. It can have a direct business tie-in, such as an escape room about a project management challenge, or it can be more fanciful, such as an escape room about an art heist.

Step 4. Create an Escape Room Flowchart

You'll need to determine the sequence of puzzles, challenges, and clues to effectively design the escape room's layout. One way to do this is by designing a game flowchart, which is simply a diagram of how learners will progress through the experience. This will help you consider timing, transitions between puzzles, and how you'll use the screen space or physical space. It will also help you decide how many and what types of clues or puzzles to design and provide an overview of how learners will find and solve clues and puzzles. The game master, or whoever is overseeing the escape room experience, will also find the flowchart helpful.

Step 5. Design the Puzzles, Challenges, and Clues

Ensure that clues, puzzles, and challenges vary in difficulty, are appropriate for the learners' skill level, and are integrated into the theme and story. You also need to align the activities with the desired instructional outcomes, ensuring that solving a clue or puzzle requires the application of specific knowledge or skills.

Step 6. Create Hints and Tips

Make sure learners don't become too frustrated. A little frustration is good, but too much will ruin the experience. They may need hints or tips to get past any spots where they get stuck. If you create a list of hints or tips ahead of time, the game master can provide them quickly; otherwise, they'll have to come up with them in the moment and may not suggest the best options.

Step 7. Assemble Assets

Now it's time to gather props. For a physical escape room, you might need to acquire hollowed-out books, distinct types of locks, keys, and other elements to match the story and theme. If the escape room is virtual, you'll need to work to develop interactive online locks, click-to-reveals, and drag-and-drop exercises that will make the experience engaging. Card games, board games, and worksheet-focused escape rooms need artwork, text, and other elements to make them engaging.

Step 8. Build the Escape Room

Depending on how elaborate your escape room is, it may take anywhere from days to just a few hours to build a physical structure. Programming a virtual experience will also be time consuming because it involves developing scoring, graphics, and other elements necessary to make the experience complete.

Step 9. Train a Game Master

Most escape room experiences have someone who watches over the learners, provides hints, and keeps an eye on the progress the team is making toward their escape. This person is the game master and needs to be trained, given a list of hints, and instructed on how to oversee the experience. A game master shouldn't be too intrusive but also shouldn't be absent when the participants need help or have a question.

Step 10. Launch a Pilot Program

If the escape room is virtual, there may be complex logistics involved in using virtual meeting software like Zoom or Teams with another software that provides the actual escape room experience. You'll need to use a pilot group to figure out how the software works together before launching the experience to a large group of people. Make changes based on the results from your pilot.

Step 11. Launch the Escape Room Experience

Invite your target audience to use your escape room. Provide an excellent experience with a well-trained game master and don't forget to include a debriefing to help learners apply what they learn to the actual situations they will encounter.

Step 12. Evaluate and Revise

After the escape room experience is over, evaluate its effectiveness in meeting the learning objectives. Gather feedback from participants and make revisions as necessary to enhance the learning experience for the next group of learners.

AI Assist

While AI tools can't yet develop an entire digital escape room from scratch, they can assist you in several ways. First, AI tools can provide ideas and concepts. When posed to an AI assistant, the following prompt can help you design and conceptualize your escape room for learning.

```
Design an escape room for learning that immerses
learners in a thematic adventure requiring them to use
their knowledge and problem-solving skills to unlock
clues and escape within a set timeframe. The theme,
puzzles, and storyline should align with the following
learning objectives [enter learning objectives here]
to reinforce educational content in an engaging,
interactive manner.
```

You may want to provide additional information to the AI assistant if you know some specifics, such as:

- ▶ **Theme.** Choose a theme relevant to the subject matter.
- ▶ **Storyline.** Choose a narrative that integrates the content participants should learn. The storyline should drive the game and motivate them to solve puzzles.
- ▶ **Types of puzzles.** Include puzzles that require critical thinking, collaboration, and application of knowledge.

This extra information will produce a more detailed design. Here is a sample prompt:

```
Design an escape room for learning around the theme
of [a Sherlock Holmes mystery], requiring the learner
to use their knowledge and problem-solving skills
to unlock clues and escape within a [60-minute
timeframe]. Include a storyline about [solving an
accounting mystery to prevent bankruptcy]. Puzzles
should revolve around the following: [using a
spreadsheet to find number combinations for a lock],
[assembling items to reveal a timeline or sequence],
and [ciphers to unlock policy information]. The
theme, puzzles, and storyline should align with
the following learning objective [effectively use
spreadsheet software to organize, analyze, and
interpret financial data to identify anomalies or
irregularities that may indicate potential issues
or areas requiring further investigation during
an audit] to reinforce educational content in an
engaging, interactive manner.
```

AI assistants can also help create digital assets. However, this can be complicated. After I entered a prompt about Sherlock Holmes, the AI assistant did not create a Sherlock Holmes office because of copyright and usage policy issues. So, I wrote a workaround prompt:

```
Create artwork for a Victorian-era office that's
appropriate for a London-based detective.
```

The result is shown in Figure 4-4.

Figure 4-4. An AI-generated image of an escape room. *Source: Image generated by DALL-E in ChatGPT 4o.*

Use your imagination when creating artwork with an AI assistant and always be mindful of ethical and fairness issues. You can experiment with AI art tools such as Stable Diffusion, Midjourney, DALL-E, Adobe Express, and hundreds more. Each one provides a slightly different stylized output, so find the one that works best for you.

Case Study: Improving Communication and Teamwork in an Escape Room

Note: The name of the firm and other details in this case study have been changed to ensure confidentiality.

SuperConsultants is a professional services firm headquartered in the eastern US with more than 100 employees. The firm provides a broad spectrum of services—including assurance, tax advising, technology consulting, and auditing—to clients across industries ranging from financial services and technology to healthcare and consumer goods manufacturing.

The firm is known for its commitment to quality, ethical standards, and continuous innovation. It works with businesses of all sizes, from startups to multinational corporations, helping them manage risks, improve performance, and achieve their strategic objectives. Its regional networks and depth of expertise enable it to offer insights and solutions that address complex business challenges and capitalize on opportunities in the ever-evolving marketplace.

The Challenge

Recently, the firm faced challenges fostering effective teamwork and communication among new employees. The leaders knew that good communication and teamwork would positively affect the efficiency and quality of client engagements and that the faster new hires could work together effectively and efficiently, the better results would be for everyone. The challenge was to enhance collaboration, communication, and problem-solving skills among new consultants to improve client project outcomes and overall firm performance. While facing this challenge, the firm was in an unusual hiring situation, needing to bring in six new junior associates, which was twice the typical number hired in a year.

Why an Escape Room?

The firm wanted to do something big and bold for the six new hires who were all from well-respected MBA programs in the eastern US. SuperConsultants had competed with two other regional companies for the area's best and brightest and wanted to stand out from the crowd and make sure the new hires told colleagues at other companies about their exciting and energetic onboarding experience. The company also wanted to drive home the need for teamwork, observational skills, and problem solving, as well as the requirement for open and continual communication with peers, supervisors, and clients to its group of new hires.

The fact that the company was onboarding double the usual number of employees forced the HR department to rethink its process. The HR team had to create activities and training experiences that engaged all six employees without disrupting too much of the daily work routine of other associates and partners at the firm.

Lidia, one of the partners, had recently taken her daughter and friends to an escape room and was intrigued by the energy and excitement it had given the group of teenagers. She thought that an experience like an escape room could be a positive new element to add to the onboarding plan, but wasn't sure how to suggest it to the other partners. Then, while at an international L&D conference, she saw an interesting session about using escape rooms as learning vehicles. The description alone was enough to inspire Lidia to move forward with the idea.

Making the Case

Lidia had to convince the other partners and the talent development director that an escape room would be an appropriate and effective method for onboarding the new hires. She did some research and made her case by highlighting three aspects of the escape room:

- The escape room experience could mirror a real-life consulting scenario. The new associates could be trapped in a client's office looking for signs of off-book activities or anomalies in financial reporting—a quasirealistic and engaging scenario.
- Forcing the new hires to work together under pressure to solve a series of problems could become an ideal crucible in which the partners could see how well the new hires acclimated to the firm's typical working conditions.
- If designed well, the escape room experience would demand the same skills as a successful client engagement, including communication, teamwork, and problem solving.

The good news was that Lidia successfully made her case. The bad news was that the company put her in charge of creating the escape room experience. She was excited but nervous and immediately rolled up her sleeves, jumped online, and found several resources describing how to create escape rooms for learning.

The Solution

Lidia recruited a team to help her, and together they decided to schedule the escape room experience toward the end of the training program as the culmination of all the learning during the onboarding experience.

The team's first task was to walk around the available office space and find a suitable location for the physical escape room. They decided to use a conference room that opened into an adjacent office. The majority of the activity could occur in the larger conference room, but the final clues could appear after participants completed a task and entered the adjacent office. The size also worked well for six people.

Lidia and her team set to work transforming the space into a realistic accounting office with desks, chairs, filing cabinets, and computers. They added decorative elements (including plants, art, and a coffee station) to enhance the atmosphere. They also planned to place one of the clues in the coffee maker's filter compartment and another in the lunch menu attached to the mini fridge.

Next, the team focused on integrating puzzles and challenges into the office setting, creating fake balance sheets, income statements, and cash flow statements with intentional errors and discrepancies for participants to find and correct. Certain numbers in the corrected documents would help participants open locked drawers or find keys. They set up a computer with a password-protected file that contained crucial information about the escape room's storyline, which would get them to open the adjacent office door leading to the final clues. The final puzzle added an element of intrigue. In the office, a secret ledger would reveal a fraudulent scheme when participants shined a black light on the pages.

Lidia and her team could monitor the progress of the new hires as they interacted and moved through the escape room challenges. Both sides—Lidia's team and the participants in the escape room—could ask and answer questions during the search for clues, puzzles, and challenges.

Before opening the escape room during the onboarding program, Lidia's team conducted test runs with volunteers to check the timing and fine-tune the puzzles, clues, and challenges, as well as to ensure the experience was engaging and instructional. They decided to eliminate several puzzles because getting to the final clues took more than an hour. Once all the adjustments were made, Lidia felt confident that the escape room was ready for the new hires.

As the clock ticked, the new hires were able to open three types of locks and find key documents hidden in drawers, under plants, and in the coffee filter. They laid all the documents across a desk, and after about 10 minutes, they asked Lidia's designated game master a couple questions. They quickly noticed a pattern of discrepancies in the numbers and realized that they would have to apply their knowledge of accounting principles to reconcile the figures. After a brief discussion, they decided that four of them would work on the documents while the other two searched for additional clues. They soon found the new clue on the lunch menu that revealed large errors in the balance sheet.

Applying their understanding of assets, liabilities, and equity to information on the balance sheet, one participant found another clue hidden behind a picture on the wall. This led them to turn on the office computer, only to discover the files were password protected. One of the participants deduced the password by applying information from the previous day's onboarding session and solving a puzzle embedded in the cash flow statement in one of the documents. After a few more moves, the participants finally opened the door to the adjacent office and discovered the ledger.

One of them realized they would need to find a blacklight to read the ledger. So, a small group worked under pressure to review a set of transactions in the ledger and identify which ones violated best practices in auditing. Once they discovered the problematic transactions, a small drawer opened to reveal a key to a larger drawer containing the flashlight they needed. Flashlight in hand, the whole group re-examined the ledger and discovered the fraud. They completed the escape room with five minutes to spare!

In the debriefing afterward, the new hires reflected on their experience in the escape room, noting how the simulated challenges closely mirrored the feelings they anticipated in real-life consulting scenarios they expected to encounter at SuperConsultants. They also discussed how the need to communicate openly and rely on one another's strengths was crucial to their success. The escape room exercise not only enhanced their understanding of the firm's operations but also reinforced the importance of teamwork and problem solving in a high-pressure environment. The participants appreciated the innovative approach, stating that it made the onboarding process engaging and memorable, significantly boosting their confidence and readiness for client engagements.

The leadership team also gained valuable insights. They observed how quickly the new associates adapted to the escape room challenges and how effectively they collaborated under pressure. This experience provided a clear indicator of the new hires' capabilities and potential areas for further development. The feedback highlighted the success of the escape room in fostering essential skills and building camaraderie among the new team members. The positive outcomes encouraged SuperConsultants to consider incorporating similar interactive and action-first learning activities in future training programs to maintain their commitment to quality and innovation.

Benefits and Results

By the time they escaped the room, the new hires had bonded as a team and applied much of the knowledge they'd gained during onboarding and in their MBA programs. This laid a foundation for success in their new roles. Lidia's team was ecstatic, and the new hires loved the experience.

Positive feedback from the participants in their evaluations demonstrated the success of the escape room experience. They reported a greater appreciation for the importance of teamwork and communication. The buzz about the experience also brought a significant increase in applications, which helped the firm recruit within the region during the next hiring cycle. When the new hires attended a recruiting event at a local campus, no one could stop talking about the escape room experience.

After onboarding, partners and associates observed a high level of teamwork and communication among the new consultants. The camaraderie they had built early on seemed to lead to more effective collaboration on client projects and enhanced project outcomes. Two years after they were hired, all the participants in that initial escape room experience remained with the firm and were solid, valuable employees.

Lessons Learned

The design team at SuperConsultants learned several lessons during the process of building the escape room for the new employees. Leverage them as you design your own action-first escape room.

- **Create a realistic scenario.** Lidia and the team focused on realism and authenticity as they created the escape room. The theme and challenges closely resembled real-world consulting scenarios, which enhanced the relevance and impact of the learning experience. The new hires examined realistic documents in the same format and style they would soon encounter on the job.
- **Add touches of work culture.** When Lidia decided to include a menu from her firm's go-to take-out lunch place, everyone appreciated the highly specific touch. The new hires also got a peak at the environment in which they would soon be operating.
- **Test, iterate, and eliminate.** Conducting test runs with volunteers was essential to identifying the timing issue and helped Lidia and her team adjust or eliminate clues, puzzles, and

challenges to ensure the whole learning experience had the right level of difficulty and could be completed within the given time constraints. It can be difficult to eliminate a cleverly designed puzzle or clue, but just because you created it, doesn't mean you shouldn't cut it if it's too hard or takes too long to solve. The only way to determine what works and what doesn't is to test your escape room before opening it to the target group of learners. Iterating based on feedback from volunteers in pilot tests will ensure a smoother and more enjoyable experience for your learners.

Key Takeaways

Now that you're ready to create an action-first learning experience using an escape room, remember these tips:

- Escape rooms are quick but intense learning experiences that provide a significant instructional impact with minimal investment of the learner's time.
- Escape rooms can be physical or virtual action-first experiences. Virtual escape rooms can be especially effective for geographically dispersed teams.
- An escape room's story or theme is a vital component of the overall experience.
- A well-planned debriefing process is crucial to ensure that learners gain the desired knowledge or skills from the experience and don't just have fun!
- Working under pressure is a critical aspect of an escape room experience, helping learners who work in high-pressure situations improve their ability to thrive in those environments. Participants can also learn how to treat others when under pressure.
- Escape rooms help learners work on their observational skills, which are often difficult to teach in other ways.

- Escape rooms are effective for helping learners think in a nonlinear way because they allow learners to explore multiple possibilities and make connections between disparate ideas or objects. Nonlinear thinking is valuable for employees dealing with constantly evolving situations on the job.

EXPLANATION OF THE ACTION-FIRST ACTIVITY

Did you escape? How long did it take? What feelings did it evoke? How much fun or frustration did you encounter?

Action-first learning is about engaging learners in an activity and allowing them to experience and grapple with the task at hand as a method to spark learning and engagement—an escape room accomplishes all those goals. An escape room is an ideal setting for action-first learning because it places the learners directly into the action. If you don't act, you can't escape. You need to work with incomplete data, unknown answers, and an uncertain path forward. Going through an experience in which you need to escape (whether it's a book, cards, or a board game) provides you with the same feelings and experience that learners will encounter when they participate in your escape room design.

Record how you felt during the process, including what was frustrating and what worked well. Then, use the puzzles and experiences that went well as sparks for your own creativity to help you create an escape room learning experience.

Tool 4-1. Tips for More Effective Escape Room Learning Experiences

✓ Use fanciful or more realistic, business-focused themes depending on the tone you want to set and training goals. A more imaginative scenario, such as looking for hidden treasure, can be just as effective for learning as a more serious theme, such as reacting to a competitor introducing a new product.

✓ Always provide a wide variety of clues, challenges, and puzzles and vary the level of difficulty.

✓ When creating a virtual escape room, allot enough time for testing to ensure the virtual meeting software and escape room software can mesh as seamlessly as possible.

✓ Commercial escape rooms built for entertainment can provide effective instructional experiences if they're framed correctly for your learners.

5
Super Storytelling
Instructional Comics for Learning

Kevin Thorn
E-Learning Designer and Developer

We see the comic medium in its simplest form—a visual sequential narrative with simple icons and metaphors— every day conveying messages and instructing people about their behavior. For example, during the COVID-19 pandemic, three simple icons were used to change the behavior of an entire planet: a face mask, human silhouettes separated by a double arrow, and a hand under a faucet.

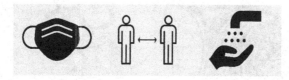

The icons instructed people to wear face masks in public, observe a minimum social distance of 6 feet (or 2 meters), and wash their hands. Icons like these are referred to as a visual narrative.

Now, take a minute to sketch a visual narrative about how to make a grilled cheese sandwich (use simple icons and minimal or no text). This is not about the art or being able to draw. It's about conveying a visual message. *(Find the explanation at the end of this chapter.)*

At the end of this chapter, you should be able to answer these questions:

- What elements make instructional comics effective for learning?
- What types of learning outcomes are best served by instructional comics?
- What design principles should you consider when designing comics for learning?
- What are some examples of comics used effectively for learning?

A group of 15 veteran warehouse workers gathered in their break room for a new training program. On tablets loaded with the training software, the workers watched a short, digital comic-style video about a hero called Captain Safety, who asked for their help in identifying, reporting, and eliminating safety hazards. The setting of the comic was strikingly familiar, with all the features of their warehouse—down to the placement of doors and the color of the forklifts. After laughing about Captain Safety's superhero costume, the facilitator put the workers into small groups. They were asked to list as many sources of back injuries in the warehouse as possible. Bonus points for illustrating the dangers with their own drawings!

When they rejoined the larger group, it became clear that three dangers topped everyone's list. After reporting back to Captain Safety on an interactive screen, the workers moved on to a new interactive video in which the captain asked for their help to stop the "villains" they'd identified as responsible for more than 90 percent of back injuries every year. While these three villains were exaggerated characters, all the workers represented in the video were familiar and real. By the end of the 55-minute activity, Captain Safety had exiled the villains, and every warehouse employee had practiced reporting potential injury hazards to managers. Even more importantly, they had learned and practiced safe lifting techniques to prevent injuries. In the following months, employees would invoke Captain Safety or one of the three villains as a reminder to co-workers to use proper lifting techniques. It was a low-conflict method of encouraging safe practices among peers and managers.

* * *

Instructional comics have been used for training as far back as the 19th century. In these visual stories, information, guidance, and educational content are presented through sequential art and narratives. Instructional comics combine elements of traditional comics—including panels, speech bubbles, and heroic and villainous characters—to share information and skills with learners. They often present complex topics in ways that are easier to understand than text alone, traditional lectures, or even slide presentations. And, their visual nature makes instructional comics practical tools for action-first learning.

Why Are Comics Effective as Learning Experiences?

Using comics as an action-first learning tool improves knowledge retention because they communicate information about complex topics in a simple, visual narrative format. Comics convey the authenticity of a problem or topic, demonstrate cultural representation, and transcend time and space, promoting connections and increasing knowledge and skill retention. This, in turn, helps encourage learning transfer. Comics accomplish these goals by presenting learners with a visual narrative with which they can connect directly and emotionally, especially if they can see themselves in the environment of the narrative or as one of the characters. And besides, who doesn't want to be a superhero?

Authenticity and Attention to Detail

Being *authentic* means being genuine, factual, and reliable. Designing authentic training is about more than just content or visual design; it also means having a cohesive overall approach. You may be familiar with a stock photo of a brightly lit conference room showing a table surrounded by a group of well-dressed people with giant smiles. If learners see a photo like this in a slide deck, they'll disengage immediately if it does not reflect the reality of their environment. When designing instructional comics, authenticity is one of the keys to effectiveness, but this requires research about the learners' environment and personas.

Authenticity and attention to detail lead to engagement, which, in turn, increases knowledge and skill retention. For example, imagine you are ditching the stock photos and designing a comic for your learners with a scene showing employees gathered for a meeting. Does the room have windows? Is the floor a hard surface or carpet? What color are the walls, and are they blank or covered in artwork or signs? Does the room have fixed whiteboards, a TV screen, a ceiling-mounted projector, or other hardware? Every detail matters—down to the placement of switches on the wall and which way the door swings open—because they ensure your instructional comic is seen as authentic. Without that realistic environment, learners will be less engaged.

Comics often use metaphorical visuals. For example, in the story at the beginning of this chapter, dangerous practices in the warehouse are represented as villains in human form. Attention to the essence of the concept being conveyed in these kinds of visuals is critical in many applications of instructional comics, such as supporting employees' mental health or keeping customers safe.

Relatability and Representation

To become successful action-first learning experiences, instructional comics—which are sometimes called "serious comics"—must consider learners' emotions and feelings and respect their identities. *Relatability*, or demonstrating an understanding of learners as people, helps us connect and engage with them. This is similar to how pursuing authenticity in a story's details creates a connection with the reader. Respectful visual representation of the learner's culture, nationality, and other markers of identity helps ensure the creation of an inclusive and effective narrative.

Many companies and organizations lack a style guide to help employees navigate and fairly represent company culture. Yet, when creating comic-focused learning experiences, it's just as important to understand the organization's culture in detail as it is to depict the details of the physical space. For example, if the learners in your audience wear company-branded uniforms, you should study the colors, logo position, style, and other features to represent them accurately. In multinational organizations, accurate representation may involve careful study of the range of employees' physical characteristics, culturally significant objects or rituals, differences between formal and informal dress, and much more. Relating to learners personally and respecting their cultural representation will ensure more engagement with the serious comic.

During the character design phase, artists often use culturally relevant research and photographic references, such as those shown in Figure 5-1.

Figure 5-1. Kevin Thorn uses photo references to sketch culturally relevant character designs for an instructional comic. *Source: Kevin Thorn. Used with permission.*

Transcending Time and Space

The educational effectiveness of instructional comics often depends on their ability to transcend time and space both in creation and conceptually. Other media can be limited by what is practically possible, with only a few poses for a digital character, a small special effects budget, or other physical, practical, or aesthetic constraints. Visual narratives in the comic medium are limited only by your imagination.

Let's consider the children's book and TV series *The Magic School Bus*, in which Ms. Frizzle transcends the ordinary world to take children on educational journeys that would be impossible in the real world. They travel through the human body or into a volcano or back in time. In this case, many more learning opportunities are possible in the comic medium than in a live-action production. Ms. Frizzle is not limited by time or space, and the magic school bus can take its passengers anywhere in its cartoon format.

Now, recall Captain Safety and the safety hazard villains as metaphorical characters from the opening of this chapter. The villain for proper lifting procedures is a fearsome, imposing character named Backbreaker, who carries a club. Anytime Backbreaker sees an employee performing improper lifting procedures, he hits them in the back, and they immediately feel pain. Backbreaker can travel throughout the organization and appear anywhere he's needed to reinforce good lifting practices.

Characters like Backbreaker, who embody a serious concept, can transport the learner into a fictional but familiar world. In this case, the villain demonstrates the real-life consequences of improperly lifting boxes in an effective way that doesn't require hiring actors and stunt coordinators or building elaborate sets. The visualization of the concept of back pain makes a more memorable impression than simply listing the consequences of improperly lifting boxes on a slide or paper handout. Think about your next training project as an instructional comic and imagine where you could take your learners if the sky were the limit.

An important element of transcending time and space is altering the learners' perspective when teaching them about complex concepts. Comics often use metaphorical characters to represent emotions when instructing learners in skills such as how to overcome fear or be more aware of their egos. For example, Figure 5-2 uses bugs to represent self-doubt, fear, and defensiveness.

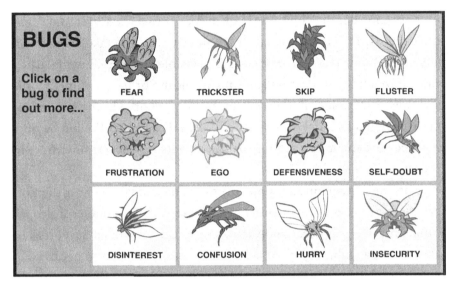

Figure 5-2. Instructional poster of emotions represented as bugs. *Source: Kevin Thorn. Used with permission.*

What Skills Can Comics Teach?

Comics leverage visual language to teach a variety of decision-making skills through visual recognition of colors, shapes, and patterns. The simple comic panel in Figure 5-3 shows a teacher asking a student to answer a math question while the student forms a mental image of counting on their fingers to find the sum.

Figure 5-3. In this two-panel comic, a teacher asks a student to do a math equation, and the student imagines counting on his fingers to come up with the correct answer. *Source: Art by Kevin Thorn for On Track Numeracy for Math Recovery Council. Used with permission.*

As a storytelling medium, comics can teach soft skills for deeper learning around empathy, self-efficacy, and other emotions. Comics also effectively teach abstract concepts, perspectives, and attitudes, such as situational awareness. And, like many other action-first learning experiences, comics are ideal for troubleshooting and emergency preparedness training.

Critical Thinking and Decision Making

Comics can provide an avenue for learners to experience critical thinking and decision making by visualizing the benefits of correct choices and the consequences of poor choices. Comics consistently demonstrate they can improve learners' confidence levels when making rapid decisions more readily than text-based media. For example, in the military, instructional comics can be used to help participants learn rapid decision making under pressure. Comics can also be an effective form of learning in healthcare, manufacturing, transportation, and other industries that require quick response times.

Emotional Empathy

Comics can enhance learners' understanding of how others feel. For example, in a scenario in which a healthcare provider is learning how to inform a patient they have been diagnosed with a serious illness, a comic-focused learning experience can be used to show what the patient hears in addition to what the provider says. The healthcare worker in the training course can then better understand and empathize with what the patient is going through. Comics often illustrate a character's internal dialogue, which is an effective way to show what another person is thinking but would never say aloud.

Self-Efficacy

Many learners lack confidence in their ability to execute specific behaviors on the job. In a positive, safe environment, comics can depict what it's like to fear failure and how to transcend that feeling. *Self-efficacy*, or confidence in your ability to control or influence outcomes, often depends on your perception of what others think. For example, a financial analyst who identifies a co-worker's costly error may fear retribution if they report it. A comic can visualize a cause-and-effect timeline of the error. During the learning experience, the analyst's supervisors could discuss ways that reporting errors will save the company money, helping the participants believe in their skills and capacities.

Situational Awareness

Comics use both dialogue and images to identify potential harm and make audiences more situationally aware. In the Golden Age comics of the 1940s and '50s, superheroes often perched above a skyline to spot and alert readers to potential danger. The illustrated landscape established the environment, and a dialogue bubble showed what the superhero said or thought. More recently, as I mentioned earlier in this chapter, images of masks, footprints, and soapy hands taught everyone to become more situationally aware of social distancing and the need to wash their hands to stop the spread of infection during the COVID-19 pandemic.

Diagnosing and Troubleshooting Problems

Narrative instructions in the form of flowcharts can aid learners in diagnosing and troubleshooting problems in software, machinery, and other physical tools, because the current and future state of a situation can be visualized, exposing potential challenges. For example, imagine a company is planning to build a new manufacturing plant that will create several hundred new jobs in a community where residents are concerned about noise, water, and air pollution. You could design an action-first learning comic that follows a new employee as they tour the future plant and explains the technology that will mitigate pollution. In this case, a comic will likely educate the local community more effectively than traditional corporate messaging.

Emergency Preparedness and Action

Everyone can benefit from instruction about emergency preparedness. A comic-focused learning experience offers a vast array of visual and illustrative styles to convey messages about what to do in case of emergencies.

For example, the typical airline safety card is a sequential visual narrative—a comic—that uses pictograms to instruct passengers about what to do if there's an emergency on board an airplane. One of the main benefits of comics is their ability to communicate universally across language and cultural barriers, as demonstrated in these safety cards, which are easily understood by passengers no matter what language they speak.

The Mechanics of Comics and Digital Storytelling

Comics leverage several theoretical constructs to guide their overall design and development. Visual Language Theory can help you consider the grammar of sequential visual narratives, the Cognitive Theory of Multimedia Learning reminds you that learners perceive information through two channels (their eyes and ears) and the principles of digital storytelling can guide you through proven development techniques (Cohn 2018; Cohn and Magliano 2020). The mechanics of digital comics also include the design decisions and digital assets you will need to develop your story, including various treatments, interactive elements, and animation effects.

Multimedia Elements

The first models of instructional comics that people usually think of are comic books, graphic novels, or comic-style television shows or movies. However, leveraging the digital realm and multimedia creates vast opportunities to convert an instructional comic into an interactive learning experience with sound, animation, and other interactive elements. For example, trainee sales associates in a home DIY retail store could interact with products visualized as metaphorical characters to learn about which tools would be most appropriate for different customers' needs.

The Cognitive Theory of Multimedia Learning suggests that we process information through auditory and visual channels, so it makes sense to leverage audio and graphics to maximize the learning experience. Spending more time in the design phase to sketch a scene and include notes in your storyboard regarding animation or motion, background music or sound effects, and audio dialogue is especially helpful for making learning more accessible (Figure 5-4).

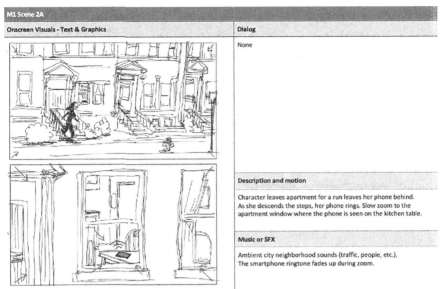

M1 Scene 2A	
Onscreen Visuals - Text & Graphics	**Dialog**
	None
	Description and motion
	Character leaves apartment for a run leaves her phone behind. As she descends the steps, her phone rings. Slow zoom to the apartment window where the phone is seen on the kitchen table.
	Music or SFX
	Ambient city neighborhood sounds (traffic, people, etc.). The smartphone ringtone fades up during zoom.

Figure 5-4. A sample storyboard scene with roughly sketched layouts of how the scene will look, move, and sound. *Source: Storyboard and art by Kevin Thorn. Used with permission by Artisan Learning*.

Taking extra care in the storyboard phase to ensure the design is appropriate, culturally relevant, and accurate will increase its educational value. Consider using the Scalable Vector Graphic (SVG) format when sourcing or creating visuals. SVG files allow for embedded text descriptions, metadata, and the ability to zoom and resize without losing quality.

Narrative audio alone doesn't set the mood or ambiance of a scene. Think of a time when you read a novel in which the author wrote a narrative description to establish the scene, explaining the environment, smells, tone, and mood. In a comic, you can write dialogue for a narrator that establishes the scene and sets the mood. The added benefit of a character narrator is ensuring all learners understand the comic's artistic style and that key elements are expressed clearly and unambiguously.

Digital Storytelling

Digital storytelling combines graphics, images, text, and sometimes audio narration or music to bring a narrative to life. Learners become actively engaged in the dialogue and pacing of the narrative. To support higher-order learning experiences—such as analyzing, evaluating, and creating—digital storytelling typically incorporates short-form videos focusing on content from various perspectives to communicate complex situations.

Stories are how we give meaning to our real-world experiences. Moreover, they are themselves shared experiences that inspire reflection and motivation. From a learning perspective, digital stories can provide explanations that require less passive reading. Within contextualized training, digital stories can also improve cause-and-effect reasoning and decision making. A comic's sequential nature helps learners move smoothly through the story's narrative.

Comics and Visual Language

Visual language is similar to written language in that when we think of the word "chair," the idea of how the letters look appears in our mind as something cognitive psychologists call a *schema*—or a mental representation of an object or concept. In the case of written language, it might be a schema or mental representation like "c.h.a.i.r." In visual language, the word "chair" is visualized in the mind as a mental image of a physical chair. We actually *see* an image of a chair when we read the word "chair" because we can summon previous knowledge (schema) of what it looks like. You're probably thinking of a chair now. I hope it's a comfy one.

Not only can we see a chair or other objects in our mind's eye, but the same concept also works for motion, like the flow of images, pictures, and diagrams. So, if I ask you to visualize going back in time, you might envision a blurry view of your current environment and then a fading, dissolving, or changing color tone, followed by a new clear image in front of you announcing your mental arrival back in time. Your ability to visualize how that mental visit to the past would look is a form of visual language.

When we combine traditional written language with visual language, we have a powerful structure for immersing learners in a story and helping them see patterns and predict what might occur next. The combination of written and visual language is an effective tool for action-first learning. Comics leverage our ability to visualize concepts, ideas, and objects and add meaning by providing a sequential narrative that we can follow and understand easily based on prior experience. An instructional sequential visual narrative can be as simple as a set of instructions for building flat-pack furniture or LEGO models, which use no words, only line drawings. Or it could be as complex as a set of visual cues from an embedded intelligence agent that indicates a community is in danger from a hostile group.

Let's Design an Instructional Comic

Instructional designers often claim they aren't artists or videographers and dismiss the notion of using the comic medium in their designs. Yet, much instructional and e-learning content today employs imagery in the form of graphics, audio for voice-overs, or videos produced by dedicated videographers. The design will dictate the type of comic art, and artists are as easy to find as other talented creators. Designing an instructional comic still requires the same instructional design process and good scriptwriting as other kinds of action-first learning experiences.

You can use stick figures and simple shapes to visualize your ideas during the storyboarding phase, similar to the way you might use stock photos and rudimentary graphics to explain instructional content. The animation industry has used this approach for more than 80 years as a way to test ideas before committing to creating artwork and moving on to full-scale production. A stick figure with a simple sketched scene and a brief explanation is typically all an artist needs to bring that scene to life. Many digital tools have a library of characters, objects, and environments to help you quickly lay out scenes.

Each training topic and situation will dictate your design flow and how you approach it, so there is no one-size-fits-all approach. Instead, consider the steps detailed here as design and development principles that you can adapt to your own workflow and organizational environment. You don't need to follow the order precisely. Designing and developing instructional comics blends art and science in an iterative process that requires fluidity, but the listed steps will lay the groundwork you need to get started on your action-first learning comic experience.

Step 1. Study Your Audience

Good instructional design begins with analyzing the audience, including the learners' context and personas. Take extra time to study and fully understand your learner population. Because comics are highly visual, learners will examine the smallest details for correctness. This is especially important when designing for multicultural audiences.

Step 2. Study the Environment

Environmental factors in instructional comics go beyond background imagery. Knowing where your learners work and their surrounding environment is important. For example, if you are designing a scene in which two characters meet in an open space at their workplace, you should understand the components of that environment. What kind of tables and chairs are in this space? What does the space's interior design look like? Sleek and modern or more traditional? Pay close attention to details such as light switches, door handles, and lighting. If feasible, do a location scouting trip and take photos for reference. If you can't travel to the location, ask others to take photos for you.

Step 3. Design the Story

Story design is an art as well as a science, and there are many approaches to good storytelling. The hero's journey, coming-of-age tales, and battles between good and evil are simple models you can follow. In comic-focused e-learning, most dialogue is written for a first-person narrator who is telling the learner about the content. An alternative would be to tell the same story through multiple perspectives, creating characters out of certain objects or abstract ideas like honesty or greed. Recall the introductory example of using comics to decrease safety claims. In that situation, safety hazards such as improperly lifting heavy objects became abstract characters who teamed up to disrupt the environment. At a training event for hardware store employees, a variety of hammers might debate which one is best for a specific customer's task.

Step 4. Develop Your Characters

Whether the characters are people, animals, things, or ideas, your goal is for learners to connect with and relate to them. To ensure you capture key details, create a design matrix that includes height, body type, skin tone, hairstyle, clothing, and accessories. If you were designing a phone company field technician character, you would need to decide their height and the type of clothing they wear on the job. Does this character need a hard hat and accessory belt? Details matter when it comes to continuity and consistency.

Step 5. Design the Interaction

Designing an instructional comic differs from designing an interactive digital comic for an e-learning activity. For example, in a static comic, a passive scene might show two characters talking with volleying dialogue. In an interactive comic, the learners might control the pace and appearance of the dialogue by interacting with each character's speech bubble. Interactive navigation allows learners to delay scenes and move at their own pace through a story. Think of it as a holistic experience that includes interacting with a navigation button, a button to play or pause media, and a button that initiates a choice. The key is to design a cohesive and balanced interactive experience.

Step 6. Design the Art

Designing the visuals for your comic starts with choosing a style. This can be overwhelming, so remember that the style needs to support the context of the instruction and should be informed by your analysis of the content, characters, and environment. An illustrative style is the simplest to create, and you can use digital tools to convert photos to that style. If you create custom art, choose a style that will enhance the overall mood and tone of the story, and don't be afraid to mix disparate genres and styles. For example, using the superhero genre but set in Bollywood or a detective story that leverages the steampunk style. This can be the most creative and time consuming phase of the design process, so plan extra time.

Step 7. Review for Accessibility

Ensure that you have included cues and descriptions of characters and environments in the narrative and respect accurate representation of the learners' cultures. Font choice is key for those with reading disabilities such as dyslexia. Comic Sans is known as one of the best comic-style fonts for dyslexia because it has fewer repeated letter shapes, which makes the letters easier to distinguish. When using speech bubbles, provide sufficient contrast and thick borders so the text stands out from other visual elements. Ensure all elements are discoverable and navigable using different inputs, such as a touch screen, keyboard, and mouse.

Step 8. Test Early and Often!

In addition to traditional e-learning, which has project timeline milestones, designing instructional comics should also include multiple release dates. Plan for a release schedule that includes the story draft and additional revisions. In addition, use a character development release schedule along with early character model sketches to refine their look and feel. When you're happy with both the story and the characters, assemble a storyboard with instructional context, scene design, navigational path, and other elements. Depending on your workflow, several of these releases can run in parallel with the main storyboard phase as a dependency of the others. The additional artwork involved in a comic project requires planning extra time to manage the overall design and production. Testing each phase with a pilot group of learners will ensure its accuracy and relevance.

AI Assist

If you are just getting started with instructional comic digital storytelling, don't worry about the art or style; you can hire a talented artist when the time comes. A vital aspect of designing an instructional comic is developing the characters. You can leverage AI tools for this task, allowing you to generate simple, minimalistic characters for initial storyboard designs. You can also use a variety of AI art tools to help create first drafts of characters.

In this example, the following prompt was entered into the AI tool OpenArt to create an image of a female character talking on a phone (Figure 5-5). You can substitute your own information in the brackets.

```
Create a [minimal black-and-white icon] of a [woman
talking on a smartphone], [SVG], [flat minimal line
vector design], and [white background].
```

Figure 5-5. An AI-generated black-and-white image of a woman talking on a smartphone. *Source: Image generated with OpenArt's DALL-E.*

Sometimes, you may need multiple poses and expressions for the same character in different settings. At the time of this writing, AI tools still have trouble generating the same attributes for several outputs of the same character. Try this prompt, substituting your own information for the information in square brackets:

```
Create three minimal black-and-white illustrations of
the same [elderly man]. In the first icon, the man is
[entering a hospital]. In the second image, the man is
[greeting a male nurse]. In the third image, the man
is [having his blood pressure checked by the nurse].
```

Case Study: Nursing Simulation Training in India

This case study is based on a project I carried out in partnership with nonprofits funded by the Gates Foundation. The details of the project are briefly summarized here.

In late 2018, a research university that had partnered with nonprofit organizations funded by the Gates Foundation recruited me for a project to reduce infant mortality rates in low-income, low-literacy populations. From 2019 through the end of 2022, I worked with an international team to design and develop a scalable solution that increased retention and knowledge transfer. The solution was an instructional interactive digital comic story about two college nursing students who had completely different experiences and points of view. After graduation, they separated to begin their careers. Divya vowed to create a compassionate and caring learning environment for all who followed her and later became known as Super Divya. Agni, however, vowed to disrupt learning environments to dissuade others from choosing a career in nursing, and she became known as Professor Agni. Figure 5-6 shows the cover art for the first episode of the digital comic, *The Adventures of Super Divya and Professor Agni*, which detailed their origin story.

Figure 5-6. Cover art for episode 1 of the instructional comic *The Adventures of Super Divya and Professor Agni. Source: Kevin Thorn. Used with permission.*

Nursing training often takes place in person in a simulated clinical environment. These simulations allow the student nurses to fail in a safe space. The brief for this project was to explore innovative ways to improve and augment nurses' obstetrics training, and the result of the collaboration was a comics-focused action-first learning experience based on video recordings of simulations and debriefings.

The Challenge

About 700 female nurses from Bihar, India, attended a multiday video simulation-based train-the-trainer program to become nurse facilitators in obstetric care. After the training event, the nurses returned to their home clinics to disseminate the information to others as nurse facilitators. Bihar is a low-resource, low-literacy region where facilitators use various techniques to ensure knowledge and skills retention. Unfortunately, after taking their course with a video simulation, many of the nurses reverted to pretraining practices within a few months, creating a lack of consistency in procedures. The challenge for instructional designers was to create a novel approach that was more relatable, scalable across the region, and communicated effectively to a low-literacy audience.

Why Instructional Comics?

The trainers had a successful simulation training program in place and believed that adding an asynchronous, interactive instructional comic would bring additional benefits. The first benefit would be that the digital story could reach a wider audience and add more nurses to the program with little additional effort.

The second benefit would be that nurses could interact with the characters in the story as often as they wanted, retaking the lessons multiple times. In this way, simulation participants could connect with the characters and scenarios on a deeper level, leading to higher retention.

The episodic lessons depicted real-life scenarios, but the third benefit was that the digital space meant incorrect choices were met with positive, helpful feedback, rather than dire consequences. These interactive practice scenarios fostered critical thinking, encouraged self-efficacy, and bonded the learners as peers. They all understood the consequences in real life would be much more serious.

Last, by crafting a story of real-life scenarios in a visual environment that respected cultural representation, nurse participants were much more engaged when attending live simulation training. They could explore each of the 10 episodes in sequence as a complete story or in any order they chose to refresh their knowledge about specific tasks based on the learning objectives. Feedback showed that the comic had connected with learners, who shared that they could see themselves in the story. A few said they wanted to work hard to be more like the protagonist!

Making the Case

The project lead and researchers knew that pitching a digital instructional comic was risky. The comic medium requires more time and logistical planning due to the amount of artwork and digital assets that need to be created, and it is often perceived as much more expensive than traditional asynchronous learning programs as a result. The project team prepared by analyzing costs associated with scheduling, travel, and attending in-person simulation training. They discovered that the cost of designing and developing an instructional comic would be far less than holding multiple in-person simulation training sessions per year. They were also confident that this innovative approach would improve knowledge and skills retention.

The team explained to stakeholders that after the initial investment, a digital instructional comic was scalable at no additional cost, and they'd save money if nurses didn't have to travel to training sites. The instructional comic would be deployed before and after live simulation training sessions. As a result, nurses attending live training would have pre-existing knowledge on which to build, and after live training, the instructional comic would become a job aid for review.

After presenting all their data and a persuasive argument, the project team received full approval.

The Solution

The audience of nurses was surveyed about potential designs for the instructional comic, and they chose a superhero genre in Bollywood style. The story follows Divya and Agni, two nurses who were college roommates and best friends. After college, they went their separate ways to begin their careers. Divya, the protagonist, recalled an enriching experience during her schooling and vowed to ensure that more nurses had the same experience. Agni, the antagonist, had the opposite experience and vowed to disrupt the training of other nurses to dissuade them from choosing a nursing career.

Divya, later known as Super Divya, designed advanced tools in her lab to help new nursing facilitators overcome anything that stood in the way of successful training. Agni, later known as Professor Agni, developed synthetic metaphorical insects—including *fear*, *disappointment*, and *hurry*—sending them swarming into the simulation training event whenever Super Divya was teaching.

Each episode began with Professor Agni describing her excitement about a new bug she had created—declaring with villainous glee that this bug would finally end simulation training for all nurses. Super Divya would then reveal a new tool to eliminate each new bug and bring back the nurses' confidence in training. The end of each episode showed Divya flanked by Professor Agni, who was hanging her head in defeat—but with a hint of a diabolical grin as she considered plans for her next attack.

The character designs in this instructional comic related to the learners both culturally and personally thanks to the believable, although exaggerated, story. The interactive story leveraged reusable learning objects in new and creative ways to support a low-literacy audience and implemented interactive scaffolding practice with visuals that foreshadowed obstacles and guided the learners in a well-structured case for good decision making and problem solving.

Benefits and Results

Using comics to communicate about serious and complex topics significantly improves knowledge retention. The benefits of the comic medium include a low barrier to entry in regions with a low-literacy audience and low-fidelity deployment.

Leveraging instructional comics to teach observation and soft skills to nurse facilitators led to significant improvements for those who participated. The comic increased self-confidence, self-reflection, and self-awareness. The results also showed an 82 percent overall increase in retention and a 15 percent increase in overall knowledge transfer (Kalra et al. 2022).

Before training, participants said they were not confident in their current ability to perform the tasks. The most significant result after experiencing the instructional comic and attending simulation training was a 67 percent increase in self-confidence scores (Steil et al. 2020). Research also supports the use of instructional comics for serious topics in retention, knowledge transfer, and self-efficacy improvements (Whiting 2020).

Lessons Learned

The overall lessons learned during this project were to shorten the length of the instructional comics, pay close attention to the relatable details of the characters, and thoroughly research the technological infrastructure of the regional environment. In addition:

- **Shorter modules are more effective.** The initial pilot design was a two-module course with an average 45-minute seat time per learner. Although there was a high degree of feedback, the module was too long and had zero impact on retention scores. Based on this information, the entire format was redesigned into 10, 15-minute episodes. The second pilot release showed improvements in retention scores. They also leveraged spatial learning by releasing one episode at a time.

- **Details matter in designing relatable characters.** Character design was the most challenging phase of the overall project. Because the artist came from a different culture, they had to do extensive research and pay careful attention to detail. The smallest details mattered, including skin tones, jewelry, and clothing.
- **It's important to understand technological limits, especially in low-income regions.** Using technology in a low-resource environment was challenging because broadband speeds in the region were equivalent to older dial-up modem speeds. Early testing led to a change in the deployment plan from hosting the episodes on a server with access via an internet connection to publishing the episodes on portable drives for offline access. The evaluation plan also had to be redesigned because this technology pivot eliminated the ability to capture real-time data.

Key Takeaways

Now that you're ready to create an action-first learning experience using a comic, remember these tips:

- Authenticity begets engagement, which leads to an increase in retention. Achieving authenticity in a comics-based learning experience requires research about the learners' environment that goes beyond learner personas.
- Comics can transcend time and space by exploring alternative perspectives in storytelling and transporting learners into fictional worlds that are often believable enough to be real.
- Comics have no limits in terms of what they can portray. They can convey anything from the nuances of abstract ideas to diverse cultural representations to intense emotions. They can also leverage universal design to address details that are difficult to capture in other media.

- Comics can increase learners' awareness, deepen meaning, and challenge critical thinking skills.
- Using images in sequential narratives, comics leverage the same schematic knowledge patterns that people usually recognize in writing.
- Through stories, humans create meaning from their experiences and learn to make decisions, which is why they can become helpful tools for teaching causal reasoning.
- Digital storytelling requires less cognitive effort than exposition because of the narrative framing of an experience.

EXPLANATION OF THE ACTION-FIRST ACTIVITY

Show your iconic sequence to a friend or family member and see if they can identify that you are trying to show how to make a grilled cheese sandwich. Actual artwork aside, did the sequence make sense? Do you see the importance of order, sequence, and simplicity of message? This can help you think about distilling complex processes into simple, universally understandable icons to create visual comics that promote clarity and efficiency. As an instructional designer, you will discover that visual storytelling is a tool for creating clear, concise, and engaging visual content.

Tool 5-1. Tips for Effective Comics-Based Action-First Learning

✓ Build in extra time during the planning process to carefully consider character attributes to ensure cultural representation.

✓ Create characters that learners can relate to, which will increase learner connection and engagement.

✓ Study the learner environment and pay close attention to physical details so learners recognize the comic environment as an authentic space.

✓ Leverage the power of the comic medium and strive to design wordless pictures.

6
Choose Your Path
Branching Scenarios for Learning

The advent of voice-activated AI and natural language interfaces make it possible to create a voice-based conversation with an AI character that has almost unlimited branching and built-in feedback. To experience how this works, you'll need an AI tool that accepts audio input, which is typically a mobile app downloaded to your smartphone.

If you haven't already, download ChatGPT or another AI mobile app. Then, initiate the role play through the voice interface using a verbal prompt. Say to your AI assistant, "I'd like to conduct a sales role-play scenario. I'd like you to act as a potential client. I will be a salesperson attempting to sell you an e-learning solution. You are interested but a bit reluctant. When I say, 'Stop role-playing,' you will evaluate how well I conducted myself during the sales process. I'd like you to start now." Then, enjoy the discussion. *(Find an explanation at the end of this chapter.)*

At the end of this chapter, you should be able to answer these questions:
- What elements make branching scenarios effective for learning?
- What type of learning outcomes are best for branching scenarios?
- What basic design principles should you consider when designing branching scenarios for learning?
- What are some examples of branching scenarios for learning?

Priya was staring at her computer screen, engrossed in a branching scenario designed to help her navigate difficult conversations as a manager. This scenario presented a particularly challenging situation: providing

BRANCHING SCENARIOS

constructive feedback to Damire, a great employee, who had just made a mistake that cost the company $100,000.

One option was to address the issue head-on. She could schedule a meeting with Damire and calmly explain the mistake and its implications. Another option was to discuss the mistake in a team meeting without singling out Damire, initiating a more general discussion about mistakes. A third option was to ignore the mistake altogether. And, her final option was to fire Damire, which she eliminated right away. She then narrowed her choices and made her decision: Have a one-on-one meeting with Damire.

As the scenario continued to unfold, Priya watched the consequences of her choice play out. She saw that speaking to her employee privately led to a more open and honest dialogue, helping to resolve the issue and strengthen their working relationship.

She was pleased but couldn't help wondering what would have happened if she had mentioned the mistake in the team meeting. She clicked back in the scenario and selected the team meeting choice—it did not go well. The results were confusion, frustration, and mistrust among the team members. The scenario provided feedback about why the team meeting was the wrong choice, highlighting the importance of clear, direct, and personal communication in difficult situations.

By the end of the scenario, Priya had gained valuable insights about how to handle difficult conversations as a manager. She had learned that the most difficult conversations can be the most important ones to have, and that being honest and transparent with team members is the key to fostering a culture of growth and development. Armed with this knowledge, Priya felt more confident in her ability to manage similar situations in the future, relying on the branching scenario training as a guide.

✹ ✹ ✹

A branching scenario allows the learner to become part of a story that includes many opportunities to choose certain paths or solutions over others. As the learner progresses through the learning experience, they are required to make decisions based on what is happening within the scenario's story. Providing an array of choices and forcing the learner to decide which option is best develops the knowledge and skills they can use when confronted with a comparable situation in real life.

In a branching scenario designed for learning, some choices will be correct, some may be incorrect, and some will be neutral. The learner decides which branch, or path, to take through the scenario, and each branch results in a different outcome. The decisions force the learner to become active, always making a choice before moving forward. They can't passively sit back and daydream or wait until an answer is provided. They must commit to a decision.

The consequences of each decision become evident once the learner commits to their choice. Because it's a fictional scenario, time can be accelerated or slowed down, which means consequences that might normally take months will be clear right away. For example, in a scenario for project managers in the construction industry, a learner might decide to cut costs by using a cheaper grade of steel. A branching scenario can accelerate time to show how this choice would eventually lead to a structural failure requiring expensive redesign and repair. In the real world, the material's weakness might take months to manifest, but in the scenario, it would take only a few minutes. In another kind of scenario, a learner might opt to push a web design team to work overtime to meet a deadline, only to discover the long-term consequences are a decline in morale, increased errors due to fatigue, and high turnover among team members.

Well-designed branching scenarios force each learner to solve problems and think critically while providing behavioral and contextual cues. The environment, characters, and situation should be as realistic as possible in the scenario so the learner is better prepared to interpret and respond when faced with a similar real-world situation. By experiencing a branching scenario, the learner builds expertise in an environment where mistakes don't cost money, customers, or employee morale.

Why Are Branching Scenarios Effective for Learning?

Branching scenarios are effective because they simulate real-life decision making and consequences within a controlled, safe environment. By presenting learners with different choices, branching scenarios encourage critical thinking, problem solving, and the application of knowledge in context. They also accelerate the building of expertise because learners can practice repeatedly in a controlled environment with targeted feedback. Let's consider several key reasons branching scenarios make great action-first learning experiences.

Immersing Learners

Within a branching scenario, learners participate in immersive decision-making processes that closely mirror real-life situations. They can't passively watch what's happening on a screen; they must constantly respond and make choices. The learners are genuinely part of an unfolding story in which their decisions alter the outcome.

The interactive structure of a branching scenario engages learners more deeply than many other kinds of training. They can feel as invested in the consequences of their choices as they would in a real workplace scenario, such as the one presented in Figure 6-1.

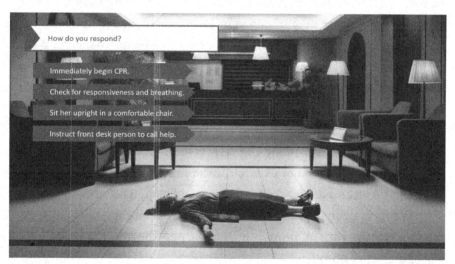

Figure 6-1. How would you respond? You come across a person passed out in the lobby and must make a choice quickly in this branching scenario, which is designed to teach emergency response techniques to hotel employees. *Source: Image courtesy of Karl M. Kapp.*

Simulating Real-Life Challenges

In everyday work situations, employees constantly make decisions. Can I offer a refund to this customer? Should I accept or reject this insurance claim? Is it a mistake to scold my best performer when they continually arrive late to work? Do I ask the next question or let the client speak? How do I handle this emergency?

Learning how to properly act and react at critical times (such as in an emergency) or in more mundane activities (such as in conversations with customers, clients, and employees) is critical to individual and organizational success. An e-learning module or classroom lecture can teach the best steps to take, but it's different when you must apply that knowledge on the spot in unique situations. Branching scenarios bridge that gap, allowing learners to practice applying knowledge in a realistic setting with realistic characters and then—crucially—to observe and react to the consequences of their decisions.

Highlighting Delayed Effects

In real life, cause and effect are sometimes separated by weeks, months, or even years. It may take months for the effects of a poor decision, such as taking a shortcut in manufacturing a car or airplane, to catch up with company decision makers. Sometimes cause and effect are so far removed that it's hard to know which action or decision was most directly related to a bad outcome.

Branching scenarios can help learners understand the dynamics of cause and effect because time can be accelerated to quickly show the results of a poor decision. For example, in a branching scenario designed to train physician assistants, skipping one small step in a standard protocol for patient care can lead to a series of events that culminate in a negative outcome for the patient, reinforcing for learners the importance of adhering to the proper protocol.

Making Mistakes Safely

No one wants to make a mistake in front of a customer or client, especially if the life of a co-worker or patient or thousands or millions of dollars are on the line. In a branching scenario, learners can make mistakes safely without worrying about real-world consequences. In the controlled setting of a branching scenario, learners have the freedom to experiment, take risks, and explore different outcomes without fearing real-world repercussions. Instead, mistakes become learning opportunities.

A CEO might decide to invest heavily in the marketing department of their company, only to realize later that this unbalanced approach hampers critical areas like product development and customer service. A mistake like this, if made during a branching scenario focused on long-term leadership strategies, can lead to valuable real-time feedback and new insights. The learner could analyze where their decision making went awry and how to bring balance to their business plan. The ability to safely make mistakes and then try again is one of the biggest strengths of branching scenarios as action-first learning tools.

What Can Branching Scenarios Teach?

Branching scenarios are an exceptionally dynamic action-first technique. They teach a range of skills and concepts essential for professional growth and effective decision making. By presenting learners with a series of decisions and their consequent paths, branching scenarios replicate the complexity of real-world situations. The learner's active engagement in problem solving and decision making helps hone their skills like critical thinking, judgment, communication, leadership, and empathy.

Decision Making

Decision making is the most obvious and important skill learners practice in branching scenarios. We make multiple critical decisions each day, but we rarely have a chance to practice or get feedback on our decision-making skills. How can we grow and improve professionally without feedback and practice?

Branching scenarios provide immediate, clear feedback, which allows learners to see the direct results of their actions. An immediate feedback loop is crucial for learning and improving decision-making skills because learners can see the impact of their choices and adjust strategies accordingly—then go back to practice more variations around a particular skill.

Using digital branching scenarios, a company can invest time, money, and energy in developing experiences that can then be scaled easily and inexpensively to train as many people as many times as necessary.

Empathy

Branching scenarios based on emotional narratives, characters, and situations can leverage the *affective domain*, or emotional aspect, of learning. A scenario in a healthcare setting might involve interacting with a patient who has a specific medical and personal background. As the learner makes a series of decisions, they quickly see the direct impact on the patient's health and emotional well-being. In another scenario, a learner might have to adopt a patient's persona to observe how casual comments or ill-timed help by a healthcare professional influences their mental health. Both types of scenarios would provide the learner with a deeper sense of empathy for the learner's patients.

Branching scenarios are uniquely effective for teaching empathy and fostering emotional connections because they can place learners in another person's shoes, prompting them to experience and better understand different perspectives. In any well-designed branching scenario, learners will encounter situations in which they must make decisions based on not only logic or policy but also on the emotional and personal impact of their choices.

Self-Reflection and Self-Assessment

An instructional element of branching scenarios that is sometimes overlooked is that they allow learners to stop and think about the challenges they face.

In a real-life situation, we often rush to make a decision. In a branching scenario, on the other hand, we can usually take our time to consider our options. We can stop at each decision point to ponder outcomes, predict what might happen based on a particular answer, and then consider alternative perspectives as we determine the most appropriate choice.

This means that as learners, we can reflect and assess our motives, responses, and biases as we progress through multiple branches and decision points. When we take time to reflect upon our decisions and ponder possible results, we are improving our self-reflection and self-assessment skills—two of the most valuable soft skills for leaders and employees.

Situational Awareness

Situational awareness is a person's capacity to recognize and assess a situation, collect pertinent data, evaluate it critically, and choose the best course of action to mitigate any risks or challenges that may arise. In short, situational awareness allows us to observe and interpret our surroundings accurately. Branching scenarios are effective tools for teaching situational awareness because learners can be placed in an environment where they must observe, interpret, and react to a variety of cues and unfolding events. When they take action, they are then evaluated on how well they observed and interpreted the simulated environment.

Branching scenarios also allow learners to experience the consequences of *reduced* situational awareness. For instance, someone might miss a critical warning sign in a scenario about workplace safety that leads to an injury, emphasizing the importance of vigilance and attention to detail.

Diagnosis and Troubleshooting

Branching scenarios can be designed to simulate the intricate process of diagnosing and fixing problems. For example, you could present learners with a malfunctioning piece of recording equipment and a set of symptoms and then ask them to diagnose the specific problem by choosing between various methods for testing and analysis. You might also ask them to decide which tools to use when presented with the problem, which parts to replace, or which adjustments to make. Each decision would lead to different outcomes and reveal new information or additional challenges.

Many branching scenarios in medical fields ask learners what tests should be requested for a patient with particular symptoms, what the correct diagnosis would be, and what course of treatment would be the most appropriate. Branching works in these situations because the learner can return to the decision point and try again if they're incorrect. In the process, they'll learn the right questions to ask and which tests to run next time.

Sales Skills

Sales training programs often include branching scenarios as part of the instructional package because they effectively teach sales skills. Branching scenarios simulate the dynamic and interactive nature of real sales situations, allowing a sales professional to work on their decision-making abilities, communication skills, and overall effectiveness in closing deals. In a typical sales interaction, the outcome is heavily influenced by how they handle various customer responses and objections. Branching scenarios replicate this by presenting learners with a simulated sales conversation in which they must make choices at key points in the dialogue. Sales people can experiment with different techniques and strategies in a risk-free environment.

Branching Scenario Mechanics

When creating a branching scenario, we can use essential design principles and concepts to maximize the learning experience. The choices can be text based or audio based using AI. In an audio interaction, AI generates responses for the other characters, allowing the learner to engage in a realistic conversation. This type of branching scenario is growing in popularity as more e-learning tools incorporate AI. Regardless of the interaction between the learner and the branching scenario system, the following design principles apply.

Leverage Multimedia Elements

Think beyond silent, still images of two people talking by carefully using multimedia elements to create the environment, mood, and narrative you're seeking. Consider using images, graphs, charts, and animations to illustrate the concepts. For example, in a branching scenario designed for emergency response training, you might include an animated map showing how a fire spreads in a building, the location of all exits, and which ones are blocked by fire or debris. This visual aid helps learners better understand the urgency and scale of the situation.

Visual cues can be used to represent characters' emotions or reactions, adding depth to the narrative and enhancing the learner's empathy and understanding. To increase the sense of urgency, you could consider adding the sound of a door slamming to signify an angry person in a negotiation scenario or the background noise of an ambulance in a medical emergency scenario. Involve as many of the learner's senses as you can to immerse them deeply and make each scenario as authentic as possible. Of course, you always want to keep accessibility issues in mind, so don't rely solely on sound to convey information. Refer to chapter 11 for more detailed information about accessibility.

Provide Nuanced Choices

Our choices are rarely obvious in most professional dilemmas; we have to make trade-offs and compromises and balance a variety of factors. If all the answers in a branching scenario are obvious, learners will lose interest. You'll want to incorporate nuanced choices in any scenario you create.

Nuanced choices force learners to think critically and analyze deeply, considering multiple points of view before deciding what to do. When learners must explore different pathways to see the consequences of their actions, they gain a deeper understanding of the subject matter and greater self-awareness. They often reflect on their personal values, biases, and decision-making styles. In a training scenario for physicians, for instance, the learners might need to choose how to communicate sensitive information to a patient. The scenario could allow them to explore several communication styles to see how each one affects the patient's understanding of the prognosis and emotional response. The results would be better communication skills for the physicians, greater empathy, and more patient-centered care.

Build in Reflection Points

We can't take for granted that learners will stop to reflect on their own. So, we need to strategically place reflection points at key moments in a scenario, such as after significant decisions or outcomes or at the end of the experience. At each reflection point, you should prompt learners with thought-provoking questions that encourage them to examine the reasoning behind their choices, as well as the effectiveness and emotional and practical implications of those choices.

You should also provide feedback and insights at these reflection points. The feedback, which could include expert analysis or additional insights, should help the learner understand and learn from the broader implications of their decisions. Encourage self-assessment by allowing learners to evaluate their performance and understanding.

The pauses should include time for emotional and intellectual reflection. You can ask learners to consider how the characters in the scenario might feel or how their mental health could be affected by decisions made within the scenario. Consider including opportunities for learners to take notes or create a learning journal. Another option in larger training programs is to form smaller group debrief sessions or asynchronous chats. These groups or chats can be incredibly valuable, offering a space for learners to share experiences and learn from one another.

Keep Branching as Simple as Possible (But Not Too Simple!)

Carefully balance the number of decision points and the complexity of the branching. Some novice designers create overly complex scenarios, which can lead to frustration for learners and cost overruns for the organization. Learners can find it difficult to track the consequences of their choices if there are too many branches, resulting in diminished learning outcomes. On the other hand, too few branches might oversimplify the scenario and make it uninteresting for learners.

Effective branching scenario design means ensuring that each decision point is meaningful and effective. Every branch should offer a unique learning opportunity and contribute to your overall learning objectives. Never add branches for the sake of complexity, but carefully consider how each decision and its consequences add value to the learning experience and your desired learning outcome.

Let's Design a Branching Scenario for Learning

Designing a branching scenario is not as difficult as it seems. You can sketch out initial designs and storylines using simple paper and pencil or sticky notes, and markers to draw lines linking branches. A paper-first approach allows for easy modification and refinement of the scenarios. Designers can even cover an entire wall or whiteboard with sticky notes to visualize how each decision within a branch links to the next. If you prefer not to go "old school" with sticky notes and whiteboards, you can use digital tools to help design, plan, create, and distribute branching scenarios. Some options include:

- Adobe Captivate
- Articulate Storyline (Rise also has some branching)
- BranchTrack
- Colossyan
- ELB Learning Lectora
- iSpring Authoring Tool
- Near-Life Platform
- The Regis Company Simulation Platform
- Synthesia
- Vyond

Now we'll review 10 basic design steps for creating a branching scenario. Remember, you'll often need to blend different stages, revisit previous ones, or contemplate multiple branches simultaneously. This is an iterative and sometimes messy process, but by following these steps, you'll lay an effective foundation for your branching scenario.

Step 1. Define Your Instructional Goal

Determine what learners should achieve by the end of the scenario. Break the goal into teachable subgoals, which could be a series of decision points within the scenario or a branch of the scenario. You may want to consider more than one goal at a time, such as a knowledge application goal *and* an emotional goal. For example, if you're teaching project managers how to resolve team conflicts, the instructional objective requires learners to apply their knowledge of conflict resolution techniques, communication strategies, and team dynamics. The goal may also require empathy and emotional understanding of teammates. The knowledge application goal and emotional or affective domain goal are both at work in this objective.

Step 2. Create the Setting, Environment, and Characters

Branching scenarios should be based on real or highly realistic fictional situations. To convince learners they are in a real situation, you need to identify the types of people in the setting, what they would be doing, their titles, and their points of interaction with the learner. Ensure you have the most effective sights and sounds to immerse the learner in the scenario. The more realistic the branching scenario, the more likely a learner will behave as they would in a real-world situation instead of trying to outthink or outguess the design.

Step 3. Create the Correct Path First

Establishing the correct path first will help create a sturdy foundation for developing decision points and less-optimal branches. It also helps ensure a focused narrative and that your key learning objectives will be met.

Step 4. Create Alternative Branches

After your correct path is established, it's time to create alternative branches. These should realistically represent the kinds of mistakes learners might make or misconceptions they would have in a real-world situation. By integrating these wrong choices in the scenario, you expose learners to a broader range of potential outcomes, fostering a more comprehensive understanding of the subject matter.

Base your alternatives on common errors. For example, in a medical training scenario, alternative branches could include the most common diagnostic errors or misconceptions about treatment options. In a business negotiation scenario, you might include typical pitfalls like miscommunication or misunderstanding terms. Your alternative branches should challenge learners to think critically and apply their knowledge to identify and correct mistakes.

Step 5. Determine How to Give Feedback

There are two main types of feedback in a branching scenario. *Realistic feedback* is the kind that would naturally occur in a real situation, such as a customer smiling when the learner tells them they are getting a refund. *Artificial feedback* is only visible to the learner because they are in a branching scenario. An example of artificial feedback is a *mood meter*, which indicates the general disposition of a character, such as happy, sad, angry, or puzzled (Figure 6-2). It sends a clear message about how the character in the scenario is reacting to the learner's choices.

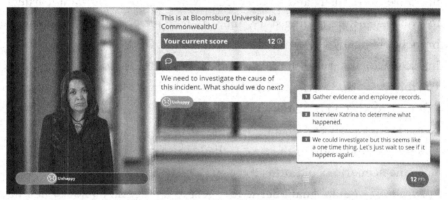

Figure 6-2. The mood meter for the character in this scenario indicates she is unhappy. Choosing the correct answer can improve her mood. *Source: Branching scenario created with the Branch Track tool. Image courtesy of Karl M. Kapp.*

After deciding on the type of feedback, determine if it should be delayed or immediate. *Immediate feedback* occurs the moment a learner makes a wrong decision and might tell them to start over or redirect them to make another choice. *Delayed feedback* usually comes during a debrief after the learner completes the entire scenario and might include a summary of the decisions the learner made and whether or not they were good.

Step 6. Create Reflection Points

Remember, you want learners to reflect on all the decisions they've made during a branching scenario. One option is to create strategic reflection points with thought-provoking questions that are outside the story the learner is experiencing. Or, you could also let the characters in the scenario ask questions that require the learner to reflect at several key points, or you could include a longer reflection at the end of the scenario. For example, a reporter might enter to ask the learner about their experience. What's most important is that multiple reflection points are integrated into every branching scenario to maximize learning.

Step 7. Ensure Narrative Cohesion

You have created a story, characters, decision points, and correct and incorrect pathways through the scenario. Now, it's time to ensure that the narrative flows easily and all the pieces work together. You want learners to experience an engaging story, and you need to verify that all paths and branches logically flow from the main narrative. For example, in a branching scenario about how to set up a massive crane on a construction site, you might ask the learner to first determine the best location for the crane. After correctly choosing the location, the learner might be given choices related to properly stabilizing the crane with crane mats, outrigger pads, or some combination of the two. If the learner makes choices that aren't safe, the scenario could offer the option to repeat the stabilization step. However, it wouldn't make sense to revert to the decision about where to place the crane, because that step was completed successfully. Go through all branches of your scenario to see if you need to correct any logical errors in sequencing. Make sure the sequence of events naturally and logically moves from one decision to another.

Step 8. Address Accessibility

Ensure that your branching scenario is as accessible as possible by following these tips:

- **Verify that the online branching scenario is fully compatible with screen readers, which are essential for visually impaired users.** All text—including instructions, feedback, and branching options—should be screen-reader friendly.
- **Include descriptive alt-text for images and meaningful link text.** If possible, the scenario should be navigable using a keyboard alone, with a logical tab order and accessible controls.

This means ensuring that all interactive elements, like buttons for making choices in the scenario, are operable without a mouse. Providing keyboard shortcuts for common actions can enhance usability.

- **If the branching scenario includes audio or video elements, you should include closed-captioning.** Captions should accurately reflect spoken dialogue, choices the learner needs to make, and other relevant sounds. Descriptions should be included in the audio track or provided as a separate, optional track. This ensures that all users have equal access to the media's informational content.

- **To accommodate users with cognitive or motor disabilities—and everyone else—ensure that the design of your branching scenario is clear, intuitive, and free of unnecessary complexity.** Avoid time-limited tasks or provide the option to extend time limits, which can be a barrier for some learners. You may also consider a mechanism that gives users hints or help.

Step 9. Test and Iterate

Develop a prototype of your scenario and test it with a sample group of the target audience. Use their feedback to refine and improve the scenario before a large-scale launch. This will help you catch any gaps in logic or ineffective or incorrect branches.

Step 10. Release and Track Progress

Release the branching scenario to your pool of learners and check to ensure it's being properly completed. Monitor any problems with the larger group of learners.

AI Assist

The following prompt can help generate content for a branching scenario using an AI assistant. Adjust the content within the brackets to include relevant information for your branching scenario.

> You are an instructional designer tasked with creating
> a branching scenario on the topic of [*business or
> academic topic*] in [*name type of industry*]. Include
> [*number of characters*] named [*character one*] and
> [*character two*]. Provide dialogue for the branching
> scenario. Indicate which branches are preferable, which
> branches lead to dead ends or undesirable outcomes,
> and which lead to desirable or positive outcomes.

Case Study: VenaMedTech's Innovative Branching Scenario

Note: The name of the firm and other details in this case study have been changed to ensure confidentiality.

A large Canadian company, VenaMedTech, specializes in the production of high-quality intravenous (IV) tubes that are essential for a wide range of medical procedures. The IV tubes are known for their reliability and safety and are crafted from high-quality materials that ensure durability and flexibility. VenaMedTech's IV tubes and sets are specially engineered to ensure a consistent, controlled flow of medications and fluids. All products undergo rigorous quality control checks according to stringent international medical standards to guarantee patient safety.

The company serves a diverse international client base, including hospitals, clinics, and emergency medical services. When VenaMedTech sales representatives go to a hospital, their goal is to create a customized IV set that meets the hospital's needs in most areas. If a hospital's IV sets are standardized within 80–90 percent of the hospital's functions, costs will be minimized for both the hospital and the manufacturer. This approach to customer service and customization results in high-volume sales and a high level of satisfaction for the company's clients.

The Challenge

VenaMedTech had a successful sales training process that included a live in-person classroom role-play exercise, but it was labor intensive and not scalable. They also included discussions and Q&A sessions with three trainers, an observer who monitored the conversations, and a facilitator who coordinated the entire event.

However, in an effort to create a program that was more efficient, the company decided to convert the four-hour, face-to-face role-play exercise into a branching scenario. This new program would require fewer trainers and increase the number of sales reps trained each month.

The training development team faced a daunting task. Role plays can go in many directions, and it can be hard to create enough branches and options in a branching scenario to mimic the freedom of a live role play. They also knew it would be hard to mimic the subtlety of human interactions and to ensure the scenario didn't feel fake or inauthentic.

Why a Branching Scenario?

The training development team decided a branching scenario would most closely mimic their already successful live role-play exercise. Learners would venture into a fictional hospital and ask questions, receive responses, and work with their clients to assemble the best configuration for an IV set to meet the hospital's needs. The decision making, critical-thinking process, and interactions during this branching scenario would closely match existing training but they would also be scalable.

It was easy to see the immediate benefits of an online branching scenario, including the time savings, by comparing it to the existing training program. With the branching scenario, all sales reps could be trained in less than a year rather than the 26-month training time required for in-person role plays. In addition, the branching scenario could be repeated multiple times, allowing sales representatives to explore different decision pathways and outcomes to deepen their understanding of how to interact with various hospital departments.

Making the Case

To get executives on board and help secure funding for their project, the training team analyzed what it would cost to continue the current live, in-class training versus the full cost of developing a branching scenario. Current training costs included flying sales reps to headquarters, paying for hotel rooms, factoring in an hourly rate for each trainer, and calculating the opportunity costs of lost sales. The team also determined the potential increase in sales that would occur once all sales representatives completed the training process, based on previous results after live training sessions.

The results? Converting to an online, branching scenario would save a significant amount of money and increase revenue. Soon after the team presented their carefully researched business case to upper management, the executives gave the go-ahead.

The Solution

The training development team created a large-scale branching scenario in which each learner entered a hospital and chose which departments to visit. Within each department, the learner entered a conversation with the appropriate professional to understand the department's needs related to IV sets. A total of six department heads were available to meet, but only four were important to the final decision; if the learner understood this, they could skip the meeting with these two department heads. If sales representatives skipped the wrong hospital professionals, however, they wouldn't get the necessary information to recommend the correct IV set. If they spoke with everyone, they wasted time. This realistic scenario required the learner to think about how to use their limited time and reinforced the need for critical thinking and analysis.

When a sales rep asked the right question or gave a correct response, they would continue down a branch and receive all the necessary information. If they selected a less-than-optimal choice or asked the wrong questions, they kept going in the scenario but their potential to make the wrong final choice increased because they had received limited information. The wrong choices never doomed the sales reps but did make the job much more difficult—just like a real-world sales situation.

The training developers added another twist to help mimic the in-class exercise: The learner had to indicate how confident they were in their response. The training team wanted to make sure the sales representatives were not overly confident if they chose the wrong answers. Whenever that happened, the sales representative had to play through the branching scenario again. The team also wanted to know if a salesperson knew the right answer but said they were not confident. The goal was to engineer the right level of confidence and product knowledge among the participants.

Throughout the entire branching scenario, the sales representatives received feedback from two characters. One was an inside champion who worked in the hospital's administration department. They would meet with the sales representative before every department conversation and give them the lowdown regarding key issues and pain points related to the IV sets in the department. Sometimes, the champion had solid information; other times, they had little helpful information. However, all the information they offered was accurate.

The other character was a sales manager who introduced the learner to the hospital scenario and provided critical information and subtle hints about the process. They gave feedback on each element of the conversation the sales representative had in a department and guidance on how their choices departed from the desired goals. The sales manager character also shared closing comments about the sales process after every encounter and encouraged the learner to make notes for later use.

In the end, after the sales representative assumed they had spoken to everyone—surprise! Another person appeared who turned out to be the procurement manager. If the learner's conversation with the procurement manager wasn't successful, the entire opportunity at the hospital was lost, and the learning scenario started over. At every moment, the outcome of the branching scenario depended on the learner's choices.

At the end of the scenario, the learner had to select the correct IV set elements from a matrix of options. There were two correct choices, but only one was ideal. As in real life, more than one option worked, but one was better than the other. The learner's confidence score was calculated to ensure they had the right balance of confidence and knowledge. Choosing the incorrect IV set or having a poor confidence versus knowledge balance meant the learner had to retake the branching scenario. The whole simulation took about two hours.

Benefits and Results

Overall, VenaMedTech's branching scenario was a huge success. They achieved the following results:

- Almost 81 percent of the learners agreed or strongly agreed that the learning objectives were met.
- Nearly 90 percent agreed or strongly agreed that the scope of the material was appropriate to meet their needs.
- More than 76 percent agreed or strongly agreed that the use of multimedia and audiovisuals enhanced the activity.
- More than 70 percent agreed or strongly agreed that they learned new knowledge from the activity.

While these results are impressive from a learning perspective, the most dramatic one was the new business growth that occurred after sales reps completed the branching scenario. Growth increased twelvefold from the original baseline measurement. The branching scenario met the goals of the organization, saving time and money and increasing revenue.

The team interviewed sales representatives after the experience, and one of their main comments was that before completing the branching scenario, they hadn't realized how important it was to visit all relevant departments within the hospital and how much that would influence the final sale, even though this point had been discussed throughout previous training programs. Until they experienced failure or success in the branching simulation as a result of speaking to the right departments, the sales representatives didn't fully understand how significant that simple technique was to their overall success.

Lessons Learned

VenaMedTech's team encountered some obstacles during the development but overcame them and developed a list of lessons learned. These lessons can help you develop an action-first branching scenario.

- **The most challenging task in the project was writing the sales conversations in a way that seemed natural but optimized learner time.** The training team's goal was to capture the essence of conversations but not all the ins and outs of typical face-to-face discussions. This was a delicate process. Fortunately, because a few members of the design and development team had conducted many face-to-face role plays, they knew the desired learning outcome, the direction the conversations tended to go when they went wrong, and various responses expected of hospital personnel. Even then, the team needed to focus continually on the desired learning outcomes—the branching could not go on indefinitely, so they worked hard to make the conversations realistic but short and to the point. Several times, the development team decided to end a conversation that was going too far in the wrong direction. That might not happen in a live event, but it made the branching scenario more manageable for the learners and development team.
- **Negative feedback doesn't mean the design is bad.** The sales representatives did not like having to replay the branching

scenario if they got something wrong. They also did not like having to retake the scenario if they were right, but their score indicated a lack of confidence. The design and development team viewed the negative feedback about replaying the scenario and confidence levels as reinforcing the goals they were attempting to achieve. Learners didn't have to be happy to learn; sometimes, difficulty and struggle leads to better learning outcomes than getting everything right on the first try. Just like in real life, if sales reps lacked confidence or got a move wrong, they might fail, so the design team wanted learners to understand this on a visceral level.

- **The branching scenario provided an instructional bonus not available in the live classroom role play.** Specific, targeted feedback on individual performance was missing from the live role play. In the branching scenario, on the other hand, when a sales representative reached a particular area, their decision was evaluated and they received two levels of feedback. The sales manager was one source of feedback, and the other was the customer or hospital professional with whom the learner was interacting. The customer feedback about what did and didn't work well was especially helpful. The sales manager's feedback helped point learners in the right direction for future attempts at securing sales. Targeted, personal feedback is not always possible in a live event.

Key Takeaways

Now that you're ready to create an action-first learning experience using a branching scenario, remember these tips:

- Branching scenarios provide an interactive and immersive learning experience. When learners are put in the driver's seat—making decisions and experiencing consequences—they become more engaged and invested in the learning process.

- Branching scenarios can simulate real-world situations so learners can practice making decisions in a risk-free environment. This helps them develop critical thinking and problem-solving skills.
- Learners receive specific and targeted feedback about their decisions in a branching scenario, which is crucial for reinforcing learning and correcting misconceptions. This instant feedback loop helps learners understand the implications of their choices and promotes reflective learning.
- Online branching scenarios provide access to a wide audience, regardless of location or time constraints. This scalability ensures that effective training is not limited by geographical barriers or limited resources.

EXPLANATION OF THE ACTION-FIRST ACTIVITY

This is an early generation of a voice-activated branching interface with almost unlimited branching because you, as the instructional designer, don't need to design any of the branches. It provides a rich practice opportunity for learners. You may want to create a chatbot and preload your company's information on a sales or leadership model (or another topic) that you want to create a branching role play for. To do this, check to see if you have internal AI resources—you don't want to post critical corporate information into a public AI model like ChatGPT. Also, keep in mind that AI still makes mistakes and isn't perfect, but the ability to have voice-based conversations and allow learners to practice dialogue is an important action-first development and something you should be exploring. If you're having trouble finding the sound wave icon, it's in the lower-right corner of the image in Figure 6-3.

Figure 6-3. Use verbal interface for role-play with an AI tool. In the ChatGPT mobile app, tap on the headphones to initiate a verbal interface and start the role play.

Tool 6-1. Tips for Effective Branching Scenarios

✓ Create branching scenarios to help correct potential common mistakes. By offering these options, you can correct learners before they make mistakes in the field.

✓ Highlight cause-and-effect relationships. This is especially critical when the effect of an action or decision is not revealed in a timely fashion in real life.

✓ Use branching scenarios to teach learners how to diagnose and trouble-shoot problems. This can apply to anything from fixing a malfunctioning piece of equipment to treating a medical condition to determining why a star performer is suddenly underperforming.

✓ Teach learners about the affective or emotional domain by using branch-ing scenarios to develop empathy for other people.

✓ Carefully weigh the depth and detail of dialogue when writing a branch-ing scenario to keep the length manageable.

✓ Always build reflection points into your scenario and carefully consider what types of feedback you will provide for learners.

7
Live and In-Person
Live Interactive Experiences for Learning

 Grab a piece of paper and a pencil or pen. Write down three reasons you believe that live interactive learning sessions are effective. Keep the list next to you as you read this chapter and see if any are listed here. *(Find the explanation at the end of this chapter.)*

At the end of this chapter, you should be able to answer these questions:

- What action-first elements will make live learning experiences more effective?
- What types of learning outcomes are best for live learning experiences and events?
- What basic design principles should you consider when designing a live learning experience?
- What are some examples of action-first exercises and activities to facilitate learning in live events?

Ramón entered the training room ready to participate in an interactive learning exercise on marketing concepts for small companies. Over the past few months, he had been frustrated in his new role as project lead in the organization's growing marketing department. He'd signed up for the training course hoping to gain some essential skills and find support from others in similar roles.

The trainer, Nicholas, greeted Ramón and the other participants warmly and explained the session's format. He divided the class into small

groups, each tasked with developing a marketing campaign for a specific product line at a warehouse supply company. Ramón's group was tasked with promoting industrial shelving units to small businesses.

Ramón and his group brainstormed ideas, drawing on their knowledge of marketing principles and the description they received of the shelving units' unique features. They discussed target markets, messaging strategies, and promotional tactics, including social media campaigns and trade show appearances. Nicholas circulated among the groups, providing guidance and feedback. He encouraged them to think creatively and consider all the practical aspects of implementing their ideas.

After 45 minutes, each group presented their marketing campaign to the class. Ramón's group outlined a comprehensive plan that impressed Nicholas and the other groups. They identified the shelving units' key selling points, such as durability and customization options, and developed a compelling advertising strategy to reach their target audience. Nicholas praised the group for their innovative ideas and thoughtful approach. He highlighted the importance of understanding your target audience's needs and tailoring a message to resonate with them. He then led a final discussion of all the lessons learned that day in training.

As the day concluded, Ramón felt a sense of accomplishment and connection. He had learned valuable marketing concepts and gained practical tips, techniques, and ideas from the trainer and his peers. He immediately started thinking about how to leverage the new information back at the office, and he made plans to meet with several members of his group later in the month for an informal follow-up discussion and mutual support.

※ ※ ※

Humans are inherently social creatures. We actively seek out others to work and connect with in a variety of ways, from chatting over coffee to Zoom meetings to conversations via LinkedIn or Slack. Psychologists who study self-determination theory emphasize the importance of human relatedness—along with autonomy and competence—as a fundamental psychological need. *Relatedness* is our need to feel connected to others, to care about them, and be recognized by them. These connections provide emotional support and a sense of belonging and play a critical role in—among other things—creating an organizational culture.

The most effective method of bringing people together and supporting human connections is a live learning experience, which could take place in person (with everyone gathered shoulder-to-shoulder in the same room) or in a high-tech virtual classroom (Figure 7-1). In either case, however, the default teaching method is often an old-fashioned lecture. While lectures can certainly serve a purpose, more interactive methods can fully engage learners, enhance their feeling of relatedness, and encourage better learning.

Figure 7-1. An AI-generated image of learners interacting through a virtual meeting software. *Source: Image generated by Karl M. Kapp using ChatGPT 4o.*

In this chapter, we'll consider what makes live learning experiences so valuable and how to make yours the best they can be. In any live learning environment, you'll want to establish a safe, inclusive atmosphere where learners feel comfortable expressing their views. You need to provide clear communication about learning goals and expectations and create participatory, relevant, and dynamic experiences—the hallmarks of a great action-first experience.

Why Are Live Experiences Effective for Learning?

Like many other action-first learning experiences, live interactive learning helps foster communication, soft skills, and problem solving. A distinct advantage of live events is that they can go beyond transferring knowledge by tapping into the affective domain of learning to bring people together to share an experience and create a common frame of reference to build organizational culture. In live events, it becomes easier to clarify gray areas and foster understanding among participants. Learners themselves are more likely to network with peers and share their real-world experiences, including best practices.

Building Organizational Culture

Live interactive experiences bring together learners from various locations and backgrounds to solve problems and build bridges within an organization. These cultural and social exchanges are valuable assets for learning and improving business operations and strategies because employees from diverse backgrounds and departments bring a wealth of perspectives and experiences to the table. Live interactive gatherings are especially valuable in global, multinational organizations, but they can also forge important connections in a nationally dispersed organization in which people in different parts of a country have very different perspectives.

Let's assume you want to create a more dynamic, comprehensive understanding of your multinational company's marketing strategies. You believe an upcoming training event about global marketing at your headquarters in Atlanta, Georgia, would benefit immensely from the insights of employees in Germany, France, and Italy, so you invite them to a live online session. Your US–based marketing team's approach to digital advertising differs significantly from the European team's approach, which emphasizes data privacy and regulatory compliance. Bringing the European team into the live interactive training program enriches the immediate learning experience for everyone and directly contributes to shaping company strategies on a deeper level. In addition, the American and European team members are able to forge new professional relationships that extend beyond the confines of the training environment and build a more supportive organizational culture.

Clarifying Gray Areas to Enhance Understanding

Live interactive experiences facilitate real-time participation and feedback; unlike self-paced or solo learning experiences, live sessions also allow for immediate clarification of policies, questions, and misconceptions, which helps the learning process. So, when a learner poses a question or expresses confusion, instructors can provide instant clarification and more detailed explanations or examples.

Immediate responses from instructors can stop misconceptions from taking root and also allow learners to progress in their understanding of a concept and maintain the flow and continuity of the learning process. Any clarifications or answers are shared with everyone else in the live learning experience—diminishing the chances of misunderstandings and uncertainty for the whole group.

Networking With Peers

As I previously mentioned, live learning experiences offer abundant opportunities for learners to engage with their peers and the instructor, share experiences and ideas, collaborate, and learn from one another. Leadership programs frequently use live experiences to ensure that leaders across an organization know one another and can work well together as peers. Ideally, these interactions allow individuals to share insights, comfortably challenge one another's understanding of problems and problem-solving strategies, and build solutions collectively.

When networking with peers in a live setting, each participant brings unique knowledge and viewpoints to the table, which improves the learning process for everyone involved and often leads to deeper comprehension and more innovative thinking. Each participant also finds new opportunities for collaboration, career advancement, and building broader networks within the organization.

Sharing Experiences

An organization's community is built on a foundation of common experiences and knowledge. For instance, we often see colleges forge community among first-year students by using a common cultural reference point. Sometimes called the "freshman experience," it involves bringing first-year students to campus before other student cohorts to engage in games and activities that allow them to meet one another and create shared memories. The students refer to the events over the next few weeks and months, providing common reference points and conversation starters. In the corporate world, the equivalent experience might be a ropes course, in which members of a department go off-site for an afternoon to learn to work together by making it through a series of obstacles. However, these are often controversial and sometimes alienate attendees, especially if they aren't able to participate.

Live classroom learning experiences that are designed properly can offer the same sorts of community-building events on a much smaller and more accessible scale than outdoor bonding activities. The goal of these classroom or virtual events is to nurture a sense of camaraderie and cohesiveness in a brief time with a focus on business or academic outcomes and goals. One of the most effective ways to jump-start the process of developing a classroom community is for learners to play a board game or card game, as I described in chapters 2 and 3.

What Can Live Interactive Experiences Teach?

It's becoming more difficult to bring employees together for live learning experiences in many organizations. So, when people do manage to get together, it's important to leverage those opportunities to teach critical soft skills—including communication, collaboration, and improvisation—and include hands-on practice time.

Communication

Live learning experiences are particularly effective for enhancing communication skills, such as speaking, listening, and even understanding body language. For example, during a live classroom debate on corporate ethics, participants might be asked to articulate their thoughts clearly and persuasively. They would also be required to actively listen to others' viewpoints, ask clarifying questions, and respond thoughtfully. This real-time interaction would allow learners to practice their skills before applying them back on the job.

Although it can be challenging to interpret body language in virtual learning settings, technology has advanced enough to make nonverbal cues more discernible through video. In face-to-face sessions, gestures, eye contact, and posture play an even more significant role in conveying messages. In both contexts, learners can develop a keen awareness of the subtleties of communication, learning to effectively read and respond to nonverbal signals. A small group assignment, such as a think-share-pair exercise, allows participants to practice one-on-one and one-to-many communication.

Collaboration

Group activities in live learning sessions can provide a safe environment for understanding and practicing collaboration. During these projects, participants work as a team, simulating real-world scenarios. In a live project management session, a small group of participants could plan and execute a mini project. This would require delegating responsibilities and coordination that mirrors the complexities of teamwork in a professional setting. In live learning experiences like these, participants can learn firsthand about the nuances of group dynamics and better understand how individual roles and personalities affect the team's collective performance.

Understanding the complex dynamics of collaboration is crucial for those who have to manage diverse teams in a workplace where blending different skills and temperaments is a key to success. By engaging in live learning experiences that promote collaboration and cooperation, participants discover that the success of their team depends on each member's contribution and ability to work harmoniously toward a shared objective.

Improvisation

We don't often think of improvisation and spontaneity as business skills, but they can be invaluable for leaders, managers, and frontline employees.

Improvisation is crucial for negotiations, client interactions, and crisis management. In a live interactive learning experience, a participant can be engaged in real-time discussions and debates in which they must quickly process information, adapt their thinking, and articulate responses on the spot. Such interactions mimic the fast-paced and often unpredictable nature of the business world.

The ability to improvise and think on your feet is essential to becoming an effective leader. Leaders frequently encounter situations in which they must provide immediate guidance or make decisions without extensive deliberation. Training in a live learning environment where participants can practice and refine their improvisation skills can prepare them for similar real-world challenges.

Hands-On Practice

Many jobs—from computer repair technician to pharmacist to nuclear engineer—require hands-on skills and knowledge. For these jobs, there is no substitute for hands-on training and practice. Would you want to go to an auto mechanic who had never physically interacted with a car's engine, specific auto parts, or diagnostic tools? Direct engagement is crucial for understanding how a complex piece of machinery works. During live learning sessions, auto technician trainees can learn to diagnose problems, perform repairs, and replace parts. They get to handle and become familiar with the proper tools and equipment and build their confidence.

A hands-on, live learning approach is vital for fields in which tactile skills and precision matter most. Live interactive learning experiences ensure that when trainees enter the workforce, they are well-prepared and knowledgeable professionals.

Live Interactive Learning Exercises

Lectures are often the go-to method for delivering content in live learning experiences, but there are other more engaging and effective ways of sharing content. Of course, you can incorporate the action-first experiences discussed in this book—including card games, board games, and escape rooms—but any method that immerses learners in creative activities is valuable. They need to think about and manipulate the ideas and concepts the course is focused on. The following sections detail four proven interactive techniques you can try in both virtual and face-to-face live learning sessions.

Think-Pair-Share Exercises

A *think-pair-share exercise* should begin by giving each learner a question, a diagram to draw, or an activity related to your topic. Provide a difficult assignment so the learners must think deeply before responding. Give them time to perform and think about the assignment. Next, divide them into pairs (or groups of three, if necessary). Use breakout rooms for virtual sessions or move groups into different corners of the room if you are in a face-to-face session. In pairs or trios, learners should engage in a thoughtful conversation about the topic.

The third and final step in the think-pair-share process is to share ideas. Ask the groups to come back together to share their conversations, answers, drawings, or other products of all that thinking with another learner. This encourages learners to interact with each other and the content at the same time. In the end, each learner will have applied their own thinking to the question or task, shared ideas with one or two fellow learners, and then shared those ideas with the entire group to get feedback. They may have received validation for their ideas or had an opportunity to defend their thinking. All these activities result in increased learning and retention.

Construction Activities

A *construction activity* asks learners to build a model of a concept or theory. This type of activity is based on the instructional theory constructivism, which suggests that learning occurs when people have to actively work to construct their own path to understanding instead of relying on someone else to tell them what they should know. Here again, we're moving away from traditional lectures and toward more action-based learning.

To create a construction activity, pick a model or concept you want your learners to understand. This could be something like a sales model, a leadership concept, or a hybrid work model. If you are operating in a virtual classroom, create a slide listing all the elements of the model but without a clear visual representation; just include the text in scrambled order. If you're in a physical classroom, write each element of the model on a piece of paper.

Place learners in teams of three or four, and ask each team to arrange the words into their own version of a model and to illustrate it with any icons or other embellishments they deem helpful. Encourage them to use shapes, images, and arrows with whiteboard tools in the virtual classroom or good, old-fashioned paper and markers in the physical classroom. The embellishment process helps learners understand and construct their models.

Allow this exercise to go on for 20 to 30 minutes. When their time is up, recall the learners from breakout sessions or various corners of the classroom and ask each team to explain their model to the entire group. After all the teams have presented their versions of the model, point out which elements match the official model and which ones diverge from it. Any cognitive dissonance or confusion can serve as critical discussion points and learning opportunities.

Interactive Narratives

An *interactive narrative* combines storytelling with audience responses. The instructor creates a case study based on a common industry challenge and adds a series of questions that can be answered by an audience response system. This can be done virtually or face-to-face.

The instructor divides the group of learners into two teams. Each team listens to the instructor's narrative, and then, at appropriate moments, they are presented with questions related to the narrative. Each person responds to the questions, and answers are tabulated according to team affiliation. Teams create a form of friendly competition and provide the instructor with real-time feedback about whether or not the learners understand the case study and can respond correctly. If the majority of learners don't understand or answer incorrectly, the instructor can pause to clarify information. This is an effective way for an instructor in a live session to measure understanding while presenting content. If you want to get more sophisticated, the group's answers could lead to different branches.

Problem-Based Learning

In *problem-based learning*, participants are presented with a problem that is similar to a dilemma they might encounter on the job. During the live session, learners need to find a way to solve the problem. To do so, they conduct research using the company's intranet; discuss and apply principles, policies, and processes; and find a solution. The instructor's role is to guide and facilitate learning rather than directly provide information.

If you were training auditors, you might present them with a scenario in which they are asked to audit a manufacturing company that has discrepancies between its physical inventory count and records in its computer system, as well as misalignments between taxes paid on versus the actual amount of on-hand inventory. Determining the exact nature and cause of the problems forces learners to apply auditing standards, ethical considerations, and analytical skills to address and resolve issues at the manufacturing company. In this approach, each learner works to solve the problem, or groups or teams could work together to solve the problem, like in Figure 7-2.

Figure 7-2. An AI-generated image of learners collaborating in person to solve a problem. *Source: Image generated by Karl M. Kapp using ChatGPT 4.*

Let's Design a Live Interactive Learning Experience

Whether you conduct your live interactive learning experiences in a physical classroom or a virtual online setting, the focus should be action first. Design each event to encourage immediate involvement and participation. Yes, lectures can still play a role—but it should be diminished. Instead of beginning with long lectures or another method of content delivery that allows your audience to passively consume information, start by encouraging participants to act, make decisions, and interact with the learning materials.

Regardless of whether you're using hands-on exercises, construction activities, problem-solving scenarios, or other approaches, the development process follows the same steps. Remember, you want to create an event that is engaging, educational, and effective.

Step 1. Define the Learning Objectives

Clearly articulate what you want participants to learn or which skills you want them to develop in the live learning experience. Remember that live interactive experiences can be effective in the affective or emotional domain and for connecting learners.

Step 2. Determine What Content You Want to Highlight

A live experience helps learners with communication, peer-to-peer connections, collaboration, spontaneity, and other aspects of relatedness and human-to-human contact. Determine which of these is most appropriate for your live learning event. Content is always important, but it can be conveyed in a variety of ways. Because live interaction is becoming rarer in most organizations, it's best to consider how to take advantage of this valuable opportunity in the best way possible.

Step 3. Review Content to Determine Which Exercises Will Work Best

In a live learning situation, you have a variety of interactive options available, so look carefully at the content you want to cover and determine which exercises offer the best match. This will help you figure out how best to configure the live event for the most effective learning outcomes.

Step 4. Create the Right Timing and Organization

Because you'll be dividing the class into small groups, providing instructions for activities, and including a great deal of movement in your face-to-face or virtual session, you need to work out the timing and organization in advance. Decide how you'll create breakout groups and provide instructions, as well as how much time you'll need for each activity. Running a smooth event creates a positive overall experience. If the event does not run smoothly, the overall learning outcome can suffer.

Step 5. Train Facilitators and Provide Good Support

The instructor or facilitator needs to understand the content and learning objectives. If the person who created the content is not the person who will deliver it, then you should provide instructional scripts, lesson plans, and tips and techniques related to the content to the person who will be conducting the session. If it is a live virtual event, make sure the facilitator is trained to handle the technology platform and do basic troubleshooting. You may even want to consider adding a producer or someone else to help run the technical aspects of the software while the facilitator manages the instruction. This is often helpful for large groups of learners. For live and virtual events, the facilitator or instructor should be trained to encourage participation, manage group dynamics, address diverse viewpoints, and create an environment in which all learners feel comfortable contributing. If you can make support personnel available to deal with problems, this can improve the instructional process.

Step 6. Create the Necessary Collateral

For a live event, accompanying materials or collateral can be presented digitally via a link or physically if the event is face-to-face. Create the necessary materials, test the links, and have them ready to distribute in the session.

Step 7. Adapt for Accessibility

Making live learning events accessible to people with physical, sensory, and other disabilities or impairments requires thoughtful planning and implementation of inclusive practices. Above all, ensure the physical or virtual venue is accessible. For physical locations, this requires wheelchair ramps, accessible restrooms, and appropriate seating arrangements. For virtual events, choose platforms that are compatible with assistive technologies like screen readers. Provide materials in various formats to cater to diverse needs such as large print, braille, and digital copies for screen reader compatibility. During presentations, use high-contrast visuals and clear, legible fonts to aid those with visual impairments. Incorporating captioning and sign language interpretation will make the content accessible to participants with hearing impairments. Facilitators should speak clearly, use descriptive language, and avoid relying solely on visual cues. They may want to provide extra time for responses and use multiple communication methods.

Step 8. Conduct a Dry Run

Whether you're conducting a virtual or face-to-face session, test all the equipment, have the facilitator rehearse presentations, and run through the interactive exercises. Your dry run can help identify confusing content and steps that are unclear. You'll then have a chance to rectify any potential problems before the live event. While this is especially important for virtual events, it's also helpful for face-to-face events. If a room turns out to be too small for breakout groups, for example, you'll have to quickly make other arrangements. Or if your classroom is in a building that, because of connectivity, prevents the audience response systems from working properly, you'll need to make last-minute adaptations. This is why it's important to conduct the dry run in the actual space you'll use for the live session.

Step 9. Create a Follow-Up Strategy

Devise ways to keep in touch with your learners and allow them to connect with one another after the class. You may want to create a peer-to-peer email list (just make sure to get permission from everyone before sharing their emails). Consider sending follow-up emails, sharing additional resources, or creating an online location for ongoing discussions. These options will help reinforce the learning and build community.

Step 10. Build in Time for Reflection and Projection

Learning experiences are most effective when the learner has time to step back and reflect on what they've learned. Unfortunately, many learners have busy schedules and don't take time to reflect, so you should build this time into every interactive live learning event to ensure they can reflect on what they learned throughout the activity. Ask the learners to project themselves into the future and talk about what they will take from the learning event and use in their work. If learners project the application of lessons learned during the live event, they'll be more apt to apply those skills when they return to their jobs.

Step 11. Evaluate and Assess

It's always important to assess the effectiveness of an action-first learning event, but it's particularly key for live events. As I previously mentioned, it's not always easy to bring people together, which means these learning events have to be high impact. Evaluate your events to determine the level of impact and whether the desired learning and connection goals were met.

Also, remind participants what they learned. Sometimes, it's difficult for learners to gauge how much they've learned in a live session, and they may appreciate having a way to evaluate their progress, such as through an exercise or quiz.

AI Assist

The following prompt can help you ask an AI tool to generate ideas for live learning sessions. Adjust the content within the brackets to include relevant information for your needs.

```
You are an instructional designer who specializes in
using interactive class activities to engage learners.
You are teaching the subject of [leadership] in a [live,
virtual online] setting. Provide [three] activities
```

the learners can do to engage with each other and with the material. These activities need to include peer-to-peer interactions as well as interactions between the participants and the facilitator.

Case Study: Enhancing Sales Training With an Interactive Narrative

Note: The name of the firm and other details in this case study have been changed to ensure confidentiality.

In the competitive field of orthopedic medical device sales, Super Ortho has been a leading producer of orthopedic solutions for more than 40 years. The company is recognized for its innovative products and technologies aimed at improving musculoskeletal health. Super Ortho develops and manufactures a wide range of orthopedic devices, including joint replacement implants, specialized surgical instruments, and related medical equipment. Leaders and employees are proud of the organization's long-standing focus on advancing patient care and surgical techniques.

The Challenge

Super Ortho's sales team is highly skilled in traditional sales techniques but has struggled to effectively communicate the complex product features and benefits to potential clients—primarily orthopedic surgeons and hospital procurement teams. Traditional training methods have been insufficient to equip the team with a nuanced understanding of the products and the persuasive skills needed in this specialized market.

A two-day national sales meeting, known internally as a plan of action (POA) meeting, was planned to bring together sales representatives who would be trained, motivated, and informed of key details about Super Ortho products. The planning team decided to create an activity to motivate and train the sales team about product features during the POA meeting.

Why a Live Interactive Experience?

The team wanted an event that could motivate *and* train sales representatives. They decided that the best method was an interactive narrative technique because it is engaging and can closely simulate a real-world sales scenario with the question and answers going back and forth between the sales representatives and the healthcare professionals involved in purchasing decisions.

Making the Case

The planning team explained that the interactive story technique would motivate and engage sales representatives by providing a competition the sales team would enjoy and allowing them to practice and refine their skills in a controlled, yet dynamic environment.

The interactive narrative approach, with its combination of storytelling and real-time feedback, mimics the unpredictability and complexity of actual sales situations. It also provides a sense of anonymity because the audience response system can be configured to show team responses without tracking to individual sales representatives. The planning team hoped this would lead to more honest responses and provide accurate mapping of which questions the sales representative got right and struggled with. The instructors could use this information to quickly configure subsequent sessions at the two-day event to address specific areas of need.

The Solution

The training program was built around a detailed case study crafted by the training department with help from an outside consultant. The training team interviewed several different sales representatives, their regional managers, and their district managers to create a realistic scenario related to the product.

The story depicted a common scenario in orthopedic device sales involving an innovative knee replacement device. It included various stakeholders—surgeons, hospital administrators, and patients—each with distinct needs and concerns, and evolved based on responses from the sales team to mimic the fluid nature of real sales negotiations.

At the POA meeting, the planning team divided the large sales force of more than 100 representatives into smaller subgroups of 20. In breakout rooms, each group was further divided into two teams—a red team and a blue team (the two corporate brand colors). Each team used their smartphones and the audience response software in a product called UMU (which is an AI-powered performance learning platform that allows polling and tracking of audience responses, among other capabilities). The audience members responded to questions embedded into the sales story narrative in which competing sales reps tried to secure a contract with a fictional hospital.

As the narrative progressed, the teams addressed questions and challenges that required them to apply their previous knowledge and skills. Their responses were recorded, and the results were displayed on the projector in the front of the room. The instructor and sales reps could watch as questions were answered in real time.

This session was held on the first day of the two-day event. In the evening, the training team analyzed the results from the five different interactive narrative events. At the larger meeting the next morning, they focused on reinforcing any concepts that were either missed or not retained as well as they should have been. They also used the UMU software platform to create modules that could access the sales team when they returned to work. The modules were based on gaps or misunderstandings discovered during the interactive session.

Benefits and Results

The implementation of the interactive narrative technique at Super Ortho's POA meeting provided several benefits, with the most notable being a heightened level of engagement among the sales representatives. The competitive nature of the training event and narrative feedback kept them fully immersed, highly engaged, and deeply motivated throughout the learning process. The narrative format also played a significant role in helping the sales team better understand how to act and react when visiting a potential client, as well as how to effectively address concerns. Both skills helped improve their overall sales approach.

For the training team, the structure of the interactive narrative provided actionable feedback that they could address quickly. The team was able to identify and address misunderstandings and confusion regarding product representation and create remedial instruction by the next day.

In the four months following the event, Super Ortho observed a substantial increase in the acquisition and use of their products, underscoring the success of the interactive narrative technique in enhancing sales efficacy, as well as the effectiveness of the overall POA meeting.

Lessons Learned

Super Ortho learned several lessons that you can use as guidelines for creating live interactive instruction:

- **Context is important.** The sales representatives indicated in feedback after the event that the realistic scenario helped them apply their knowledge to real-world situations and understand how specific sales scenarios related to the product might occur. It also gave them a good understanding of the types of questions they might be asked during a sales call.
- **Interaction is key to engagement.** Much of the feedback related to the interactive narrative was about how engaged the learners felt during the live session. They believed that they needed to pay attention and didn't want to let their teammates down by answering incorrectly. This meant many of the learners were more highly focused than usual on the narrative and on applying their knowledge to correctly respond during the activity.

- **Competition was motivational for this group.** The learners enjoyed bragging about how well their team performed and how well they had done individually. This type of competition might not work with every type of learner, but it was a hit with this particular sales team.

Key Takeaways

Now that you're ready to create a live interactive experience for learning, remember these tips:

- Interactive learning events can build a stronger organizational culture by bringing peers together to get to know one another and network.
- Live interactive experiences can enhance participants' communication skills and provide opportunities for collaboration.
- Shared experiences often foster community and become shared points of reference.
- Live learning events can answer questions for participants and help clarify gray areas or address uncertainty among learners.
- Leaders often gain a sense of spontaneity and improve their ability to improvise during live learning experiences. Participants in live learning engage in real-time discussions and debates, requiring them to quickly process information, adapt their thinking, and articulate responses on the spot.
- Live interactive events are highly effective for hands-on instruction. Learners can touch and manipulate equipment and understand much more about physical tools, instruments, and machinery than is possible during virtual events.

EXPLANATION OF THE ACTION-FIRST ACTIVITY

Asking you to write down your reasons for using active learning in a live session before you read this chapter provides several instructional benefits:

- **It activates your prior knowledge and taps into your existing under-standing of live learning experiences and active learning.** This activa-tion of prior knowledge helps create a mental framework for integrating new information from the chapter, facilitating deeper understanding.
- **The process encourages you to actively participate in the learning process while reading this chapter.** Active involvement helps you retain information and make the learning experience more meaningful, as we've been discussing throughout this book.
- **Writing down your thoughts early on provides a sense of ownership of the learning.** When you articulate your own ideas and reasons, you take ownership of your learning, and that sense of ownership increases moti-vation and engagement with the material.

Consider using this action-first learning technique the next time you lead a live interactive session.

Tool 7-1. Tips for Effective Live Interactive Learning Experiences

✓ Use proven methods for both face-to-face and digital environments, including interactive narratives, think-pair-share exercises, problem-based learning, and construction activities.

✓ Always rehearse the logistics related to running a live session, whether yours is digital or face-to-face.

✓ Create a follow-up strategy to keep in touch with learners after the live event is over. When learners get back to work, they often forget some of the key information covered in the live event. Providing follow-up reminders can help spur memories and enhance learning.

✓ Create time for learners to reflect on their live learning experience and to project how they could apply information in the event to future tasks on the job. Learning experiences are most effective when participants have time to step back and reflect on what they've learned.

8

Get Real

Augmented Reality for Learning

 Go to your smartphone's app store and download the game *Pokémon Go*. Capture at least one Pokémon. Walk around (but be aware of your surroundings). See how many additional Pokémon you can catch. How does it feel to catch a Pokémon? *(Find the explanation at the end of this chapter.)*

At the end of this chapter, you should be able to answer these questions:

- What elements can you add to an augmented reality experience to make it effective for learning?
- What type of learning outcomes are best for leveraging augmented reality?
- What basic design principles should you consider when designing an augmented reality experience?
- What are some examples of augmented reality for improving employee performance?

Only six weeks into the job, Juan arrived at a customer's site ready to help troubleshoot problems in the large extruder his company sold them 14 years ago. He stepped onto the factory floor and walked to the extruder. He tapped the side of his glasses, activating an augmented reality (AR) heads-up display. A graphical image appeared in front of him floating on top of the physical extruder. The display highlighted potential areas of concern based on historical maintenance records of similar extruders manufactured by Juan's company.

Juan began to work on the large piece of equipment and his AR display guided him through each step of the troubleshooting process. As he

inspected the extruder, virtual annotations popped up, providing detailed information about each component's status and performance history. With the assistance of the AR interface, Juan quickly identified a faulty valve that had caused the malfunction. His heads-up display highlighted the elements of the machine to disconnect and showed him the appropriate tools to use for each step in the repair process. The tools appeared as glowing apparitions hovering above the equipment. He could also see digital replicas of the physical equipment he had brought with him.

Juan matched each physical item in his toolbox with its digital twin and methodically walked through the process of replacing the valve, grateful for the precise instructions in front of him as he worked. In less than two hours, he had replaced the faulty valve, tested the extruder, and had the whole system up and running again. Instead of relying solely on a bulky paper manual or trying to recall every detail from his classroom training, Juan used his AR glasses to see step-by-step instructions, safety guidelines, and relevant schematics while working on the actual equipment.

✸ ✸ ✸

AR is a technology that overlays digital information (such as images, text, videos, and 3D models) onto a real-world environment. It *augments the user's perception* of the real world by blending it with virtual elements. This integration allows users to interact with the physical and digital worlds simultaneously, creating a unique, immersive experience.

AR technology can come in the form of glasses, phones, or other screens that display and link reality and digital elements. Think about a familiar example from televised sports. At the 2022 FIFA World Cup, fans downloaded a special app that allowed them to point their phone cameras at the pitch to view information about each player's movements, speed, and performance statistics. In American football, a yellow first down line is often projected digitally onto the field to help fans watching on television see how far the offense has to go to reach a first down.

In an action-first learning scenario, AR enables learners to access information and guidance directly within their physical environment, enhancing their ability to perform complex tasks. By integrating AR technology into L&D initiatives, organizations can create dynamic and engaging training experiences that promote skill mastery and more effective on-the-job performance. Embracing an action-first approach with AR cuts training times, provides just-in-time instructions, and makes training a real-time experience because learners apply what they are learning directly to tasks in front of them.

Why Is Augmented Reality Effective for Learning?

AR is ideal for an action-first approach to learning because it can sit on top of real-world prompts. An individual can learn and do things at the same time, which creates an engaging learning experience. Afterward, they are more likely to recall knowledge and skills than if they were simply reading or listening to the content in a lecture. AR reduces the learning curve, makes the invisible visible, helps learners change the perspective and scale of a problem, and allows them to visualize abstract concepts. In all these ways, AR provides a bridge between theory and practice that can lead to higher levels of comprehension, retention, and application.

A Reduced Learning Curve

Because of its immersive and interactive nature, AR reduces the time it takes for a learner to apply a skill. For example, while viewing a piece of equipment in AR through a screen, the learner can hear step-by-step instructions matching the precise context of their current environment. By presenting instructions in a contextualized manner, AR eliminates the need for learners to decipher manuals or attend lengthy training sessions. Instead, they can access guidance and support precisely when and where they need it and apply that knowledge directly to the task at hand.

With this instant access, it's less likely learners will forget or lose track of the steps they need to take. Rather than passively consuming information, learners can actively apply the knowledge gained via AR to whatever physical tools or equipment is in front of them, reinforcing their understanding through practical application. This active learning approach accelerates skills development and enhances knowledge retention and transferability. It's as if a mentor were standing behind the learner's shoulder, walking them through the process to complete the job.

The Invisible Becomes Visible

If you're training a mechanic to fix a piece of equipment, they'll often benefit from being able to see the inner workings of the equipment. The same is true for physicians learning how to heal a patient—they typically need to see what it looks like inside, but that's often not possible without causing harm. For example, a surgeon in training needs to know what a heart looks like from all angles before attempting an operation. By using AR, things that are normally invisible can be made visible in three dimensions. AR technology allows the surgeon to overlay a realistic, 3D model of a human heart over a patient's chest, providing a comprehensive view of all its components without invasive procedures. As in the example that opened this chapter, AR can also reveal the inner workings of machinery through digital representations of valves, bearings, axles, splines, fasteners, seals, belts, and more. Anyone who has completed an AR training session will know precisely what to expect when it's time to put their skills to work in real life.

Changes in Perspective or Scale

AR alters the learner's perception. If you want to help someone experience what it's like to have poor eyesight, you can distort their vision through AR. Or, it can be used to conjure up an enormous, clear image of a blood vessel that could ordinarily only be seen through a microscope, allowing a learner to examine it from different angles. The image could even be animated to show how a certain drug might affect the blood vessel.

On the other hand, AR could show learners a miniature version of an armored vehicle so they could walk under it to point out potential vulnerabilities. AR's ability to change the scale of objects to fit learners' needs is one of its most useful characteristics.

Visualization of Abstract Concepts

Abstract data can be difficult to understand on a 2D sheet of paper or computer screen. AR offers many ways to visualize data and concepts to make them easier to grasp. For instance, in sales training, AR can visualize sales performance data in interactive charts, graphs, and heatmaps overlaid onto physical spaces. Learners can explore these visualizations spatially, gaining insights into trends, patterns, and correlations that may not be apparent in traditional spreadsheets or reports. For example, they could walk around a virtual heatmap overlaid on a 3D map of their sales territory to more easily identify areas of high and low sales activity.

By visualizing abstract data spatially and interactively, AR enhances comprehension and retention, enabling learners to make more informed decisions and take targeted actions. AR can also be used to facilitate collaborative learning experiences in which team members share and discuss visualizations in real time, fostering a deeper understanding of the data and allowing for more knowledge sharing.

What Can AR Teach?

AR is a valuable tool for teaching about the affective or emotional domain because it helps learners empathize with and understand others' perspectives. It's also ideal for practicing step-by-step procedures and providing virtual tours and orientation training. The versatility of AR and its variety of delivery systems—glasses, tablets, and phones—means it can break through the traditional classroom's four walls and move learning scenarios (including vital emergency response and safety training) to the learners themselves.

Empathy and Understanding

We all know that experiencing a situation through another person's perspective is incredibly valuable for learning about anything in the physical or emotional realm. For example, AR glasses could provide an overlay on top of a hospital room highlighting the possible dangers to patients, such as the railing on the bed that should be up to help prevent falls. For employees in the hospitality industry, AR can simulate the experience of navigating hotel premises as a customer with an impairment. In a reconfiguration of a work cell on a factory floor, AR can be used to project a piece of equipment and show how it's placement might influence worker movement or possibly cause repetitive strain injuries.

By using AR, learners can gain a deeper appreciation for others' experiences and increased empathy, compassion, and awareness of the diversity of patients, customers, and clients. To put it simply, AR helps learners step into others' shoes, which can often drive positive change.

Step-by-Step Procedures

AR can overlay digital information onto the physical environment to guide a learner through complex tasks with interactive visuals, audio instructions, and real-time feedback. With AR, knowledge application happens in real time as the AR trainer walks the learner through each step they need to perform. For example, an AR application for workers in a manufacturing plant could provide step-by-step instructions for assembling a car engine, overlaying virtual annotations and animations onto the physical components to guide them through each stage of the assembly process. As workers follow the instructions, they can visualize and then execute the correct sequence of actions, identify potential pitfalls or errors, and receive immediate feedback on their performance. This step-by-step approach allows them to efficiently and accurately complete tasks, which can be especially valuable for technicians in the field who are tasked with troubleshooting, like in the first scenario in this chapter.

Orientations and Location Specific Information

Imagine you're a new employee at a large corporation. Your interviews were conducted remotely, so your first day on the job is also the first time you've entered corporate headquarters. You step into an open lobby with a six-story atrium and marble floors. You know you're supposed to make your way to the fifth floor to find the talent development division, but when you get off the elevator, you just see an enormous space with dozens of cubicles. You're overwhelmed and have no idea what to do next—or where to find the coffee, printers, or restrooms.

AR to the rescue! Many AR apps allow for the creation of location specific information, which means that when you approach a certain machine or location, the information appears on your phone, glasses, or tablet. With an AR-enabled tablet or smartphone, you could navigate the physical space of your new workplace from the moment you enter, allowing you to explore departments, facilities, and amenities in the workplace, as well as access relevant information from HR, accounting, and your new manager. It's also possible to overlay safety protocols and photos of key staff members on your virtual tour.

You can also use interactive tours to streamline the orientation process. A well-structured virtual tour allows employees to access on-demand guidance, interactive AR information, troubleshooting guides, and schematic overlays relevant to specific tasks and responsibilities. This kind of real-time support enhances productivity and empowers employees to independently overcome obstacles, reducing their reliance on traditional training materials and support channels.

Safety Instructions and Emergency Responses

AR is perfect for visualizing safety protocols and procedures. By leveraging AR technology, organizations can transform static safety guidelines into interactive visualizations that provide learners with a clear and tangible understanding of safety practices. For example, in the construction industry, workers often encounter complex environments with multiple hazards and safety regulations. AR applications can overlay virtual safety barriers, signage, and guidelines on construction sites, which allows workers to visualize restricted areas, hazard zones, and emergency exits in real time. In a laboratory setting, AR applications can overlay virtual representations of chemical containers, hazard symbols, and safety equipment, letting technicians easily identify and interact with different types of chemicals and learn their associated risks.

When visualizing potential hazards in a realistic context, learners will gain a deeper understanding of safety principles and the importance of following established protocols. AR can also be used to simulate an emergency in the actual physical space in which it might occur—even adding virtual damage, such as a hole in the wall as a result of a virtual explosion, to help learners feel immersed in the situation while practicing the correct responses.

Complex Concepts

As we've already discussed, complex or abstract concepts can be difficult for learners to grasp or visualize, especially in the context of real-world variables. AR can help here, too. In the finance industry, for example, a learning designer could use AR to transform abstract financial data into immersive visualizations that enable learners to gain deeper insights into market trends, investment opportunities, and portfolio performance, as well as enhance their comprehension. AR can also transform abstract logistics data into visualizations that could help a learner understand inventory management, warehouse operations, and distribution networks. In this case, the learner would use AR-enabled devices to overlay virtual representations of inventory levels, shipment routes, and warehouse layouts onto physical supply chain facilities. The result would be a clear view of the flow of goods in real-time, clarifying an otherwise complex, abstract process.

AR Mechanics

To create an action-first learning AR experience, you need to carefully consider which mechanics are the most appropriate for your design. Safety should always be your first concern. Don't forget to incorporate bright colors, interesting sounds, and vibrations to provide feedback to the learner. Consider where and how you want to orient the learner to the experience—whether in a large social space or alone and focused on a single piece of equipment. Some mechanics you'll need to consider include haptic and sound-based cues, safety protocols, bold and contrasting colors, and AR orientation.

Haptic and Sound-Based Cues

Haptic and sound-based cues are often overlooked elements when creating AR experiences. These cues enhance the learner's immersive experience and make it more accessible. *Haptic feedback,* which involves using vibrations to convey information, providing a feel of a tangible interaction with digital objects in the AR environment. When a user reaches out to touch a virtual object, a phone or tablet can vibrate. This creates a sensation of contact or tangibility of the item and simulates the sensation of contact, adding a powerful layer of realism to the experience. This is particularly effective when touching or manipulating tools.

Sound-based cues can play equally important roles in enhancing an AR learning experience. For instance, the sound of rattling can alert a learner to what a malfunctioning piece of equipment sounds like. Sounds and spoken instructions can provide essential feedback. For example, a clicking sound might indicate the learner needs to look around the area to find the piece of equipment they need to work on next when troubleshooting.

Develop a Safety Protocol

AR overlays digital content onto the physical environment, which has the potential to distract learners from their surroundings and increase the risk of accidents or collisions with objects or other people. Always design AR experiences that don't compromise the learner's safety or pose physical hazards, particularly in high-risk environments, such as construction sites, manufacturing facilities, or outdoors. Provide appropriate warnings, set up safety protocols, and make recommendations to facilitators for safe use.

Prolonged use of AR devices, or smart glasses, can lead to ergonomic problems, including eye strain, neck pain, or other discomfort. Even holding up a smartphone to view instructions could, over time, lead to muscle fatigue, so design your AR interface with ergonomic considerations in mind. Optimize display placement, minimize visual clutter, and provide adjustable settings for user comfort. You may also need to include reminders to the learner to take a break or stretch after a certain period.

Go Bold With Colors and Contrast

In an AR environment, you can't usually control where the learner will be when they use the application. For example, they could be facing a multicolor background, a continually changing background, or the static background of a piece of machinery. This means that the assets in your AR experience must provide the maximum amount of contrast between the physical environment and the digital overlay. Leveraging bold colors and high-contrast elements enhances visibility, accessibility, and spatial awareness. By prioritizing contrast and color selection in AR asset creation, designers can create more effective and user-friendly AR experiences for all learners. Neon is often a good choice for making items stand out.

Determine Your AR Orientation

There are four types of orientations—intimate, personal, social, and public—to consider when designing an AR experience for learners, and each one is suitable for specific applications:

- **Intimate space experiences** focus on a person's face, head, or hands. They're ideal for face-tracking applications, such as a virtual try-on of safety glasses, sterile gowns, or other personal protective equipment.
- **Personal space experiences** involve real objects, people, or the surrounding area; for example, when a mechanic is troubleshooting a machine.
- **Social space experiences** allow a wider panorama so the camera can include more people and objects. This orientation is ideal for shared AR experiences like team building.
- **Public space experiences** are anchored to specific locations with plenty of space for augmentations and on-screen explanations. This orientation could work well for an augmented employee tour of a new office building or manufacturing plant.

In your designs, always consider which spatial orientation will work best for your learning goals. Also consider how you will trigger the experience, whether through proximity to a location, scanning a code, or scanning an object (Thykier 2023).

Let's Design an AR Learning Experience

Designing an AR learning experience involves many steps to ensure the content is engaging and educational and safely leverages the AR technology's capabilities. This is especially important because they're typically used outside a classroom or monitored environment. The learners will be on their own with an AR app. Let's discuss some essential steps for designing an AR learning experience.

Step 1. Define Learning Objectives

Don't start with the technology. Start with the problem you're trying to solve. Is the machinery too critical to take offline for training? Are you providing step-by-step instructions? Does the learner travel frequently and need to interact with virtual customers on the road to practice critical sales skills?

Clearly define the learning objectives and desired outcomes of the AR experience as well as why AR is better than another approach. Determine the knowledge and skills learners should acquire or improve through the AR learning experience.

Step 2. Create Storyboards of the Experience

It's important to synchronize the learner's experience and the content. If you're going to visualize key data, how will that experience unfold for the learner? If you're providing step-by-step instructions, do you have a complete set? How will you ensure you aren't missing any key steps? Storyboarding the learning experience will help determine what assets you need to create and what steps and actions the learner needs to take during the instruction.

Step 3. Choose the Appropriate AR Technology

Select the most suitable AR technology platform or device for delivering the learning experience based on the target audience, learning objectives, and available resources. Will you leverage smartphones, tablets, or AR-enabled glasses? What software will you use to create the AR experience? Consider device compatibility, ease of use, accessibility, and any features required for the intended learning activities.

Step 4. Create the Required AR Assets and Content

Many AR software platforms require developers to import assets into the AR application and then place those assets appropriately. You will need to dedicate time to acquiring or creating your assets and content before you can integrate them into the AR platform. This process can be aided by your storyboards, which should call out the assets needed at each point.

Pay attention to images and text. For example, to fix part of a machine, you might need an overlay of a screw (which AR can show learners how to remove) and some text or audio instructions to use as they work.

Step 5. Make Your AR App Accessible

Making an AR-enabled experience as accessible as possible for all learners can create challenges, but there are always ways to overcome them. In a growing body of research on accessibility, two aspects of AR interface design have begun to emerge as essential: Scalable Vector Graphics (SVG) and haptic and audio feedback.

SVG is a text-based graphics language that's an open standard specification created by an initiative of the World Wide Web Consortium (W3C). SVG gathers real-time spatial data and converts it into an accessible representation of items and space. Haptic and audio feedback are also both immensely helpful in expanding accessibility. Haptic feedback uses touch to communicate with the learner, including the vibration or pulsing of the device. As we discussed in the previous section on mechanics, sounds of various kinds can be used as cues (Hollier 2019).

Step 6. Develop With Safety in Mind

Keep in mind the locations where learners will be using your AR app and any safety concerns you need to address. You will need to provide safety instructions before learners use the app.

Step 7. Prototype and Test

Gather a small group of users to test the AR experience. During this process, look for any safety and accessibility problems and measure the learning outcome from the experience. Check to see if any critical steps or elements were unintentionally omitted from development. Gather feedback from learners, instructors, and other stakeholders to identify areas for improvement and refine the design accordingly. Don't forget to check compatibility and ease of use across any device you plan to use.

Step 8. Set Up a Deployment Plan

How will the learners gain access to the AR experience? Will it be through a code they scan with the camera in their smartphone? Will they need to download an app? How is the app updated? How are changes made? The creation of the AR experience is critical, but deployment is just as important. Ensure that the proper mechanisms and procedures are in place for a smooth deployment.

Step 9. Monitor and Evaluate

Monitor learner engagement, performance, and satisfaction with the AR learning experience over time. Collect data on learning outcomes and assess the effectiveness of the AR experience in achieving the intended learning objectives. Use feedback and analytics to make continuous improvements.

AI Assist

As of the time of this writing, AI tools can't create an AR environment with a simple text prompt, but that capability could develop soon. In the meantime, we can still use AI to generate ideas and concepts for designing AR-based training.

Try using the following prompt to generate ideas for AR-based training. Adjust the content within the brackets to include relevant information for your particular scenario.

```
Give me ideas about creating augmented reality-based
training for [equipment operation]. Keep the suggestions
practical and focused on the safe use of AR.
```

Case Study: Using AR to Enhance Sales Representatives' Essential Knowledge

Jessica Angove, Vice President of Experiential Learning, Tipping Point Media

A global pharmaceutical company with a division dedicated to ophthalmic products that address various eye conditions and diseases was struggling to provide training in critical skills for its sales team. The company operates in a complex landscape where its sales representatives are a vital link between innovative products and the healthcare professionals (HCPs) who prescribe them. Sales reps must have expert knowledge of the products they represent and a deep understanding of the diseases they treat. The company came to our experiential learning team to develop a new training approach that would equip sales representatives with the expertise and confidence to navigate discussions with HCPs that included anatomy and physiology as well as the features of the pharmaceuticals.

The Challenge

The primary business challenge centered on a gap in the company's new-hire training program for sales representatives, specifically related to the anatomy and physiology of the eye. Initial training was delivered remotely before moving on to in-person sessions. The sessions relied heavily on modules with PDFs and 2D images, which fell short of conveying the full shape, size, and spatial arrangement of structures in a 3D human eye.

The remote training program was intended to lay the groundwork for in-person sessions, but the sales reps were arriving at on-site training events with only a limited understanding of the eye's anatomy. They required significant time to review information during their valuable in-person training time, diverting attention from key advanced topics.

The goal for our experiential learning team was to enhance the remote training experience by leveraging a more effective modality to convey the intricacies of human eye anatomy and ensure that the sales team arrived on-site with a solid foundation, ready to participate in more advanced training sessions. The key learning objectives focused on identifying anatomical structures in the eye, describing their function, and pronouncing their names correctly.

Why AR?

AR emerged as the ideal solution for this initiative because it could transform traditional 2D images into dynamic and interactive 3D experiences. By immersing learners in a fully rendered 3D model of the eye, AR would allow them to engage, explore, and dissect anatomical structures, creating a deeper understanding. This hands-on approach led to a richer learning experience, because users could visualize and actively participate in the exploration of the eye. This kind of interactive engagement promotes the retention of complex information, making AR an ideal action-first solution.

AR provided both engagement and accessibility for remote learners. Deployable on widely accessible devices like phones and tablets, it aligned with the company's goal to bridge the anatomy–education gap and enrich the remote training experience. With AR, the company was able to transform eye anatomy education into a dynamic and memorable experience.

Making the Case

To gain organizational buy-in for the adoption of AR, the company liaison, Michael, played a pivotal role. He had previously collaborated with our organization on a successful initiative at a different company when he spearheaded the launch of their first virtual reality experience for training new hires on inflammatory bowel disease. The positive outcomes of that endeavor—demonstrated in favorable data from Level 1 surveys—positioned Michael as a strong proponent of leveraging innovative technologies to educate learners about anatomy and physiology.

Recognizing the impact and value of his firsthand experience, we gave Michael a fully functional prototype to present to his stakeholders. By immersing them in the AR technology, we could best showcase its effectiveness for bridging the gap in anatomy education and its potential to enhance the overall training experience for sales representatives.

If an organization doesn't fully understand the value of an innovative solution, investing in a working prototype is often crucial for gaining support. Through this approach, we effectively communicated the value proposition of the AR solution, aligning our client organization with the success Michael had previously witnessed and creating a compelling case for the adoption of this innovative approach.

The Solution

The AR application developed for this initiative provided learners with an immersive 3D representation of the eye for interactive exploration. It featured two distinct modes: exploration and challenge (Figure 8-1).

Figure 8-1. Explore the Eye is shown on the left and Challenge Zone is shown on the right. *Source: Image courtesy of Tipping Point Media.*

In exploration mode, learners interacted freely with a fully rendered 3D model of the human eye, starting with the external structures and navigating down to the cellular level. Key structures were labeled, and tapping on a label opened a text panel with a definition of the structure and an audio pronunciation button. A consistent user interface ensured that learners were always aware of their location within the eye, and a menu provided easy access to jump to specific structures. This learner-controlled navigation empowered them to establish connections and better grasp the spatial arrangement of eye structures.

In challenge mode, learners demonstrated their knowledge of eye anatomy by answering 15 questions based on the content of their entire home study curriculum (Figure 8-2). Through a scavenger hunt format, learners navigated the 3D eye to select the anatomical structure that correctly answered the question. This gamified approach kept learners engaged while reinforcing their understanding of eye anatomy.

Figure 8-2. Answering questions about the eye. Learners can explore the eye or enter the challenge zone to answer questions using the AR tool. *Source: Image courtesy of Tipping Point Media.*

Design and development were a collaborative effort led by a multidisciplinary team that included instructional designers, medical writers, medically certified illustrators, 3D animators, and Unity programmers. This diverse team ensured a comprehensive approach that blended educational expertise with medical accuracy and technical proficiency.

The AR application was loaded into the organization's internal app store for learners to download onto their phones or tablets. To seamlessly integrate the AR application into the existing training structure, QR codes were added to the existing PDF training modules. They served as interactive gateways, encouraging learners to open and engage with the AR content at specific points in their training. This integration aimed to facilitate easy access and create a cohesive learning experience in which AR augmented and supported the existing training modules.

Benefits and Results

The official launch of this solution is pending, but initial feedback has been positive. We anticipate several benefits based on similar experiences in the past:

- **We expect the adoption of AR to result in higher engagement with the home study materials.** AR's interactive nature offers a novel and engaging approach to learning, which increases enthusiasm and participation.
- **The app's integrated data tracking will allow managers to monitor learner usage and interaction, enabling targeted interventions.** Additionally, data analytics on question responses will inform trainers about commonly misunderstood topics, allowing for more focused attention in live training sessions.
- **We also anticipate a higher level of knowledge about eye anatomy when representatives enter live training sessions.** Enhanced foundational understanding will contribute to a more efficient and productive live training experience.

Feedback from learners who have experienced immersive technologies, including AR, has been positive. Comments such as, "It's a great new way to process learning," and "It's nice to have the opportunity to learn with a different tool," indicate a favorable reception and suggest that this solution has the potential to positively affect the learning experience.

Lessons Learned

Reflecting on the project, there are two key lessons learned that can be used to inform the development of similar projects.

- **Prioritize the design of the user interface (UI) or user experience (UX).** The success of an AR solution hinges on thoughtful UI and UX design. Addressing the challenges of integrating AR "world space" assets with static "screen space" elements, especially on smaller devices, demands careful consideration. Grayboxing and prototyping (methods of testing and validating a learning experience before finalizing it) played a crucial role in our process. They allowed for rapid iteration of the interface, which was instrumental in achieving a design that not only appealed to learners visually but also proved to be intuitive and user friendly.
- **Storyboard thoroughly.** Implementing an AR solution with a large multidisciplinary team, especially in a remote work setting, requires strict attention to detail during the storyboard phase. The storyboard serves as the foundation for clear communication and alignment throughout subsequent stages, including 3D illustration and asset creation, animation, and programming. A well-defined storyboard is key to ensuring everyone on the team remains on the same page, facilitating effective collaboration and the successful execution of the AR solution.

Key Takeaways

Now that you're ready to create an AR experience for learning, remember these tips:

- AR is a technology that overlays digital information (such as images, videos, or 3D models) onto the real-world environment via a screen (such as a smartphone, smart glasses, or a tablet).
- AR can be used for learning by superimposing a sequence of steps into the learner's field of vision and then walking them through each one.
- Because AR can take place anywhere, it can be used effectively for technicians in the field as well as employees on the shop floor to provide immediate, context-sensitive assistance.
- The invisible can be made visible through AR. Images and information can be superimposed on the outside of an object (such as a machine or a human) allowing the learner to see what otherwise might be hidden inside.
- AR can provide a learner with a different perspective. It might alter their eyesight or provide a dramatically enlarged version of a key protein in the bloodstream or a miniaturized model of the solar system.
- AR can transform abstract data into visual representations that are easier to comprehend than 2D images on a computer screen. For example, learners can walk around the image and see it from different angles.
- Learning via AR can create more immersive experiences. For example, you can use immersive storytelling to make historical and cultural education more engaging and memorable.

EXPLANATION OF THE ACTION-FIRST ACTIVITY

The game *Pokémon Go* has been around since 2016. While the hype around it has long subsided, the seamless integration of AR and gameplay has only improved over time. If you haven't experienced *Pokémon Go* lately, you'll notice considerable improvements. If you've never played it, you are in for an AR treat.

As you play the game, you will notice how realistic (not to mention exciting) it is when a Pokémon comes into your field of vision. The game uses several AR elements to help you get closer to Pokémon and capture them. You get to virtually throw a Poké ball at the Pokémon to capture them as they sit in your kitchen, on your front lawn, or even in a grocery store.

You can also view a map and even take a picture of your captured Pokémon (Figure 8-3). Use the game, as well as ideas presented within this chapter, to think about how you might use AR in your own training design. How can you incorporate some of these elements?

Figure 8-3. A Pokémon named Shuckle seen hanging out in the entryway of the author's home. *Source: Photo by Karl M. Kapp.*

Tool 8-1. Tips for Effective Action-First AR Learning Experiences

✓ AR requires careful consideration of design. Always consider safety elements. Remember that you don't have control over the background a learner will see through their screen. Pay close attention to colors, contrast, and placement of information to ensure maximum accessibility.

✓ AR tools and software are rapidly evolving, so it's important to evaluate the technical requirements and limitations of each AR experience. Consider factors such as device compatibility, network connectivity, and potential latency issues.

✓ Overlay information, data, instructions, and other items on top of reality to orient and educate learners wherever they happen to be outside the classroom or e-learning environment.

9
Becoming an Avatar
A Metaverse for Learning

It's an oldie but a goodie that's been around since 2003, but it has so many leading-edge elements when it comes to virtual worlds and the metaverse. Your action-first assignment for this chapter is to create a Second Life account and do some exploration. Start at one of the community hubs and learn to walk, explore, and even fly. If you have an old, mothballed account, brush off that avatar and take a new plunge. You don't need goggles or a headset, but if you have them, the Second Life viewer will automatically detect them and calibrate the display appropriately, making your experience that much more immersive. *(Find the explanation at the end of the chapter.)*

At the end of this chapter, you should be able to answer these questions:
- What elements can you add to learning experiences in virtual reality (VR) or a version of the metaverse to make them effective for learning?
- Which learning outcomes are best for learning experiences and events in the metaverse or VR?
- What basic design principles should you consider when designing a VR or metaverse experience to facilitate learning?
- What are some examples of VR or metaverse learning environments and activities to facilitate learning?

The alarm rang in Leticia's ears. It was so loud it hurt. To make matters worse, the noise distracted her as she began to deal with the fire blazing in front of her. She knew she needed to concentrate on extinguishing the flames before they spread. Her colleague Danny ran into the room and asked what to do. Leticia knew her co-workers' lives were at stake.

METAVERSE

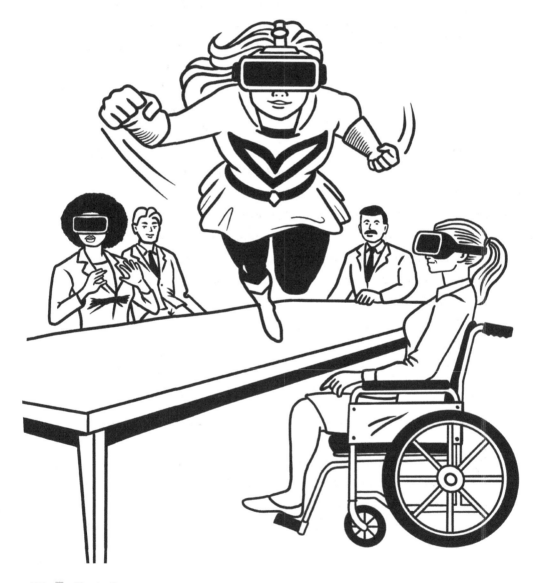

Normally calm, cool, and collected, she had been warned she might panic in this situation. She didn't believe it until now.

The fire crawling up the south wall of the warehouse was a lithium-ion battery fire. As the room started to fill with smoke, Leticia knew she was in danger of inhaling toxic gases, and the potential for an enormous explosion was real. She was now sweating and breathing rapidly.

She looked around for tools she could use to fight the fire but couldn't remember if she should use a Class A fire extinguisher or a Class D—or if she should just douse it with water. She was losing valuable time and the fire was intensifying. Leticia remembered the instructor in her safety training course mentioning something about flooding the area around the fire with water so it wouldn't spread, but that was best for small fires.

"What makes a fire small, medium, or large?" She was trying to remember exactly what the instructor had said as the fire raged closer.

Leticia first felt a vibration on her face and then heard a horrific sound before everything went black. She hadn't acted fast enough. The batteries had exploded.

"OK, Leticia," she heard the instructor's calm voice say. "Take off the goggles and headphones, and let's talk about what just happened."

While the fire Leticia and Danny had faced looked and sounded real, it was actually a training exercise, carried out in a safe, controlled environment in the metaverse designed to help warehouse employees learn to deal with the panic and stress they would face in similar real-world situations. Leticia's company used metaverse technology to create an immersive learning environment complete with the sounds, vibrations, and sights of dangerous environments. The goal wasn't to *tell* Leticia and her fellow employees how to fight lithium-ion battery fires; it was to teach them how to fight those fires in a realistic and immersive way—while they were experiencing the associated emotions and feelings—and to keep mistakes from happening later when lives were truly on the line.

* * *

In 1992, author Neal Stephenson published a science fiction novel called *Snow Crash*, in which he coined the term *metaverse*. Stephenson's metaverse was a world entered through a computer and a pair of goggles and earphones. In that world, everything was connected, and the virtual avatar could go anywhere, with no boundaries.

A similar concept furthered interest in the idea of the metaverse when *Ready Player One* was released in 2018. The movie was based on a 2011 novel by Ernest Cline in which the hero, Wade Watts, enters a version of the metaverse called the OASIS, which was created by computer genius James Halliday. Wade subsequently saves the OASIS from villains who want to ruthlessly exploit the metaverse for their own nefarious purposes.

These two works of fiction brought a great deal of attention to the idea of the metaverse, but neither the impact of Facebook CEO Mark Zuckerberg's decision to rename his company Meta in October 2021. In doing so, Zuckerberg declared that his company would create an actual metaverse mimicking science fiction. "In the metaverse, you'll be able to do almost anything you can imagine," he said.

As of the writing of this book, that ambitious version of the metaverse has not been fully created, but its tools—including goggles or glasses, headsets with earpieces, virtual world software, and computers that can power these virtual spaces—have been around for decades. Collectively, we refer to this technology and the artificial environment it creates as "virtual reality" (VR).

The concept of virtual reality includes all the elements of the metaverse but they are not interconnected, because you could have a VR experience in which you're confronted with a raging fire for safety training, and then learn negotiation skills in a different virtual environment with a different avatar. The two experiences are not connected, and your avatars are not interchangeable. In other words, you can't walk or fly from the warehouse fire to the boardroom because the two experiences are likely developed by different companies using different software. You are learning in VR in two places, not the metaverse.

However, because the term *metaverse* has gained popularity and its meaning is so similar to *virtual reality*, we will use the terms interchangeably in much of this chapter. For our purposes, I define a *metaverse for learning* as an artificial virtual space in which users can interact with a computer-generated digital environment and with fellow learners in the same virtual space, which they enter by wearing goggles or glasses.

In the metaverse or virtual reality, the learner controls a virtual version of themselves called an *avatar*. The learner interacts with the environment through their avatar, experiencing everything in a realistic way but from a safe distance. Digital "twins" of locations, equipment, and tools help recreate specific aspects of reality so learners can repeatedly practice techniques, processes, and safety protocols.

Because it exists virtually, the metaverse can track movements, record actions, and provide real-time feedback to trainees in the middle of a learning experience. Learners access the training environment using a headset and earphones to ensure their senses are fully engaged. When a participant's sight and hearing are involved, their brain can be persuaded into believing the situation is real so they behave accordingly.

In this kind of action-first experience, learning is no longer just an intellectual exercise because each participant's affective or emotional domain is also contributing.

Why Is the Metaverse Effective for Learning?

The metaverse provides an immersive environment where learners can engage with content in a highly realistic way through simulations and virtual interactions. Learning in the metaverse is especially effective because it engages multiple senses, allows for collaboration across distances, offers a safe space for trial and error, and provides infinite scenarios and resources for learners.

Engage Multiple Senses

Because the learner is isolated from the world by wearing goggles and earphones, their senses are focused entirely on the virtual experience. In some cases, they may also be wearing gloves, vests, shirts, or other haptic garments (similar to what Wade Watts wore in *Ready Player One*) that react to what is happening in the virtual environment. For example, when a participant is playing a first-person shooter game and bumps into a door frame, their arm will feel a vibration or squeeze. Sound cues can also vary in intensity and tone, depending on the participant's inter-actions within the environment.

The metaverse's immersive experience can envelop the learner in ex-periences ranging from working on an oil rig in the middle of the Atlantic Ocean to stacking boxes in a warehouse in Kenya to sitting in on a tense meeting with an unhappy client in Madrid, Spain. The fact that multiple senses are engaged creates a highly realistic action-first training session.

Allow Collaboration Across Distances

The "death of distance" refers to the fact that in the metaverse, geograph-ical distance is no longer a barrier to collaboration and teamwork. One learner in New York City can collaborate with another in Tokyo, Japan, as if they are in the same location. Unlike video calls, learners in the metaverse feel like they are all in the same space because they see each other standing or sitting nearby and have the same spatial references (such as, "On your left, you'll see the extruder machine."). This virtual proximity facilitates close collaboration and is particularly beneficial for organizations with global operations. Learning in the metaverse allows teams to pool expertise and perspectives from far and wide to address complex, enterprise-wide training issues. It opens new opportunities to learn from and with people from diverse backgrounds and allows orga-nizations to access knowledgeable instructors and facilitators, no matter their location.

Offer a Safe Space for Trial and Error

The metaverse is a safe space where learners can try, fail, and learn from their mistakes without real-world consequences. This is especially import-ant in fields such as medicine, aviation, and engineering where errors can have serious implications. In the metaverse, learners can practice com-plex procedures, troubleshoot problems, or experiment with different approaches without fear of costly or harmful errors. After an exercise or ac-tivity, they can analyze and learn from their errors by replaying situations, reflecting on their decision-making processes, and receiving immediate feedback. This iterative experience of making mistakes, understanding them, and trying again is particularly helpful for deep learning and mastery of complex skills.

Regularly engaging in trial-and-error learning experiences in a safe environment helps learners build confidence in their abilities and helps them develop resilience as they become accustomed to viewing mistakes as learning opportunities rather than setbacks.

Provide Infinite Resources and Scenarios

There is no limit to the resources and scenarios a metaverse experience can deploy. For example, training first responders with actual firefighting equipment, active police cars, helicopters, and other specialized gear is usually too expensive to stage and assemble in the real world. In the metaverse, all that equipment can be created virtually and rendered in realistic detail. You can assemble as many firetrucks and police cars as needed. First responders can experience fighting fires on an oil rig, at a chemical plant, or on a busy highway. The number, type, and complexity of scenarios are infinite because they are relatively easy to create and execute compared to staging them in real life. For instance, a manufacturing company could use the metaverse to train staff to handle advanced, dangerous machinery or equipment.

A metaverse role-play experience can also include infinite branching options. In a traditional branching scenario, the designer needs to consider and develop each branch. In a metaverse environment, on the other hand, a real person exists behind each avatar. This means any question or line of inquiry can be followed because the people controlling the avatars can instantly react to these questions and continue the discussion. Additionally, advances are being made in AI to allow nonplayer characters (NPCs), which are completely computer generated, to interact with learners in a metaverse environment using natural human language to simulate an actual real person rather than a computer-generated avatar.

What Can the Metaverse Teach?

The metaverse for learning is particularly effective for developing both hard and soft skills—from technical expertise in a field like engineering or nursing to more general business skills like teamwork, problem solving, and adaptability. Learning in a metaverse experience also includes reflecting on the experience. It can provide insights into how teams work together, how to manage people across a distance, and how to handle pressure.

Technical Expertise

A metaverse learning experience can include equipment and tools ranging from hammers and drills to scalpels. Therefore, individuals are able to practice specific technical skills using the proper equipment and tools in a realistic manner and environment. This might include performing virtual surgeries, troubleshooting communications links, testing a broken piece of equipment in a field situation, piloting an aircraft in a simulated storm, or rearranging an assembly line to help ensure the best possible flow. The scalability of the metaverse means that learners can be focused on a single tool or piece of equipment or zoom out and configure the layout of an entire factory. The ability to scale and create digital twins of equipment and places in the metaverse means learners can practice skills or experience situations in a much more cost-effective way than using physical items.

Grace Under Pressure

In many workplace environments, remaining calm in demanding situations is essential for success. A metaverse learning experience can create realistic stress and help participants learn how to cope with it. For example, a metaverse learning experience could recreate the tense atmosphere of a corporate boardroom during a critical budgetary crisis, the high-pressure environment of an emergency room, or the intensity of a dangerous military operation. These simulations would include emotional and psychological stressors to provide a holistic learning experience. Participants can practice responding calmly and effectively under pressure while learning to process information, assess options, and make swift decisions in less-than-ideal circumstances. Teams can learn these skills together, practicing personal composure while managing team stress and ensuring effective communication continues even when the stakes are high.

Teamwork

A huge advantage of learning in the metaverse is that it provides an opportunity for more teamwork. People can log in from different locations and practice working as a team. Because sessions can be recorded, learners and instructors can replay interactions to evaluate how the team worked together and identify areas that might need improvement. It's possible to replicate the team's typical workspace in detail. For instance, a team working on a construction project can operate within a simulated building site, complete with virtual models of the structure, tools, and equipment. These details enable teams to navigate the challenges and dynamics of their work—observing, learning, and then applying the lessons in real-world situations.

Leadership and Management Skills

Leadership training in the metaverse can simulate real-life leadership challenges and decision-making scenarios. Leaders can analyze complex situations, consider different approaches, and solve problems efficiently. For example, you could put someone into a situation in which they must lead a team to develop a new product to outmaneuver a competitor. In this scenario, the leader would use critical thinking, planning, delegation, and decision-making skills to ensure the product is developed properly. You could also create same kind of scenario for someone learning to manage projects in which they must allocate resources, meet with team members, and establish team deadlines and norms to ensure the project is completed on time and within budget.

A variety of scenarios can help leaders and managers learn how to communicate strategies, give clear instructions, and provide feedback. They can also learn how to handle conflicting team members or those not working collaboratively with others.

Critical Incidents

Properly reacting to emergencies is essential for saving lives and protecting property, but practicing and preparing in-depth for disasters isn't easy. The metaverse is an ideal training platform for learning to handle critical incidents because it can mimic everything from an earthquake to an industrial accident to a cyberattack. Individuals and teams can practice their response to a crisis in a real-time simulated environment. You may ask participants to make quick decisions, coordinate with others, use emergency equipment or procedures, and manage the aftermath of the incident. The immersive nature of the metaverse ensures they experience the stress and fear associated with real-life emergencies, which is crucial for developing the ability to remain calm and effective under pressure.

In addition, the metaverse allows for the repetition of scenarios, with altered variables and conditions reflecting various levels of complexity and severity. Repeated exposure is essential for learning best practices for critical incidents. The metaverse also provides an opportunity for interdisciplinary training in which different response teams (such as medical personnel, firefighters, law enforcement or operations, sales, and executive leadership) can collaborate and practice coordinated responses.

Archetypal Metaverse Learning Experiences

Don't think of the metaverse environment as simply an online learning module or a classroom. Instead, think of it as an opportunity to take the learner anywhere they need to go or put them anywhere they need to be—whether that's inside a nuclear reactor, on a distant oil rig, in front of a commercial vehicle's steering wheel, or in a potential client's office. In the metaverse, learners can be immersed in a realistic situation that requires action, exploration, and decision making as if the situation unfolding in front of them were real. Here are several metaverse learning archetypes you can use to frame learner experiences.

Go on a Field Trip or Scavenger Hunt

A *field trip* is a structured visit to a specific location to learn more about that location. It's structured because the person is not just walking around aimlessly, and there's a purpose and a reason for visiting the location. A metaverse field trip engages learners in a highly realistic, but controlled and safe environment. For example, new employees at a manufacturing plant can go on a metaverse field trip to learn about safety protocols, hazardous areas, and production processes before ever physically stepping foot on the factory floor. This experience makes their initial visit to the actual, physical manufacturing plant safer and more familiar. To add even more immersion and interactivity, you could create a scavenger hunt in the metaverse and ask learners to look for specific items, such as pieces of equipment, emergency exits, or safety hazards.

Scavenger hunts and field trips are effective methods of leveraging the metaverse to allow learners to explore places that are difficult or dangerous to access. These experiences orient learners to safety hazards, the layout of the area, and physical traits of a specific location.

Orienteering a Conceptual Scenario

Conceptual orienteering means immersing a learner into a specific situation or scenario to experience a concept that might otherwise be abstract or unfamiliar. This helps them truly understand the concept, identify with the feelings the concept evokes, and gain insights into dealing with the concept in real life. For example, you might place learners on a beach during a tsunami to witness the ocean appearing to drain away before a huge wall of water comes right toward them. This would help make the concept of experiencing a tsunami real but also safe for the learner. Or you might put the learner into an environment where everything appears blurry to simulate how the eye disease macular degeneration affects a person's vision. This can help healthcare professionals build empathy with their patients.

Conceptual orienteering can also include orienting the learner to abstract data and information. This might involve creating a virtual view of the stock market that the learner can fly over to see the different stocks color-coded with red for losing value and green for gaining. This experience could provide insights into sectors or groups of stocks that might not be as obvious if the data wasn't visible.

Preparing for a Critical Incident

Preparing learners for a critical incident helps them plan for or react to situations that are infrequent, unexpected, or too dangerous to practice in the real world. This immerses the learner into a critical and dangerous situation they may encounter someday and trains them to deal with it. It immediately captures the learner's attention and provides a realistic experience in which they must solve an issue by thinking quickly and applying the appropriate knowledge within a crisis.

Because it's the metaverse, critical incident training typically involves multiple learners working together to handle an incident and keep everyone safe. Fortunately, if something goes wrong in their response, no one is hurt or injured. An example of a critical incident learning experience could be to place learners into a situation where a hazardous chemical spill has occurred in a factory or laboratory. They would have to make decisions about assessing the situation, identifying the type of chemical, containing the spill, evacuating affected areas, and perhaps implementing decontamination procedures to prevent further harm.

Operationalizing Applications

In a metaverse learning experience, a learner can interact with and manipulate realistic objects to gain proficiency in their functionality and performance. This is a simulation of hard or technical skills, which include the operation of a piece of equipment, machinery, or vehicle. Digital twins are often used in an operational application so the user can practice with an exact duplicate of the real item, such as a steering wheel on a delivery truck or the throttle control on a helicopter. This allows the learner to complete the proper steps and procedures necessary for operating a variety of equipment.

A typical example of the operational application archetype is a virtual flight simulator. The person learning to fly manipulates and controls a digital version of the actual cockpit—complete with instruments, lights, and controls—exactly duplicating the one in a physical plane.

Practicing Soft Skills

In many situations, a person needs to display effective soft (or power) skills, including working with others, negotiating, and socially interacting. Within a metaverse learning experience, individuals can practice working together and applying these social skills in a digital environment. For example, you could place a learner in a virtual retail store, showroom, or business setting and ask them to close a sale. The potential purchaser could be the trainer role-playing a potential customer. The practice transaction takes place in the safety of the metaverse, so the consequences of failure are minimal, but the context, situation, and setting feel realistic because the environment's visual and audio cues are present. It can also be recorded, allowing the trainer to provide feedback to the learner. The social simulation design is an effective way to practice key social skills.

Let's Design a Metaverse Learning Experience

Creating a metaverse learning experience involves numerous steps. But, because it is so technology centric, one major piece is to carefully choose the platform in which the metaverse experience will reside. You also need to develop a good interactive design because it will influence learner engagement, knowledge retention, and the overall effectiveness of the experience, as well as achievement of the desired learning outcomes. To create a successful interactive design in a metaverse learning environment, you'll need to follow the steps detailed here.

Step 1. Identify Target Audience, Develop Learner Personas, and Define Learning Objectives and Outcomes

Start by identifying the target audience and developing learner personas. Determine which abilities are necessary to fulfill the job description in the real world. Clearly define the instructional goals and objectives learners should achieve within the metaverse learning environment, and strive to incorporate basic accessibility from the start. Investment in a metaverse is often large. It takes time to construct the needed assets and set up the environment, as well as money to purchase the platform and equipment to run it; therefore, it makes sense to leverage your metaverse platform to achieve multiple learning goals for a variety of learning situations. I recommend developing a list of learning scenarios or situations that you believe a metaverse will be most effective for.

Step 2. Design Instructional Walk-Throughs

Once you have determined the objectives, create a walk-through. Attempt to envision how the learner will enter the simulation (where will they be standing in the metaverse), and then consider the steps they will take to begin learning in that environment. Note whether they need to pick up any objects, turn any knobs, or manipulate any equipment. Determine how learners will communicate with one another and the instructor. Will you be teaching soft skills like communication and leadership or hard skills like how to troubleshoot a piece of equipment? Once you understand the instructional walk-through, you'll be able to determine the functionality you need in your metaverse platform as well as any necessary visual elements and spaces. At this point, you should identify the types of data you want to collect on learner performance and indicate at what stages in the learning process you want to collect it.

Step 3. Determine the Desired Visual Environment

There's one more step you should take before you look at metaverse platforms. You'll need to develop storyboards or images of what you expect the environment to look and feel like, including the visual design, layout, and interactive elements of every virtual space you'll need. If you have an idea of what the space (or spaces) should be within your metaverse learning environment, it will help you analyze and select your technology platform.

Step 4. Analyze and Select the Appropriate Platform

Carefully examine the many metaverse options and vendors that exist to find the right platform for your needs. Some have prebuilt spaces and environments that might work for you, while others allow you to import drawings to create a 3D environment. Discuss accessibility capabilities and limitations, as well as any advanced levels of compliance your organization might need. You should also look for a platform that supports your organization's required level of interactivity, realism, accessibility, and user engagement. Make sure it's compatible with your target audience's hardware and software requirements—some metaverse platforms will run across different hardware (such as goggles) on desktop and laptop computers, and smartphones. Determine the delivery channels that you will leverage in your organization and choose an appropriate technology platform. Don't forget to involve the IT department and ensure that the software will run on your organization's network.

Step 5. Plan for Accessibility

With the target audience, objectives, platforms, and technical details established, continue to build basic accessibility into your design, as needed. One place to look for guidance in this area is the Microsoft Accessible Mixed Reality website, which provides research, tips, and techniques to help ensure that the creative environment is as accessible as possible. You can find the link to the site in the recommended resources at the end of this book.

Step 6. Gather or Create 3D Assets

Once you have purchased a platform, it's time to develop the learning environment. You'll want to use the platform's creation capabilities to build the needed spaces, or you could have the vendor perform that operation. You may need to import assets or have them created, and you'll need to develop or check the functionality of any virtual machines or equipment. Determine how data on learner performance is created and what type of dashboard or reports provide that data to the instructor.

Step 7. Create Facilitator Materials

Because the metaverse often provides a group learning experience, a facilitator is typically present. They'll need training and materials to understand how to oversee the learning experience. Should they interrupt learners in the middle of the experience or wait until after to debrief? Do you want to debrief in front of the entire team, one-on-one, or both? How will the learner receive the data on their performance? You need to work out these issues before the live event.

Step 8. Pilot-Test the Instructional Scenarios

Once you have built out all the assets and created a facilitator guide, you should test the scenario with a small group to ensure it makes sense and no one gets confused, the instructor knows what they are doing, and the metaverse platform is responding correctly. At this stage, you may also discover any confusion the learner might have while onboarding to the metaverse environment and learning how to navigate with their avatar. Note: This is usually an issue because many people are not familiar with navigating a virtual character through a virtual world like the metaverse, which means you'll need to teach them navigation techniques.

Step 9. Build an Onboarding Tutorial

After you discover the areas of friction for learners in terms of accessing the metaverse platform, create a general tutorial for the onboarding process. You don't want learners to experience the cognitive overload of trying to navigate and learn within the metaverse. You want them to be comfortable navigating and manipulating their avatar *before* the actual learning experience starts. Often organizations will create fun events within the metaverse that aren't tied to a specific learning objective but are designed to familiarize learners with the environment.

Step 10. Conduct Training

Once everything is in place, conduct the training session within the metaverse. As an important element, don't forget to build in reflection and a chance to review lessons learned from the experience. This reflection will help solidify the lessons learned.

Step 11. Evaluate and Revise

Based on observation, evaluate the effectiveness of the metaverse learning experience against the initial objectives. Gather feedback from learners and instructors and analyze any available performance data. Use this information to make ongoing improvements to the experience.

AI Assist

While AI can't yet create entire virtual worlds or metaverse learning experiences, the technology is moving in that direction. You can currently use AI tools to assist you in creating VR learning experiences in several ways, including generating content, improving sound, and creating intelligent characters. You can use text-based AI tools to develop ideas and scenes to serve as jumping-off points for storyboards or descriptions of the experience. Here's a prompt to generate ideas for a metaverse learning experience. Replace the elements in the brackets with your own content.

```
Create a metaverse learning experience for a [new
worker] in a [manufacturing organization] learning to
work a [lathe]. Indicate how to evaluate the learner's
performance within the environment.
```

Case Study: VR and Portable Gaming Boost Navy Readiness

Anders Gronstedt, The Gronstedt Group

This case study involves a project for the US Navy that converted a legacy touchscreen maintenance training program into a firewall-protected VR simulation. It completely immersed the learners, who wore headsets to enhance the sensory experience.

In brief, the sailors could step into a virtual submarine machinery room of such convincing fidelity that they had a real sense of being there in real life. While turning valves and tightening bolts, they would feel tactile vibrations from the controllers in their hands. They would hear the diesel engine roar to life. The self-paced program included tutorials, feedback loops, and learning scaffolding. A handheld gaming PC version was also available if space, comfort, or cyber security was a concern.

The Challenge

Every year, the US Navy loses $400 million due to congestion and delays in its training pipelines. It's prohibitively expensive to physically reproduce the environment in which sailors operate as well as all the complex equipment and tools they use on ships, submarines, and aircraft. It can also be difficult to realistically recreate an emergency in which sailors need to perform at a high level while under extreme pressure. The navy sought a practical solution that provided the realism of being onboard a ship or submarine while reducing costs and effectively meeting a variety of training needs.

Why VR?

One of the most important criteria for this training was to recreate the feeling and function of being onboard a ship or submarine; the sailors needed an immersive, realistic environment. The navy's ships and submarines are not ideal learning environments because they are constantly in use for real-world operations, and training has to be conducted in as safe an environment as possible. A solution using VR and digital twins of all equipment seemed like the perfect fit. The environment had to be separate from any other virtual experience due to security concerns, so we created a VR environment.

Making the Case

The Naval Air Warfare Center Training Systems Division (NAWCTSD) teamed with the Gronstedt Group under a Cooperative Research and Development Agreement (CRADA) to jointly create the technology. CRADA is a program in which the federal government and an independent third party contribute personnel, services, facilities, equipment, intellectual property, and other resources toward specific research and development efforts consistent with the mission of a particular federal agency.

Because of the need for realistic, immersive learning, the collaborative partners focused on transforming existing touchscreen training—Multipurpose Reconfigurable Training System (or MRTS 3D)—into a VR experience.

The MRTS 3D program features a detailed 3D environment deployed on 55-inch touchscreens to simulate a variety of scenarios for sailors to practice real-time troubleshooting and maintenance procedures. The implementation via touchscreens was effective, but the MRTS 3D team recognized VR's potential to provide more immersive training that could give sailors a realistic feeling of being aboard an ocean-going vessel, complete with the accompanying sights and sounds.

The team wanted to create the sensation of performing hands-on tasks under stress, such as troubleshooting a flooded diesel engine in a submarine machinery room. The goal was to create a strong feeling of presence that was so convincing that the sailors would forget they were not actually experiencing the critical incident as a training exercise. For example, instead of using abstracted, unrealistic hand gestures on a flatscreen to turn a wrench with the MRTS 3D program, the team wanted a scenario in which a sailor could pick up the wrench with their virtual hands, fit it onto the bolt, and turn it, while also experiencing everything as if they were inside a submarine. Details about this realistic experience formed the foundation of the case the partners made for training using VR, which is also known in some circles as *spatial computing*.

The Solution

Working in close partnership with the navy's team, the Gronstedt Group developed a demonstration project that put sailors into a high-fidelity submarine machinery room to work on a 688-class diesel engine. The team created hyper-realistic models, directional sound, and vibrating hand controllers. The goal was to hack the sailors' senses of sight, feeling, and hearing.

In practice, an instructor's screen followed learners through every step as they navigated the virtual 688-class diesel engine. The instructor provided videos and text instructions to guide sailors through the process of starting up the engine, and learners could grab the instruction screen and position it in midair at whatever location was most suitable for the task they were performing. Just like in real life, they used their hands to turn valves, push buttons, check gauges, tighten bolts, and pull levers. If they made a mistake, the VR scenario could easily be reset thanks to the unlimited opportunities to redo an action. A compass arrow at the user's feet showed where to walk to perform their next task, and learners had the option to physically walk around the simulated submarine (if their real-world space was large enough), or they could use controller thumb sticks to navigate a virtual space while seated or standing in place (Figure 9-1).

Figure 9-1. VR naval training in action. Hands-on VR training in a hyper-realistic submarine builds muscle memory. *Source: Gronstedt Group and Denver Headshot. Used with permission.*

The project required a team of 3D artists and game designers to optimize a high-fidelity experience for mobile headsets, along with spatial learning experts to develop guided practice with tutorials and feedback.

Headsets and hand controllers tracked everything the learners did in the VR environment, providing detailed analytics regarding mistakes, pause or confusion points, and proficiencies. The system can track an overwhelming number of metrics, but the magic happens when meaningful data is fed back into the learning management system. These reports can then be used to suggest new scenarios that are focused on the skills that need improvement.

When sailors are absorbed in the training, they lose track of time and seem to enter a state of flow, as they learn and practice skills in this safe environment. Learners and instructors from all over the world can interact with each other seamlessly, appearing as avatars to collaborate on tasks and then debrief.

The low-cost, standalone VR headsets are portable and easily deployable at the point of need, including aboard ships. They don't need cords or a PC, can be used seated or standing, are self-paced, and support multiplayer simulations. When comfort, space, or security aboard ships make using VR challenging, learners can still engage with the application on personal computers using game controllers or handheld gaming devices (Figure 9-2). Game controllers have been the prime 3D flatscreen interface for three decades and are second nature for most sailors. The accessibility of mobile VR and handheld gaming PC training will multiply reps and sets of intense, deliberate practice, building muscle memory and boosting readiness.

Figure 9-2. Handheld device for VR training. Handheld gaming PC simulations address space, comfort, and cybersecurity restrictions aboard ships. *Source: Gronstedt Group and Denver Headshot. Used with permission.*

Benefits and Results

Testers of the system gave it a near-perfect score. "You felt like you are actually working on the system and not just a screen," said one user. This resonated with leaders and sparked a flurry of ideas to enhance fleet readiness with VR learning at the point of need, whether in port or underway.

Feedback from an anonymous, voluntary user test by 23 sailors at the Trident Training Facility in Bangor, Maine, on November 15, 2023, was exceptionally favorable (as indicated in Figure 9-3).

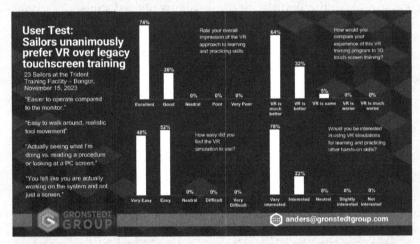

Figure 9-3. Navy VR user test feedback. The data and quotes in the graphic represent feedback from the sailors who experienced the immersive training. *Source: The Gronstedt Group. Used with permission.*

Lessons Learned

This development process provided valuable takeaways, offering practical lessons that you can apply to similar projects in the future. The lessons include:

- **Strive for visual, functional, and cognitive fidelity.** This means the experience should look right, work right, and emphasize developing crucial cognitive skills through tutorials, feedback, and scaffolding. The sailors' movements during the experience reinforced valuable muscle memory, which is highly effective in skill acquisition and retention. They also appreciated the realistic interaction with the virtual environment.

- **Plan to integrate data collection into the VR training program from the beginning.** Planning to integrate analytics into the training system allowed us to determine which data was most important to track. This also meant we could track almost every aspect of learner performance, allowing us to create personalized learning plans, which helped sailors focus on skills they needed to improve. This approach enhanced learning outcomes and overall fleet readiness.
- **Bring in experts to help with spatial learning and develop guided practice exercises, tutorials, and feedback.** Merely reproducing the environment and letting learners walk around does not have the same instructional impact as carefully planning an instructional experience within the VR environment.

Key Takeaways

Now that you're ready to create a metaverse experience for learning, remember these tips:

- The metaverse is an expanded version of VR and spatial computing. While the terms are not the same, they're often used interchangeably. The common trait is that the learner's senses are immersed in the digital experience, making them feel like they are in the actual place and situation.
- A metaverse learning experience provides a safe environment for learners to practice both technical (hard) skills and social or soft skills, like communication, leadership, teamwork, and collaboration.
- Avatars allow the learner to control a virtual version of themselves that interacts with the environment, enabling a dual learning experience of direct participation and objective observation from a safe distance. This is one of the few learning environments in which that experience can happen.

- The ability to recreate digital twins of equipment, places, and tools in the metaverse allows for realistic practice of techniques and procedures.
- The metaverse allows for almost infinite branching scenarios because a real person is operating the avatar and can respond to any question. This means dialogue and choices don't need to be pre-scripted as with some other learning delivery tools. The use of AI-powered NPCs will expand the opportunities for unscripted actions.
- With the metaverse, you can achieve total sensory immersion (through goggles, headsets, or headphones) and haptic feedback devices (like vests or a specially made jumpsuit) to enhance the learning experience and make it highly realistic.
- The metaverse allows you to create unlimited resources and scenarios. This provides the opportunity for developing scalable, cost-effective training solutions, and is especially helpful when dealing with expensive real-world setups requiring lots of resources and equipment.
- The metaverse overcomes geographical distances. The learners all feel like they are in the same physical space at the same time.

EXPLANATION OF THE ACTION-FIRST ACTIVITY

The world of Second Life is a great entry point into metaverse experiences because it can be used across platforms. When it's used with a headset and goggles, Second Life becomes a VR experience. Learning to navigate and explore in this environment will make you more familiar and comfortable with controlling an avatar and experiencing movement, social interactions, and tasks within a digital world.

The more comfortable you become within a digital world, the more you will start to see the possibilities for action-first learning. Even though VR, digital worlds, and the metaverse have been around for years, they are still not widely used or leveraged for learning. As the technology becomes easier to use and more ubiquitous, it will be integrated more and more into organizations' training curricula. If you start exploring now, you'll have a head start in this area.

Tool 9-1. Tips for Effective Metaverse Learning Experiences

✓ The metaverse allows you to create unlimited resources and scenarios. This provides the opportunity for developing scalable, cost-effective training solutions, and is especially helpful when dealing with expensive real-world setups requiring lots of resources and equipment.

✓ The metaverse can be used to simulate high-stress environments, aiding in the development of grace under pressure, a valuable skill in many professional fields.

✓ A metaverse learning environment can help train individuals and teams in dealing with critical incidents, allowing for the simulation of natural disasters, industrial accidents, and other crisis situations.

✓ Before purchasing a metaverse platform, envision the learner's experience and determine what interactions they will have with the environment, objects, and fellow learners. This will help identify the features and functionalities that you'll need to ensure proper instruction in the metaverse.

10

An Anytime, Anywhere Coach
AI-Powered Coaching for Learning

Let's interact with a chatbot. Follow this QR code or type in bit.ly/DrKappChatbot to experience a chatbot I've created. It's a virtual Dr. Kapp who can answer questions about action-first learning,

games, or gamification based on my books, presentations, and other things I've written. Try asking it some questions. What types of responses do you get? Does it feel like you're interacting with a real person? *(Find the explanation at the end of the chapter.)*

At the end of this chapter, you should be able to answer these questions:

- What elements can you add to an AI-powered coach to make it more effective for learning?
- What types of learning outcomes best leverage an AI-powered coach?
- What basic design principles should you consider when designing an AI-powered coaching experience?
- What are some examples of AI-powered coaching for improving employee performance?

Sam, a software engineer, was worried about an upcoming presentation he had to give to executive leadership. Would he be loud enough? Could he avoid the infamous "ums" and "ahs" that punctuated every presentation he gave? Could he remember to emphasize the right words—his

manager called them *power words*—to convey the proper message? If Sam could pull this off, his department would have a good chance of receiving extra funding for research. If he failed, the funding would go elsewhere. Sam struggled to figure out how to make sure his message would land, despite his subpar presentation skills.

Sam asked if he could hire a speaking coach, but the cost was high, so his manager said no. With the presentation just two weeks away, Sam's manager recommended the digital speaking coach Abbie. A company called Presentr had designed Abbie specifically to help people like Sam become better at presenting in front of a large audience. He was skeptical but desperate, so he agreed to give it a try.

Sam opened up the Abbie app on his smartphone, placed it in front of him, and gave his presentation. Abbie analyzed the presentation and noted multiple opportunities for improvement. "Duh, I already knew that," Sam mumbled. But then he got something he hadn't expected: detailed feedback and a dozen guided practice opportunities. Abbie provided information on pacing, volume level, and correcting the use of "ums," "ahs," and other filler words. The app also provided specific exercises to help Sam improve each problem area. It measured his volume (using a meter to show when he was too soft or too loud) and tagged each filler word. Following each practice round, Abbie provided more advice on how Sam could improve. He entered some of the keywords he wanted to emphasize most in the presentation, and Abbie tracked them. He especially appreciated that the app allowed him to practice the presentation when and where he wanted, not just in the office. He put in his earbuds and used the app while jogging, while making dinner, and even in his dentist's waiting room.

After just two weeks, Sam felt much more confident facing the executive committee. The presentation was the smoothest and most powerful he'd ever done, and his department got the approval and funding it needed.

Why Is an AI-Powered Coach Effective for Learning?

AI-powered coaches offer L&D professionals a valuable way to combine technology and pedagogy to help people in any work environment improve performance. Consumer-focused coaches for losing weight, exercising, and meditating have been around for several years, providing personalized feedback and motivation combined with actionable content. AI-powered coaching has now taken off in the business realm. These tools work so well because they offer personalized learning, immediate and targeted feedback, motivation and engagement, and exception-driven initiatives.

Personalized Learning

One-on-one coaching is one of the best ways to help someone master a new skill, but it's not scalable with humans as coaches because each person needs an individual coach. AI eliminates that need while still personalizing learning.

An AI coach can assess a learner's existing knowledge and skill levels through interactive activities, quizzes, and other means. Once an initial evaluation is complete, the coach will provide customized feedback and practice opportunities based on individual needs. In Sam's case, the AI targeted his mistakes, pronunciations, pacing, word choice, and personal quirks. The AI-powered coaches suggest practice opportunities that are tailored, in terms of difficulty and complexity, to align with the learner's current skill level. This adaptive approach ensures that learners are consistently challenged just enough to stay engaged and motivated without feeling overwhelmed or discouraged.

AI-powered coaching mirrors the *zone of proximal development theory*, which posits that the most effective learning occurs just beyond the person's current abilities. AI coaches can create learning experiences that are neither so easy that they are boring nor so difficult that they are frustrating. Therefore, the AI coach can provide specific, actionable counsel and guidance until the learner has mastered the desired skills.

Immediate, Targeted Feedback

If you've used an AI chatbot, you've probably noticed their speedy responses to your questions. AI-powered coaches can provide near-instant responses and guidance too, which is highly valuable as long as the guidance is well targeted.

Psychologist Anders Ericsson and his colleagues discovered that deliberate practice leads to the best results when people are trying to learn a new skill. *Deliberate practice* simply means "individualized training activities specially designed by a coach or teacher [or in this, case AI] to improve specific aspects of an individual's performance through repetition and successive refinement" (Ericsson and Lehmann 1996). In deliberate practice, feedback isn't just about correcting errors; it also involves guidance on how to better learn and apply the skill, including strategies and tips tailored to the learner's current mastery level. This facilitates deeper comprehension and more nuanced skills development, because learners are not merely told what they did wrong but are guided toward specific ways to improve their performance. AI-powered coaches can also use data from interactions with learners to improve future training sessions. By continuously updating the task difficulty and focus, the AI coach ensures that learners are always working at the edge of their capabilities—a defining aspect of deliberate practice.

Engagement and Motivation

AI-powered coaching applications allow participants to set clear, attainable goals and get immediate feedback while also tracking their progress in real time. Visible progress is crucial for motivation providing clear evidence of skill development. AI-powered training often incorporates interactive game-like elements that enhance employee motivation and engagement in the learning process. Seeing progress toward a goal by earning badges or points, especially on a daily basis, can be highly motivational for learners and heighten their commitment to the learning process.

Exception-Driven Initiatives

AI-powered coaching tools can track progress and identify patterns in employee performance. In addition to giving feedback directly to the user, the AI coach can also provide that information to managers and supervisors. By using those data-driven insights, managers are able to spend less time on general supervision and more time addressing specific needs. They can provide one-on-one attention to those who need additional assistance, maximizing the effectiveness of human coaching because they know exactly who needs the extra nudge.

Let's look at a hypothetical example. An AI-powered coaching tool might report a pattern of declining sales conversions over the past quarter for an employee named Jen. Instead of having to review every team member's performance manually, Jen's manager would receive an alert about the downward trend. The manager could then schedule a one-on-one coaching session to better understand the challenges Jen is facing and provide targeted training or resources to improve her sales technique. On the flip side, AI-powered coaching can also ensure Jen's manager quickly recognizes when she is doing an outstanding job and exceeding key performance indicators (KPIs). That manager can quickly provide kudos to Jen and any other high-performing individuals they are supervising.

What Can AI-Powered Coaches Teach?

AI-powered coaches can be effective tools for L&D professionals to deploy within any action-first learning environment. They can provide personalized instruction in almost any subject area, including technical skills, soft skills, and even complex decision-making processes. They can help managers and supervisors manage people more effectively. And most importantly, they can adapt to the varied learning needs of employees and provide motivational cues to assist in goal setting and achievement. Here are a few key areas in which AI coaches can be particularly effective.

Goal Setting and Achievement

Setting goals helps individuals maintain their focus, prioritize activities, and change behavior—all of which are crucial to achieving personal and professional success. With an AI-powered coach, an individual can set their own goals, monitor their own progress, and gain feedback and inspiration based on their own actions. An AI coach thus becomes an effective tool for guiding the user incrementally to achieve what they desire.

From a manager's point of view, an AI-powered coaching tool or copilot can help set clear, measurable goals for employees that are aligned with the organization's broader objectives. The AI tool can guide managers to provide effective feedback and support to team members, creating a productive and positive work environment. An AI-powered coaching tool's ability to alert managers to specific employee performance data, both positive and subpar, allows managers to provide proper feedback, remediation, or kudos. When key patterns in an employee's behavior are identified, managers can ensure that both individual and team performances are optimized, contributing to the overall success of the organization and individual employees.

Professional Development Anytime, Anywhere

Success in almost any career requires technical skills and soft (or power) skills, including a range of nontechnical, universally applicable abilities—such as communication and leadership—that enable individuals to interact with others effectively and productively. Keeping power skills sharp by practicing them regularly is usually a crucial factor in long-term career development. Unfortunately, many organizations lack an environment in which to practice and hone power skills with targeted, direct feedback, and our fast-paced workplaces often make it difficult to allocate time to mastering power skills.

Fortunately, an AI-powered coach can provide anytime, anywhere practice. Tools like Presentr's Abbie, LEADx's Amanda (an AI-powered coach that helps with leadership), or Galileo (an AI-powered expert assistant for all things related to human resources) are accessible on any smartphone, which means the coach can travel with the learner. No need to coordinate schedules or meet at a certain location. You can pull your coach out of your pocket and instantly start a session. AI-powered coaches can ask and answer questions, evaluate the performance of a specific skill, and analyze data from corporate systems. They can also access the employee's input in a customer relationship management (CRM) system and analyze the data to provide recommendations for better customer interactions.

AI-powered coaches can be developed to strengthen any power skill. For example, an employee could practice negotiation skills with an AI-powered coach by asking it to evaluate their statements or practice leadership skills in a simulated interaction. As we've discussed, if you are a manager, an AI coaching tool can help you track the progress of your direct reports, including those who are struggling and need assistance.

Self-Analysis and Reflection

Self-reflection is a valuable skill for most professionals. Many personal AI-powered coaches use interactive techniques—such as asking probing questions, providing feedback, and guiding users through thought-provoking exercises—to promote self-reflection.

AI coaches also offer a level of consistency and accessibility not always available in traditional mentoring or coaching relationships because they are available 24/7 for just-in-time advice and support. Their constant availability ensures that professionals can engage in self-reflection at their convenience, encouraging a habit of regular introspection.

By analyzing responses and tracking the progress of the individual, AI-powered coaches can adapt their questions and feedback to suit the learner's unique situation, making the self-reflection process more relevant and more effective. An AI-powered coaching tool can also store the learner's progress, past responses, and feedback patterns to help them reflect on what they have done in the past and determine if they are on a path toward professional and self-improvement. The coach can also set realistic, achievable goals tailored to the person it's coaching. In the process of setting and working toward goals, learners are able to see tangible results from their self-reflection efforts, thereby reinforcing the value of the AI-enabled coach.

Technical Skills Support

Imagine a technician who needs to determine how to troubleshoot a piece of equipment. A well-designed AI-powered coach could provide the instructions and guidance to accomplish the task in a manner similar to how a GPS works. The technician could engage the coach via a smartphone or wearable device and answer a series of diagnostic questions about the equipment's symptoms and behavior. Based on the technician's responses, the AI coach could suggest possible causes of the problem and guide the technician through initial checks, such as verifying power connections and looking for visible damage. If the initial solutions don't work, the coach could move on to provide detailed, sequential instructions for further diagnosis and repair. The technician's feedback at each step of the process provides additional data that the AI coach can react dynamically to, which leads to further instructions—much like a GPS recalibrating a route after a wrong turn. When the problem with the equipment is resolved, the AI coach could also help prepare the final documentation to provide a complete record of the problem and resolution process for others to reference in the AI's knowledge base.

By continuously updating its database with the latest information from each troubleshooting session, an AI coach can become increasingly accurate in diagnosing and guiding repairs. In this way, an interactive feedback loop between an individual and an AI coach ensures more precise, effective troubleshooting throughout an organization.

Wellness Skills Improvement

Providing health and wellness skills for employees is an important, but often overlooked, responsibility in most organizations. In fast-paced, high-pressure work environments, creating a culture that prioritizes health and wellness can lead to benefits for employees and their organizations—and AI-powered coaches can help.

An AI coach can help mitigate the effects of job-related stress, prevent burnout, and promote a healthier, more engaged workforce. For example, an AI wellness coach can design individual wellness plans, addressing specific health goals like stress reduction, cardiovascular fitness, and nutrition. It can also be available anytime and anywhere to encourage consistent participation in healthy activities at the employee's convenience.

The coach can also serve as a confidential resource with whom employees can discuss health issues. Confidentiality and anonymity factors may encourage employees to interact more freely with an AI-powered coach than a human one. Additionally, an AI coach can offer resources like cognitive-behavioral techniques and motivational inspiration, as well as direct employees to professional support services when needed.

An AI coach can provide aggregated data on health trends within a company to help leaders identify the most common wellness problems and refine workplace strategies to mitigate them. The implementation of an AI wellness coach in a corporate setting not only supports individual health but also cultivates an organizational culture that values everyone's well-being.

AI-Powered Coaching Mechanics

When designing an AI-powered coach, it's important to consider how people interact with a human coach. You'll want your app to include features similar to what a person can do, but then, when possible, go beyond that to leverage the value of AI.

Important features for every AI-powered coach include the ability to interact constantly with the learner, provide motivation, report data visually, and continually report on a learner's progress. These action-first elements of AI-powered coaches should be at the forefront of your mind when creating your tools.

Be Interactive

A human coach always interacts and exchanges information with the other human they're coaching. An AI-powered coach should do the same, including initiating conversations, asking probing questions, sending reminders, and responding to the learner's inputs in real time. This two-way communication allows a coach to assess a learner's understanding, clarify concepts, address concerns, and provide targeted guidance.

If a learner is struggling with a particular concept, the AI coach should be able to diagnose deficiencies through intelligent, adaptive questioning. Based on the responses, it should then offer resources, simplify explanations, or help the learner modify their goals and targets. If the learner is advancing quickly, the coach should introduce more challenging tasks. It can even suggest games and other activities to help the learner practice. For example, Presentr's Abbie uses games in which the learner must meet certain volume and pacing goals. Games can help make almost any activity more fun and engaging.

Include Motivational Elements

An AI-powered coach should be designed to provide effective, motivational feedback and include algorithms capable of understanding and responding to individual user needs and progress. This involves developing the coach so it can accurately interpret user inputs and deliver personalized, context-sensitive feedback that's constructive and positive, focusing on reinforcing strengths and guiding improvements, instead of just pointing out mistakes.

If possible, the AI-powered coach should adapt its feedback style to suit the user's preferences and help ensure that its encouragement and guidance are meaningful and motivational to the specific person using it. A personalized, supportive approach not only fosters skills development but also boosts confidence and motivation, making the learning experience more engaging, effective, and meaningful.

Be Visual

An AI coach should be able to provide feedback and instructions in the form of graphics, charts, and other visual elements—from progress bars to pie charts and interactive diagrams. Visual elements can enhance the learning experience and make it more intuitive and effective, providing a clear, immediate understanding of performance, progress, and areas that need improvement.

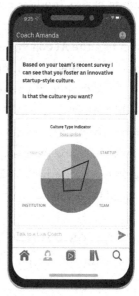

Imagine you're creating an AI-powered leadership coach. Wouldn't the people using this tool appreciate graphics that show their progress toward each target and highlight trends and patterns in their performance? If possible, include the ability for learners to personalize the visual feedback (Figure 10-1). Some learners respond better to detailed graphs, while others prefer simple, color-coded indicators.

Figure 10-1. The Coach Amanda mobile app uses personalized graphics to enhance users' engagement.

An AI-powered coach should be able to adapt the visual feedback it provides based on a learner's interactions, preferences, and progress to ensure that it remains engaging and effective.

AI-powered coaches can also use visual instructions such as flowcharts, step-by-step diagrams, and animated tutorials to guide learners through complex tasks or concepts. These kinds of visuals help reduce cognitive load and enhance comprehension.

Track and Report Each Learner's Progress

Knowing where you've been and where you're going is an important aspect of coaching. Any app used for coaching needs to keep track of what the learner has done in the past and compare it to what they need to do to achieve future goals. An AI-powered coach should have multiple mechanisms for collecting data on the learner's activities, interactions, and performance, such as quiz scores, completed tasks, and time spent on desired versus undesired activities. The coach should then be able to analyze the data to assess the learner's progress, identify areas of strength and weakness, and track and report improvements over time. Based on the learner's progress, the AI coach should offer personalized feedback and recommendations, highlighting strengths and pinpointing areas for improvement.

For example, if you're developing an AI-powered sales coach app, you could collect data on all sales representatives' activities, including completed training modules, the number of deals closed, and the number of cold calls made over a specific period. The app could then provide feedback and recommendations to help each sales rep make better progress toward their goals.

Let's Design an AI-Powered Coach

Developing an AI-powered coach should follow a deliberate, careful process that not only involves instructional design principles to ensure learning occurs during the coaching process, but also requires attention to motivation, types of interactions, and feedback. Here's a step-by-step guide for developing an AI-powered coach.

Step 1. Define Objectives and Desired Outcomes

The first step is to determine the problem you want to solve with the AI coach. Do you need to improve employee presentations? Allow for better troubleshooting at a customer site? Sharpen sales or negotiation skills? You want your AI coach to be *focused*. If you try to teach all things to all people, it will not work.

Narrow your AI-powered coach's focus to one or two related areas or skills, such as technical training or leadership behaviors. Establish clear goals for what the AI coach should help someone achieve. To select the right technology, you need to understand the specific requirements of the AI coach.

Step 2. Create a Paper Prototype

Develop a paper-based prototype to assess the content, feedback, and overall flow of the coaching experience. Working out the design on paper will help expose any flaws in your thinking, gaps in the coaching, and other problems that might not be visible until you have this prototype.

Step 3. Research Users

Conduct thorough user research to understand your target audience's needs, including those with certain conditions or divergent needs. Where do you envision the learners using the AI-powered coach? At their desks? On their smartphones? At a client's location? You'll need to conduct research and analysis to determine any possible usage scenarios.

Step 4. Consider Accessibility Requirements

You will also need to define accessibility requirements in line with standards like the Web Content Accessibility Guidelines (WCAG) to ensure your tool is usable for as many people as possible.

Step 5. Select the AI Technology

When selecting the actual technology with which you'll build your AI-powered coach, consider the type of coaching it will provide, desired outcomes, target audience, and desired functionalities. For instance, if you're creating an AI wellness coach, technologies that support health data analytics and personalized feedback mechanisms would be essential. This can also be true if you want to connect to corporate databases, learning management systems, or learning record stores. Ensure the selected technology is compatible with assistive technologies such as screen readers and speech-to-text software.

Step 6. Consult Experts for Help With Legal Compliance and Ethical Considerations

AI can contain biased and inaccurate information and approaches to feedback. You'll need to invest a great deal of effort to ensure your AI coach complies with relevant data protection and privacy laws. Consider ethical aspects of AI-powered coaching, particularly in terms of data usage and the fairness of AI algorithms. The perception of unfair, biased, or unethical practices will quickly render any AI coach useless from the learners' and managers' perspective. Transparency and the highest ethical standards are required for successful development and deployment.

Step 7. Design an Intuitive User Interface

The user interface (UI) and user experience (UX) are crucial for ensuring that your AI coach is easy to use and engaging for learners. Technologies that allow for the development of intuitive, user-friendly interfaces are essential. This includes considering multimodal interfaces (text, voice, and visual) that can cater to user preferences and needs.

Step 8. Design Effective, Motivational Feedback

At this point, decide what types of motivational feedback and encouragement you are going to program into the coach. For example, you might want feedback to acknowledge progress and highlight milestones, such as completing 50 percent of a training course. Create feedback to reinforce that a person is doing the right thing. You might choose to remind learners that mistakes are part of the improvement process and that they need to stay focused on their ultimate goal to build resilience.

Step 9. Implement Analytics and Connect to Databases

Implement analytics to track user progress and engagement. Use this data to further personalize the learning experience and develop insights into enterprise-wide patterns. Consider which corporate databases, such as a CRM system, the AI coach you are developing will need to connect with.

Step 10. Include Practice Activities

An AI-powered coach should not just provide feedback, but should also include practice activities and exercises so the learner can hone the skills the coach is helping them develop. As in Sam's experience, which we discussed at the beginning of the chapter, the coach should encourage practice, provide feedback on practice activities, and use those activities to improve the learner's skills.

Step 11. Pilot Test the Coach

It's important to conduct thorough testing with a diverse group of users, including those with disabilities or neurodiversity, to ensure the AI coach is accessible, user friendly, and achieves the desired goals. Testing in a small group will help you work out any inevitable bugs and problems that arise.

Step 12. Deploy the AI-Powered Coach and Conduct Training

Don't assume everyone will automatically know how to use the coach or how to integrate it into their daily routines. This is especially true when deploying an AI coach to assist managers. A few targeted training sessions can help make the process more transparent and accelerate the adoption curve.

Step 13. Develop a Maintenance and Update Plan

You will need to update your AI coach regularly to incorporate the latest advancements and instructional approaches. Continuously monitor and improve accessibility features to ensure compliance with evolving standards, user needs, and expectations. Create a feedback loop so those who use the coach can provide ideas and recommendations for changes to the experience.

AI Assist

Creating your own AI-powered chatbot is easy and fun, and it can become a valuable action-first learning tool. To create your own chatbot, scan this QR code or type bit.ly/MyOwn Chatbot into your browser.

Here you'll find a video that provides instructions for creating an interactive chatbot using ChatGPT. Experiment and have fun with your chatbot. Consider how you can use the chatbot's conversational element to create your own action-first learning experience.

Case Study: AI-Powered Coaching Boosts a Corporate Rewards Program

Natalie Roth, Employee Engagement and Experience Expert

This case study is based on real events. Details, including the company name, have been fictionalized, but the achieved results are real.

Dormiro, a multinational hospitality company with thousands of properties worldwide, wanted to increase sales conversions and customer satisfaction scores. Its team of in-house and outsourced customer service and sales (CSS) representatives is dispersed in remote and hybrid contact centers around the globe. The CSS reps are responsible for booking and managing reservations across many hotel brands.

In an environment of increasing global travel, Dormiro wanted to grow sales and customer loyalty metrics linked to its rewards program. In most companies, rewards program enrollments are a measure of customer loyalty, and they can be an especially effective tool in the hospitality industry. According to Skift Research—which provides proprietary research, analysis, and data tools for the travel industry—loyalty members account for 30 to 60 percent of hotel room revenue and tend to pay higher average daily room rates than nonmembers (iSeatz 2022). Dormiro's CSS reps were consistently asked to take advantage of every opportunity to turn guests into rewards program members while also providing a high level of service to support future bookings and hotel stays.

The Challenge

The company was struggling to motivate its CSS representatives to promote the rewards program and effectively convey its benefits to guests. Performance metrics, especially customer satisfaction scores, were inconsistent across in-house and outsourced CSS teams. Team leaders were responsible for motivating CSS reps to achieve loyalty enrollment goals and enabling them with knowledge and skills to provide high-level customer service, but they faced several significant challenges:

- Data was dispersed across numerous tools and platforms, requiring time-consuming manual analysis.
- Team leaders found it difficult to identify who needed coaching and the best ways to address individual skill and knowledge gaps.
- External providers struggled to promptly share brand and loyalty membership policy updates with outsourced CSS representatives, which led to customers receiving outdated information.
- The fully remote working environment exacerbated these problems because it was difficult for leaders to build rapport with their teams and create a positive coaching culture.

These challenges combined to produce inconsistent, infrequent coaching that failed to address each team member's unique needs.

Why Use AI-Powered Coaching?

The company knew that effective performance across its dispersed teams required consistent, continuous, and scalable coaching practices that could be personalized and adapted to each individual. The solution also needed to include elements of gamification to motivate team members to develop their skills and change their behaviors, as well as to recognize and reward their progress.

Stacy, the new vice president of L&D, came into her job looking for ways to connect training to performance. The L&D team had traditionally been evaluated based on training efficiency (completion rates and completion time), but Stacy wanted to move beyond those metrics to measure the impact of training on CSS team *performance*. In partnership with Erik, the company's global vice president of operations, Stacy embarked on a journey to transform the company's training and coaching practices to achieve these goals.

Making the Case

In his previous role at another company, Erik had implemented a software solution that gamified performance metrics and connected employee performance to relevant learning and coaching through personalized, AI-powered experiences. The tool leveraged operational data, including customer interactions, to automatically trigger relevant learning and coaching based on an individual representative's performance.

After reviewing several options, Stacy and Erik were convinced that the best choice was from a company called Centrical, which offered a frontline employee performance experience software solution. Erik had previously used this platform and believed it would provide the most holistic solution and allow them to optimize team leaders' time spent on gathering performance data to develop their teams and on administrative duties to manually manage rewards and recognition. At the same time, it would improve the overall experience for each CSS representative by making goals and progress visible in real time and supporting them with personalized training and coaching.

To get executive buy-in for their solution, Stacy and Erik decided to run a six-month pilot implementation with a subset of in-house CSS reps and their team leaders. They then planned to compare their performance improvement and employee satisfaction survey results to teams not participating in the pilot. If the pilot turned out to be successful, they would ask to roll out the solution to all CSS representatives, including the company's outsourced service partners.

The Solution

Dormiro implemented a solution that provided an AI-powered digital coaching experience to both the CSS reps and their team leaders. The tool became a copilot for team leaders, providing an actionable and guided 360-degree view of team member performance through a team dashboard, while also offering CSS reps real-time visibility into their performance with guided support in the flow of work (Figure 10-2).

Figure 10-2. Team dashboard showing performance. *Source: Image courtesy of Centrical.*

Stacy and Erik's teams worked closely to implement the solution. They brought in the IT department to integrate the program with existing software platforms to provide the performance data. Simultaneously, they transformed much of their existing training content into interactive microlearning modules. Centrical simplified these efforts with its generative AI content-creation capabilities. The tool also required each CSS representative to configure personalized goals and the team had to build standardized coaching templates and evaluation forms to ensure feedback and information was presented evenly and fairly to all team members.

Once the configuration and setup were complete, the CSS reps started each day by logging into the Centrical tool. Their dashboard looks similar to the one shown in Figure 10-3.

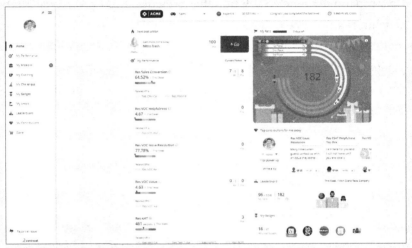

Figure 10-3. CSS dashboard showing individual performance. *Source: Image courtesy of Centrical.*

If they were behind on loyalty enrollments, the digital copilot would provide a nudge to remind them of their goal, along with a prompt to acknowledge the performance gap. This private notification was the first step in addressing the improvement opportunity. It was presented positively to provide psychological safety while also motivating the rep to step up.

Reps could track their progress in real time through the gamified dashboard. As they reached their goals, they earned game points, which meant leveling up and earning badges and rewards. In addition, the AI-powered digital coach provided each CSS representative with relevant microlearning modules based on their performance gaps. Modules included refresher quizzes on loyalty program benefits and interactive branching simulations to practice conversations with guests.

If the AI-driven training did not result in performance improvement, and a rep's performance continued to trend downward, that information would appear with other performance outliers on the team leader's insights dashboard. The team leader could take immediate action by initiating a coaching conversation, providing additional learning and support, or even creating a personalized goal challenge to motivate the rep to improve—all directly from their dashboard.

Once the rep's performance began trending upward, the team leader received another automated notification, this time prompting them to send out recognition in the form of kudos or a digital badge. The reps appreciated this feature because they could share these badges and kudos in a virtual chat, which helped create a stronger sense of community among the remote team.

As I previously mentioned, the team leader's experience included AI-powered insights that identified performance outliers and prioritized actions based on performance and business needs, including highlighting the loyalty enrollment conversion rate. Team leaders could take immediate action within the tool or start a more comprehensive evaluation to uncover the root causes driving the performance gap.

Using generative AI, Dormiro's new tool automatically evaluated relevant customer interactions for any CSS reps with performance gaps, scored them, and provided evidence to the team leader, who could then review and edit the automated evaluation, view and validate the evidence provided from recorded customer interaction, and even ask questions about the customer interaction using an interactive AI chatbot, before finalizing the evaluation.

These capabilities saved the team leaders significant time in determining who to coach and in completing performance evaluations. The team leaders and the training team reviewed automatically summarized feedback provided by CSS reps in pulse surveys, as well as their results on microlearning modules. They then used this information to identify whether additional support or training was needed.

The platform automatically reminded team leaders if they had pending messages from reps to respond to, open evaluations, and outlier insights. This helped ensure that they gave consistent and timely coaching and development. Team leaders also had gamified personal performance goals that kept them motivated to provide the right level of coaching and recognition to their teams. There were awarded points for hitting team coverage targets and providing regular coaching and recognition.

Benefits and Results

The AI-powered coaching solution was extraordinarily successful in increasing loyalty enrollments, sales conversion rates, and employee satisfaction. Within six months, the company saw:

- An 8 percent increase in customer satisfaction scores
- An 8 percent increase in loyalty program enrollment
- A 14 percent increase in premium sales conversion

The results showed a positive correlation between team leaders' engagement and their teams' results, with 35 percent higher overall scores and almost twice as much learning content completed for the teams in the pilot program.

Employee satisfaction surveys showed that team leaders strongly agreed the platform made coaching highly effective and made performance discussions with CSS reps more productive and transparent.

"Centrical optimizes time spent to gather KPI information and administrative duties for rewards and recognitions," said Erik. "We found that by letting agents know what their goals and results are, supporting them with on-the-job training and coaching, and recognizing their efforts, they help us drive improvement. I've found that agents are very responsive to challenges and competition, and so are their managers."

Lessons Learned

Here are three lesson distilled into critical insights that you can use to help guide your development of an AI coach:

- **Keep the design user friendly.** By gamifying digital coaching and learning, Stacy and Erik were able to draw CSS reps and team leaders in and create healthy competition without the AI coaching feeling like a version of Big Brother monitoring their every move.

- **Manage the change.** Communicating "what's in it for me" to all stakeholders was essential to the successful implementation. Stacy's L&D team needed to understand how connecting learning to performance could help them drive impact through learning, and their team leaders needed to understand how the new tool would eliminate low-value time spent on administrative activities while enabling them to provide more effective one-on-one support to their teams. For the CSS reps, it was important to highlight how the tool would enable their success and growth.

- **Frequently update content.** To drive sustained engagement with the solution, Stacy's team had to regularly update the content. They leveraged AI content creation tools to keep the content fresh and AI summaries to understand where employees needed additional support and content, which made the team leaders' jobs easier.

Key Takeaways

Now that you're ready to create an action-first learning experience with an AI-powered coach, remember these tips:

- The anytime, anywhere access to an AI-powered coach is a huge advantage. No need to coordinate schedules—the AI coach can help an employee whenever assistance is required. It is learner centric.

- An AI-powered coach is a terrific option for personalized learning and deliberate practice because it can adapt learning experiences to an individual employee's preferences, pace, and needs.
- An AI-powered coach can help with employee engagement and motivation, including support, nudges, and advice to help learners achieve their goals.
- AI-powered coaches can simultaneously coach a large number of employees across an entire organization, which is particularly beneficial for large or geographically dispersed teams. Unlike human coaches, AI-powered coaches don't get tired or distracted, ensuring a consistent level of training across the organization.
- AI-powered coaches should be designed to eliminate bias and harmful outcomes. AI is susceptible to human bias, which can be unknowingly or knowingly programmed into algorithms and feedback mechanisms.
- An AI coach's ability to identify outliers and automatically send messages, nudges, and reminders makes it an ideal tool for managers who want help dealing with large teams effectively.
- AI coaches can teach soft or power skills and technical skills well, so they can be deployed in a broad variety of industries for many purposes.

EXPLANATION OF THE ACTION-FIRST ACTIVITY

Did you ask an interesting question? Was the response what you expected? Did it feel like you were speaking to an actual person?

Chatbots are used in training applications to provide information and content in an interactive format. Unlike humans, chatbots are available 24/7. You can also download AI tools such as ChatGPT or Claude to your phone and interact with them using your voice—no typing required. Learners simply ask a question and receive an answer. It's like engaging in a real-world conversation with a knowledgeable instructor.

For those who have never tried an AI chatbot tool, here are some instructions for downloading the app to your smartphone and using the voice feature:

- **For Android**—go to the Google Play Store, search for and download the official ChatGPT app, and install it on your phone. Enter the requested login information. Open the app.
- **For iOS**—go to the Apple App Store, search for the ChatGPT app, and tap "Get" to download and install it on your phone. Enter the requested login information. Open the app.

To speak, press the sound icon, and then ask a question. You will see a black screen, which indicates the AI chatbot is thinking, and then it will respond. Once it responds, you can carry on a conversation.

Tool 10-1. Tips for Effective AI-Powered Coaching

✓ Take advantage of an AI-powered coach's ability to give instant guidance, clarification, feedback, and responses to queries so learners can get the assistance they need immediately in the flow of work or while they practice a new skill.

✓ Make use of the AI coach's built-in tendency toward self-reflection. In fast-paced work environments, asking an AI coach to encourage reflection and a slower pace for learners can help both the employees and the organization.

✓ Use data generated by AI coaching to track trends and organizational needs anonymously that might not otherwise be visible.

✓ Pay attention to AI-powered coaching answers and feedback to ensure that any bias is identified and eliminated.

11

Action-First for Everyone
Improve Learning Experiences Through Accessibility

Amy Pape
Instructional Designer

Think about a learning experience you recently worked on, whether it was a course, a short job aid, a workshop, or something else. When defining your participant population, did you consider whether anyone had deafness, color blindness, dyslexia, different native languages, low vision, the inability to use a mouse, anxiety, or atypical cognitive processing?

If not, examine the learning experience as if you were a participant with at least one of those characteristics. List all the required activities in the learning experience and note whether you would be able to complete them and acquire the knowledge or skills to achieve the learning objectives. *(Find the explanation at the end of this chapter.)*

At the end of this chapter, you should be able to answer these questions:

- When should you consider accessibility in the action-first design process?
- What accessibility barriers can exist for learners in an action-first experience?
- What accessibility considerations can help break down those barriers?

Renly was overjoyed to find out they had been offered a dream job at EQtech, a midsize software company with a reputation for innovation and nurturing young talent. Unfortunately, a few days before onboarding, Renly broke their right wrist and had to wear a cast for four weeks, followed

Accessibility

by another four weeks in physical therapy. The cast made it impossible to use a mouse and keyboard with the same ease as before the accident, but Renly viewed this as a minor inconvenience. They were determined to prove their worth during onboarding and start the job on a positive note.

EQtech's onboarding process included a virtual escape room designed to help new employees discover essential knowledge about company procedures. Participants learned by finding clues, deciphering messages, and solving puzzles. Upon entering the online event, Renly discovered that using a mouse and keyboard was an essential element for the experience. Many elements required instant reactions, such as rapid double-clicking, which Renly couldn't manage with their less agile left hand. Renly's temporary disability suddenly became a significant barrier that made it impossible to discover vital information, complete the event, and proceed to follow-on sessions.

The company's lack of empathy for employees with physical impairments tarnished Renly's view of EQtech. Maybe this wasn't the kind of company they should invest their time and talent in. They signed out of the onboarding session and emailed an HR representative, expressing a lack of confidence in the company and suggesting it might be better to part ways.

Within a few hours of receiving Renly's message, EQtech's directors of talent development, HR, and IT met to address the situation. They discussed the barriers Renly had encountered as well as concerns other employees had raised in recent months. They decided it was time to take action. Renly's manager called them to explain they were a valued hire and she still wanted them on her team. She said her team would update the onboarding program and discuss essential accommodations with Renly so they could complete the program as soon as possible.

Three weeks later, as Renly entered the escape room a second time, they received clear instructions for completing all tasks, including how to interact with each element via mouse, keyboard, touchscreen, and voice prompts. Renly chose the touchscreen option to explore areas of the escape room and easily used the tab key and space bar to activate certain clues. They were now able to use keyboard shortcuts to open tools and features as well as a voice-to-text tool to take notes and enter passcodes. The settings allowed for key remapping, ensuring maximum comfort and efficiency for Renly or any other participant. Renly found every clue, deciphered every riddle, and, in the process, gained the knowledge essential to begin their new position with the company.

EQtech worked with Renly to offer other accessibility accommodations when needed throughout the rest of the onboarding experience— Renly's broken wrist was no longer a barrier to completing any tasks.

The company followed up its review and revision of the onboarding experience with a year-long project to improve accessibility in all departments and job categories, including Renly and a dozen other employees in the review process. The new onboarding experience respected all employees' abilities and empowered them. HR also created a permanent committee to update systems, technology, and policies to ensure maximum accessibility and inclusion.

❋ ❋ ❋

In this chapter, I suggest some best practices for ensuring that all your action-first projects are as accessible as possible to all learners. This is not a primer on legal compliance; it's about making sure you're aware of the needs of everyone you're designing for before you jump into creating an action-first experience.

First, we'll review a few key principles and strategies, and then we'll compare accessibility needs in the digital world with those in the real world. At the end, I'll summarize the essential tips found in chapters 2–10, and share some accessible, downloadable tools.

Learner-Centric Design

As instructional designers, we want to create learner-centric experiences that increase our audience's knowledge and improve their performance. However, we can't develop our best action-first, learner-centric designs without considering all the critical characteristics of each learner, including sight, hearing, motor skills, attention, empathy, and cognitive skills. Keep in mind that accessibility in some action-first experiences is harder to achieve than in others, but we can always take small steps forward. In some cases, it may seem impossible, at which point you can think about how to provide a different but equivalent experience in terms of content and interaction.

When working to create the best action-first learning experiences, you should begin with a good design practice that is infused with accessibility. This can be summed up in six steps: empathize, define, ideate, prototype, test, and iterate.

Empathize

The first step, empathizing, is particularly important. Often, instructional designers and trainers without disabilities don't consider whether barriers exist in their designs. Others think the population who may have disabilities isn't large enough to worry about; however, this is inaccurate. About one in four people in the United States is living with one or more impairments or disabilities, which may be permanent, temporary, or situational.

It's unrealistic to try to account for every single learner profile or situation in each action-first learning project. However, we can think through an array of learner personas with general disability types to help remove barriers preventing a learner from engaging in the action-first experience. Creating learner personas is a good way to remind your team of the diversity of individuals who will be participating in your action-first learning content.

AI Assist

One place that AI can help with designing accessible action-first learning experiences is by creating learner personas. Consider using a prompt like this one to ask an AI tool to help you create personas to reference during the design process. Adjust the content within the square brackets to include the type of action-first learning you are designing.

```
Provide several personas for people living with
disabilities as those disabilities might relate
to [online learning]. Include personal background,
challenges, and remedies.
```

Define

When practicing empathy, we become aware of general disability types—including visual, auditory, motor, cognitive, and speech—and we should then be able to define the barriers those disabilities may impose on learners. With those barriers in mind, we can then choose the best *considerations*, also known as *accommodations* to incorporate into our materials. Table 11-1 shows a selection of common barriers and helpful considerations.

Table 11-1. Defining Disability Barriers and Countering Considerations

Domain	Barriers	Considerations
Vision	• Limited vision • Differentiation • Incompatibility with assistive technologies (e.g., screen readers and haptics) • Hidden information • Poor lighting	• High contrast • Larger fonts • Tactile indicators (e.g., textures or braille) • Audio indicators (e.g., feedback sound effects) • Alternative text • Assistive modality • Responsive layouts
Auditory	• Hearing impairment or deafness • Background noise • Environment	• Visual indicators (e.g., highlights or symbols) • Captions and transcripts • Manual activation of media (e.g., no automatic start)
Cognitive	• Language perception • Readability • Comprehension • Anxiety • Attention • Memory • Thought processing • Cognitive overload	• Simple language that's clear and concise • Organized structure that's logical and consistent • Simple instructions or rules • Cues, guides, and hints • Motion controls • Time constraints (e.g., learner can turn off or extend time) • Difficulty levels
Physical	• Dexterity • Mobility	• Navigable • Input modalities • Remapping • Responsive • Target areas
Speech	• Language or accent recognition • Mutism	• Alternative inputs to speech

Ideate

Now that you have a heightened awareness of the breadth and depth of your audience, it's time to brainstorm! Ideate with peers, whenever possible, to spark creativity and unique solutions. As we all know, there are no bad ideas in a brainstorm. For each solution, explore the potential barriers and outcomes, including how accessibility may enhance or hinder the intended experience. This exercise can help you find a middle ground or a unique way to accomplish your goals in an accessible way.

Prototype

Grab some simple materials (such as index cards, markers, colored pencils, and scissors) or a digital authoring tool or UI design program and create a playable mockup of your best brainstorming efforts. Be sure to remember your audience and refer to your personas for the project. Also keep in mind any potential barriers you identified, as well as the accessibility considerations you researched and aligned to your action-first experience. You may notice, as you color that index card, that certain choices—such as a color combination, lack of consistency, insufficient differentiation between landmarks or pieces, or a too-complex explanation of the rules— just won't work. Fix these obstacles as you go, and then get your action-first prototype in front of an audience.

Test

Playtest the prototype, build on what works, and improve or remove what doesn't. Over time, the best style, theme, layout, mechanics, rules, and alternatives will emerge.

Be inclusive with your testers. Recruit participants with disabilities to provide feedback at key points in the design process (including the prototype, beta, and pilot phases). They will help you identify barriers you may have missed, assess playability, and discover unintended consequences of accessibility features. With their guidance, you will be able to improve your universal design thinking.

If you don't have in-house resources, connect with communities like AbleGamers for testing support if you're creating a learning game. If you describe the learning experience you are creating, they will match you with an ablegamer who can test the game and provide feedback.

Iterate

After you have completed testing and begun using your new action-first learning experience, you'll need to continuously monitor and improve its accessibility features to ensure you are meeting the participants' needs and expectations and complying with evolving standards. Always establish a cadence for periodically reviewing and updating your learning experiences. And create a feedback loop so your learners can provide recommendations for changes.

Accessibility in Two Worlds: Physical and Digital

Some accessibility considerations, like tactile indicators, only apply in the physical world. Others strictly apply to digital assets—and many are universally applicable. As you design your own action-first learning experience, take note of the considerations that are most important for the world in which you're operating. See Tool 11-1 at the end of this chapter for help linking specific accessibility measures to specific action-first learning designs.

In the Physical World

If you are creating a board game to train a customer service team, for example, you'll need to focus on physical considerations, such as the maneuverability of tokens, dice, cards, and other pieces on the board. You should pay attention to textures, sizes, notches, and other tactile indicators. If the learning experience requires some physical movement, ensure that the locations of stations, clues, and other critical information areas have clear and easy access. If possible, keep stations relatively close so participants won't have to walk long distances.

You should also be prepared with tools, devices, or other aids to help participants reach, view, or find information. As an example, if you've created a card game, you may want to offer textured card sleeves for differentiation or to help improve grip, or you could use words and symbols in addition to different colors (Figure 11-1). In an escape room, you could provide telescoping grabbers or mirrors to assist with exploring objects on walls, shelves, or under tables. You could consider providing clues written in braille or offering both text and audio versions of clues. You may even want to create braille instructions.

 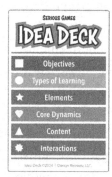

Figure 11-1. Physical playing cards that use words, symbols, and colors (not shown here in black and white) to define each of the topics.

Selected Resources

As you begin to define disability barriers and want to learn more about accessibility considerations, these resources may be helpful:

- ▶ **WCAG (Web Content Accessibility Guidelines).** Learn more at w3.org/TR/WCAG22.
- ▶ **Penn State University's Simplified Guide to WCAG.** Learn more at accessibility.psu.edu/guidelines/wcaglist.
- ▶ **Michigan State University's Tutorials and Guides to Accessibility.** Learn more at webaccess.msu.edu/Tutorials.
- ▶ **WebAIM (Web Accessibility in Mind).** This nonprofit offers accessibility training, consulting, evaluation, and certification. Learn more at webaim.org.
- ▶ **Video game accessibility guidelines.** Learn more at gameaccessibilityguidelines.com/basic.
- ▶ **3DPlayMedia's Curation of Recommended Resources for Higher Education and eLearning Accessibility.** Learn more at 3playmedia .com/blog/online-education-accessibility-policy-building.
- ▶ **Microsoft Accessible Mixed Reality.** Learn more at microsoft.com /en-us/research/project/accessible-mixed-realityanast.

In the Digital World

What about digital action-first learning experiences? If you're creating an AR experience or developing an online card game or comic, for example, you should provide accurate text descriptions for all contextual information (including captioning, transcription, and audio descriptions) as well as alternative text or captions for graphics. Representing the environment, characters, and elements of your action-first learning experience in this way will help those using assistive technologies create their own maps of your experience. You should also consider how you'll support navigation alternatives beyond a mouse, perhaps through keyboards, voice, or touch.

When in a VR simulation or an online escape room experience, ensure any flashing or blinking is dim and there are fewer than three flashes per second. Provide motion controls that allow users to change the speed of transitions, panning, and animations. To level up your learning experiences even more, increase contrast, choose fonts appropriate for learners with dyslexia, build in help and status updates, and in general, make visual elements adaptable. Allow your participants to customize the color palette and make adjustments if you are using time constraints. Always make time to playtest your designs using assistive technology and fix any bugs before you launch the learning experience.

Universal Considerations

Now, let's look at some tried-and-true design considerations that will make any type of learning experience more accessible.

Always keep your text and the experience as a whole clean and simple, using readable fonts, intuitive icons, and an intuitive structure. Never overcomplicate your language, rules, or objectives—again, keep it simple.

Visually, aim for a high contrast, simple color palette, and never rely on color alone to relay information. In fact, it's usually best to communicate essential information in at least two formats, whether that's shape and color, audio and text, or another combination.

In any learning experience, participants want to see themselves and others they can relate to, so embrace diversity and inclusivity. As you build a branching scenario or live interactive experience, use images and stories that represent a diverse audience in terms of gender, race, ethnicity, language, sexual and cultural identity, and more.

Finally, invite people of all skill levels, ages, and abilities to test, review, and suggest improvements to your designs. Review and revise your programs often based on the feedback you get.

Figure 11-2 depicts key considerations in the physical, digital, and universal worlds. Reference it as you design your accessible action-first learning experiences. Additionally, you can use the QR code for a copy of the infographic.

Figure 11-2. Design thinking. *Source: Graphic courtesy of Amy Pape.*

Key Takeaways

Remember, it's not realistic to think everything you create will be 100 percent accessible. There is also no shame in acknowledging a certain level of inaccessibility and asking learners to communicate their needs directly. This transparency will help promote trust, build a positive reputation, encourage collaboration and problem solving, and reassure learners that accommodations and alternative access to crucial information are available if needed. Remember these tips:

- Empathy is a driver of good, learner-centric design.
- Whenever possible, include people with disabilities and those who use assistive technology in a digital environment to test and provide feedback on your designs. They may uncover new barriers and elements with unintended outcomes.
- Your learning experiences will not always be 100 percent accessible, but when you consider and design for accessibility, you expand the reach, playability, and inclusivity of your designs.
- Disclose any inaccessibility in your learning experience. This transparency helps promote trust, build a positive reputation, encourage collaboration and problem-solving, and reassure learners that accommodation and alternative access to crucial information are available if needed.

EXPLANATION OF THE ACTION-FIRST ACTIVITY

If you found elements of the learning experience that aren't as accessible to all learners as you would like, use the information in this chapter to revise the experience and improve accessibility.

Tool 11-1. Essential Accessibility Tips for Each Type of Action-First Learning Experience

This tool brings together the most essential accessibility tips discussed in chapters 2–10. Use this QR code to access a downloadable version.

Experiences	Accessibility Tips
Card Games	**Visual** • Use high-contrast colors, patterns, and large, legible fonts to make textual and graphical elements more discernible. **Mobility** • Consider adding tactile feedback such as textures, raised symbols, notches, and braille.
Board Games	**General** • Don't rely solely on any one sense. • Provide equivalent experiences for learners of differing abilities. • Be prepared with alternative accommodations to mitigate common barriers (e.g., add QR codes that point to audio descriptions of visual information). • Represent information in more than one way to improve conveyance. **Visual** • Use high-contrast colors, patterns, and large, legible fonts to make textual and graphical elements more discernible. **Cognitive** • Provide clear instructions, keep rules simple, and offer game modifications for levels of difficulty. • Use simple and consistent layouts that are predictable. • Use landmarks, grid references, and buildable boards for improved orientation. **Mobility** • Use pieces with unique shapes (e.g., a hexagonal token versus a circular token) or textures for easy differentiation and maneuverability.
Escape Rooms	**General** • Create an inclusive experience without sacrificing the fun and immersive aspects of the game. • Identify potential challenges faced by individuals with disabilities. • Consider creating variations (e.g., different levels of difficulty) to ensure puzzles, clues, or challenges are readily accessible to anyone.

Experiences	Accessibility Tips
Escape Rooms (Cont.)	**In-Person** • Adding closed captions to videos or ensuring clear access to all areas of the room can broaden inclusivity. • Build in more than one way to solve a clue, puzzle, or challenge. **Virtual** • Keep the Web Content Accessibility Guidelines (WCAG) standards in mind. • Implement keyboard navigation and set an accurate tab order. • Limit speed and motion or provide the ability to adjust motion for sensitivities. • Allow for key remapping to minimize finger movement, reduce strain, and improve performance and responsiveness.
Comics	**General** • Comic sans is an easy-to-read font for people with dyslexia. • Some learners may find it hard to read words written in all capital letters. Consider using title case, which has a similar effect but is easier to read. • Say it twice—in the narrative and through visual representation, if possible. • Present digital text as true text and not as a graphic unless you're using Scalable Vector Graphics (SVG). • Provide sufficient contrast for text in the form of speech bubbles or thick borders to make text stand out on highly illustrated backgrounds (POW!). • Reflect emotions and feelings, while respecting accurate representation and culture. **Visual** • Descriptions of characters, the environment, and mood in a storyboard are a great starting point for creating alternative text and long descriptions. • Use SVG with coded text descriptions and metadata. • Offer learners the ability to zoom and resize images without losing any quality. **Auditory** • If narrating, include the details of character expressions, mood, ambiance of a room, and so on as part of the narrative (or as an audio description), especially if these details are critical to conveying the context of the story. **Cognitive** • Not everyone will understand the comic's artistic style or interpret expressions in the same way. Try to ensure key elements are conveyed using multiple methods. • Narrative framing of digital storytelling helps reduce cognitive effort. **Mobility** • For interactive digital comics, ensure all elements are discoverable and navigable using different inputs (e.g., touch screen, keyboard, and mouse).

Experiences	Accessibility Tips
Branching Scenarios	**General** • Apply built-in authoring tool accessibility options to ensure navigability (including a responsive accessibility toggle for text; reading, tab, and focus order; and alt text). • If coding from scratch, the developer should be familiar with digital accessibility standards. • Test using assistive technologies (e.g., screen magnifiers and screen readers). **Visual** • Add alternative text or a caption to describe contextual graphics. **Auditory** • Provide audio descriptions of key visual elements (e.g., facial expressions to indicate mood and signs, labels, and scene details that are important for context). • For audio or video elements, add accurate closed captions that include speakers, actions, and relevant sounds. **Cognitive** • Ensure information is clear, concise, and structured. • Use simple language and provide clear instructions at each step. • Use meaningful link text that conveys the destination. • The design of the branching scenario should be intuitive and free of unnecessary complexity. • Avoid time-limited tasks or provide the option to extend time limits. • Consider help or hint mechanisms to ensure learners don't get stuck. **Mobility** • Allow for keyboard navigation of interactive elements, ensuring logical tab order and accessible controls.
Live Interactive Events	**General** • For live virtual events, choose platforms that offer accessibility features such as live captions and are compatible with assistive technologies. • Indicate (in event details) that accessibility accommodations are available upon advance request. • Plan for and create alternatives for common barriers ahead of time. • When requested, use alternate communication methods such as a sign language interpreter within the face-to-face or virtual setting. • If exceptional situations arise, offer to work with learners individually. • Facilitators should reflect the same empathy and inclusivity for learners with disabilities that you considered during the design of the event strategy and materials.

Experiences	Accessibility Tips
Live Interactive Events (Cont.)	**Visual** • Use high-contrast visuals and clear, legible fonts in presentations. • Avoid relying solely on visual cues. **Auditory** • Ensure support of live captioning or provide sign language interpretation if it makes sense for your audience. • Speak clearly and use descriptive language. **Cognitive** • Avoid jargon and noninclusive language. • Provide extra time for responses. **Mobility** • Ensure the physical or virtual venue is compliant with the Americans With Disabilities Act (ADA) standards. For physical locations, this includes wheelchair ramps, accessible restrooms, and appropriate seating arrangements. **General** • Use bold colors and contrast to convey information on any background from any perspective. • Use SVG with coded text descriptions and metadata. • Offer learners the ability to zoom and resize images without losing any quality. • Add haptic feedback to convey information such as parameters, obstructions, warnings, or nearness. • Add sound cues for auditory feedback. • Offer a wide choice of difficulty levels. • Provide details of accessibility features on any packaging or the website. • Provide details of accessibility features in the game. • Ensure that all settings are saved and remembered. • Solicit accessibility feedback.
AR, VR, XR, and Metaverse Experiences	**Motor** • Allow controls to be remapped or reconfigured. • Ensure that all areas of the user interface can be accessed with the same input method as the gameplay. • Include an option to adjust the control sensitivity. • Ensure controls are as simple as possible or provide a simpler alternative. • Ensure interactive elements and virtual controls are large and well-spaced, particularly on small or touch screens. • Include a toggle or slider to adjust the intensity of any haptics.

Experiences	Accessibility Tips
AR, VR, XR, and Metaverse Experiences (Cont.)	**Cognitive** • Don't require multiple levels of navigation just to start playing the game. • Use simple, clear language. • Include interactive tutorials. • Allow players to progress through text prompts at their own pace. • Avoid flickering images and repetitive patterns. **Vision** • Ensure no essential information is conveyed through color alone. • If the game uses a field of view (3D engine only), set an appropriate default for the expected viewing environment. • Avoid VR simulation sickness triggers. • Use an easily readable default font size. • Use simple, clear text formatting. • Provide high contrast between the text, UI, and background. **Hearing** • Provide subtitles for all important speech. • Provide separate volume controls or mutes for effects, speech, and background music. • Ensure no essential information is conveyed through sounds alone. • If using subtitles or captions, present them in a clear, easy-to-read way. **Speech** • Ensure that speech input is not required and included only as a supplementary or an alternative input method.
AI-Powered Coaching	**General** • Define accessibility requirements in line with standards like WCAG. • Develop a maintenance and update plan to incorporate the latest AI advancements and instructional approaches. • Continuously monitor and improve accessibility to ensure compliance with evolving standards, user needs, and expectations. • Create a feedback loop so users can provide ideas and recommendations for changes to the experience.

12
What's Next?
Design Your Action-First Learning Project

Pick one of the many action-first learning methods described in this book and start designing your own experience. *(Find the explanation at the end of this chapter.)*

At the end of this chapter, you should be able to answer these questions:

- How do you plan an action-first learning project?
- How do you implement an action-first learning project?
- How do you debrief learners in an action-first learning project?
- How can you overcome resistance to action-first learning in your organization?

In the preceding chapters, I hope I've convinced you that the action-first approach is not just a design preference but a *necessity* if you're preparing learners to thrive in fast-paced, dynamic environments. Employees' ability to adapt quickly, think critically, and face challenges actively is more important than ever for organizations of all sizes and missions. Action-first learning nurtures those abilities while engaging learners in meaningful practice and knowledge application.

If you want action-first learning to enhance and improve your learning designs, it's time to take action! Sitting idly on the sidelines waiting for someone to give you permission to begin a project or waiting for the thumbs up from a manager or supervisor will not lead to success. The time to implement action-first learning is now, and as a learning designer, you can take the initiative to make it happen.

JOURNEY NEXT STEPS

Go ahead and take the plunge. Do. Not. Wait.

In this chapter, I suggest ways to advocate for action-first projects, overcome resistance within your organization, and begin designing an experience. You'll also find templates to help you navigate the process.

From Resistance to Action

Your action-first learning project begins when you identify training programs within your organization or among your clients in which traditional teaching methods are falling short or the application of skills is required. Propose action-first learning as a solution for the problem or as a way to practice the application of key skills.

Be aware that you may encounter significant resistance because these approaches are not universally accepted, especially if traditional training courses are entrenched in your organization. How you respond to the resistance makes all the difference.

Of course, one method is to ask for forgiveness after you've already implemented the solution. While this won't work in every organizational culture, sometimes it's a good way to get started. If that's not an option for you, it's usually best to create a one-page proposal outlining the expected outcome, the advantages of your chosen method, a description of why you think it will work, and a quick calculation of benefits. Decision makers rarely read beyond a single page.

Here are some steps that should help build the support you need:

1. **Look for internal champions and build a coalition of supporters.** Find like-minded peers who understand the value of action-first learning and work with them to promote its adoption. A group of advocates will have a stronger voice and more resources for implementing change than one person. Consider establishing an informal book club to read a variety of books about action-first learning (including this one!) and use the lessons learned to build an argument for change in your organization's training programs.

2. **Prepare concise, reassuring answers for the skeptics.** When faced with skepticism and opposition, be prepared to address

concerns with specific, research-based answers. Some opponents of change will worry about the feasibility of action-first learning and its alignment with existing norms and standards. Explain that you can integrate action-first learning into current practices and clarify how it aligns with your organization's instructional goals. Remember that action-first learning is about shifting the focus from passive reception of information to active participation and *application* of knowledge. I've included a chart in Tool 12-1 to help you describe the variety of available action-first techniques. (You can find it at the end of this chapter.)

3. **Suggest a small-scale pilot implementation.** To demonstrate the potential of action-first learning and gather data to support its expansion, run a small pilot program. The best advocate for action-first learning is a participant who learns, applies the knowledge gained in the action-first experience, and can explain the value of the experience firsthand.

4. **Consider a variety of techniques and choose the one that works best for your goals.** Tool 12-1 provides a quick summary of the key differences among the action-first techniques described in this book. Scan the chart to choose which one might be the most effective for the type of learning you need—from helping learners see the big picture to building organizational culture and understanding. For example, you might consider using AR to teach empathy and understanding or an escape room for communication skills.

Keep in mind that these are not the *only* action-first learning approaches; they're just a starting point. You may want to explore others, including creating video-based learning games.

Create a Plan

Once you determine which action-first design you want to use, it's a good idea to map it out on a worksheet to help think through your approach. The worksheet in Tool 12-2 at the end of this chapter provides an outline as you begin developing an action-first learning experience. You can also download the worksheet at td.org/product/book--action-first-learning/112505.

Include the following items in your worksheet:

- **Name of the experience.** The first thing you should do is decide on a name for the experience you are developing, which ensures everyone involved has a common reference point. You can use a working title and come back later once you've thought of a more meaningful or clever name.
- **Business need.** For any action-first learning experience (or any learning experience for that matter), you need to tie the learning design to business outcomes. Write down how this experience will help the organization. Be specific.
- **Desired learning outcome.** Determine what you want the learners to be able to do after the learning experience. Spelling this out clearly and sharing it with stakeholders will connect all those involved to the purpose of the experience.
- **The approach.** You are choosing a particular action-first learning approach for a reason. Spell it out. This justification will be your go-to response when a naysayer says, "Tell me again why we're doing an escape room."
- **Key mechanics.** Each action-first learning experience has many different key mechanics, and you aren't going to use every one every time. Document which make the most sense for your learning goal, the resources at your disposal, and your audience.
- **Constraints.** With any project, there are constraints beyond your control. Record them in the worksheet. Reviewing what can and can't do will help you determine if a new constraint has been put into place or an existing constraint has been lifted.
- **Your process.** Look at the appropriate chapter in this book and use the process outlined to guide you as you build the action-first learning experience. Writing out the process will help you identify any gaps or opportunities you can leverage.
- **Learner reflection plan.** The critical component of reflection will not happen magically. If you truly want learners to reflect and

take away critical lessons from their experience, you need to plan the reflection. Determine the most appropriate method or methods as well as how you want the reflection process to unfold.

- **Team members.** List the primary and secondary team members who will help make the action-first learning experience happen. Most action-first learning designs can operate with one facilitator, but the more people, the easier the task.
- **Additional notes.** Here you can add information that might be critical to designing, developing, or delivering your action-first learning experience.

Implement a Pilot Course

Once you have the design in place and you're ready to move forward with creating the action-first learning experience, the next step is to run a small pilot test and evaluate it. Remember, a pilot course is simply a preliminary test run that you conduct before the full-scale implementation of your action-first learning experience. The purpose is to identify any questions, challenges, or areas for improvement.

Running a pilot training course effectively, especially when testing new methods or content, requires careful planning and adaptability. Here are some tips to help ensure it runs smoothly and yields valuable insights.

Define Clear Objectives

Before the pilot starts, be clear about what you want to achieve. Is it a modification of the materials? Validation of methodology? Are you testing for level of engagement? Define specific, measurable objectives that you want to achieve. This clarity will help ensure that suggestions are aligned with the program's goals and not personal opinions or "nice to haves."

Prepare Thoroughly

Ensure all materials and resources are ready before the pilot course begins. This includes technology checks, organizing physical or digital learning spaces, and ensuring all facilitators are briefed on the course content and expectations. This is important because poor execution of the initial content and information may skew the actual value of what is being taught. You want to run pilot test under the best conditions possible.

Determine Your Pilot Audience

When you're testing an action-first learning approach, you need a big enough group of learners to get meaningful and diverse feedback, but this group also needs to be small enough to not overwhelm you with results and feedback. You might want to include eight to 10 individuals, depending on how large the intended audience is. If you are creating a board game that nine people will play, you probably want at least two or three test groups so you can evaluate different experiences, which would mean enlisting as many as 27 people.

Collect Feedback Continuously

Gather feedback throughout the pilot test, not just at the end. Regular check-ins can provide insights into what is working and what isn't, and people might forget their experience if you only debrief later. It's hard to notice and capture everything in real-time, so you may want to record the session with the participants' consent and analyze the recording afterward. Use various feedback methods such as direct questions, feedback forms, and structured conversations to capture the pilot participants' experiences and comments.

Evaluate and Reflect After the Pilot Test

After the pilot test, conduct a thorough evaluation based on your original objectives. Analyze the feedback to understand the effectiveness of the action-first learning experience, the engagement of the participants, and the learning outcome. Pay special attention to any unexpected outcomes, both positive and negative. Reflect and catalog what changes need to be made before rolling out the action-first learning program more broadly.

Make Appropriate Changes

Modify the action-first learning activity based on the feedback received and the observations made during the pilot. Identify which suggested changes will have the most significant ability to improve the learning experience. Prioritize those changes based on factors such as feasibility, potential to increase engagement and learning outcomes, and alignment with the overall training objectives. Also, be aware of any accessibility issues or concerns from participants. Making action-first experiences more accessible helps everyone and will ensure a smooth launch.

Evaluate the Pilot Course

The most valuable information you will get from the pilot program comes from the learners themselves. Use the worksheet in Tool 12-3 at the end of this chapter to debrief the learners and determine opportunities for improvement. You can debrief the learners individually so their biases and experiences won't influence others, or you can debrief them as a group. In that case, one person's comment can help spark others to share more feedback.

You should include the following items in your learner debriefing worksheet:

- **Name of the experience.** Recording the name of the experience can be especially helpful if you are running multiple pilot tests and receiving feedback on multiple experiences.
- **Use one word to describe the experience.** This exercise helps learners distill their thoughts, ideas, and even emotions about the action-first learning experience. Forcing someone to sum things up in a single word leads to reflection, simplicity, and clarity. It can allow them to focus on their experience and provide an easy comparison of one person's experience with another's.
- **Learning outcome.** This is the most important element of the debriefing. What did the participant learn? Was it what you intended? Did they learn lots, but not what you wanted them to learn? When you know what they learned, you'll know if your design is on the right track.

- **Engagement rate.** One of the key reasons to implement an action-first design is to encourage engagement. If the learners didn't feel engaged during the action-first learning event, something needs to change. Examine the goals, the individual elements, and the overall design to see what you can change to be more engaging. You want to score high on the engagement scale with most of the people who participated.
- **Points of confusion.** Ask the learners to identify anything they did not understand, thought was confusing, or was related to accessibility. It's often difficult to imagine every question or complication a learner may encounter. The pilot test will expose your assumptions and gaps in the design. You can then fix the friction points and gaps before moving on to a larger audience.
- **Prior knowledge.** Ask the learners if there is any information they wish they had known before the experience. Sometimes, designers incorrectly assume learners have a certain knowledge base. The pilot test debrief is a good time to find out if this is the case so you can provide extra instruction or remove unnecessary elements from the action-first learning experience.
- **Anything you didn't like.** This question allows the pilot group to play designers and give feedback on what they would like to change about the experience.
- **Reflection on reflection.** Allow learners to comment on the reflection portion of the experience. Make sure they had enough time, adequate prompts, and plenty of encouragement to reflect. Did participants understand how to translate what they learned in the action-first experience to their on-the-job activities?
- **Final comments.** Give the pilot group a chance to add any additional information, thoughts, or ideas. This is your target market and their insights will help make the experience even better.

Final Thoughts

Action-first learning helps us create dynamic, engaging, and meaningful instruction. As designers, if we are careful and clever in our use of action-first learning, we can create effective learning events that all participants will remember. The learners will gain new insights, skills, and confidence and be entertained at the same time—a win for everyone.

You now know what's possible when you choose action-first learning. The next step is up to you. Select an existing traditional course, lesson, or module and transform it from a passive "sit and get" experience into an action-first learning experience in which learners are engaged from the word *go*!

Good luck, have fun, and take action!

EXPLANATION OF THE ACTION-FIRST ACTIVITY

It's time to take the knowledge, insights, and directions provided within this book and create your own learning experiences using the Action-First Learning Framework. This chapter provided worksheets and methods you can use along with the step-by-step instructions throughout this book to achieve success. The best thing to do is get started. You'll make some mistakes but that's part of the process. If you don't take any action, you'll never create action-first learning. Stop reading and start creating!

Tool 12-1. Comparing 9 Action-First Learning Techniques

Type	Why It's Effective	What It Can Teach	The Mechanics	Key Points for Designers
Card Games	• Familiarity • Simple rules • Real-time application • Sophistication and seriousness	• Memorization of jargon, terms, and facts • Discernment and observation • Communication skills • Critical thinking • Leadership • Strategic thinking	• Sorting • Sequencing • Matching • Role playing	• Apply the right card game mechanics. • Develop the appropriate look and feel for cards. • Create rules to play.
Board Games	• Seeing the big picture • Highlighting relationships • Underscoring the nuances of trade-offs • Sharing an experience	• Systems thinking and connections • Decision making with incomplete data • Potential consequences of actions • Resource management • Avoiding suboptimization	• Create a randomized board layout. • Allow multiple actions or activities per turn. • Create a cooperative playing experience. • Encourage participation. • Design participation into the entire game.	• Create the system and interconnected elements. • Create roles and parameters around roles. • Design final artwork. • Polish the look and feel.
Escape Rooms	• Quick experience • Practice working under pressure • Safe environment to make Mistakes • Requires teamwork	• Communication skills • Fostering social connections • Nonlinear thinking • Adaptability • Observational skills	• Create a setting and theme. • Vary the difficulty and how you deliver clues. • Mix up the types of activities. • Create a plan to debrief the experience.	• Create an escape room flowchart. • Design the puzzles, challenges, and clues. • Create hints and tips. • Train a game master.

Type	Why It's Effective	What It Can Teach	The Mechanics	Key Points for Designers
Comics	• Authenticity • Reliability • Representation • Transcending time and space	• Critical thinking • Decision making • Emotional empathy • Self-efficacy • Situational awareness • Diagnosis and troubleshooting • Emergency preparedness and action	• Multimedia • Digital storytelling • Visual language	• Study the audience and the environment. • Design the story. • Develop characters and design their interactions. • Design the art.
Branching Scenarios	• Immersive learning experience • Simulate real-life situation • Highlights delayed cause and effect • Allows learners to safely make mistakes	• Decision making • Empathy • Self-reflection and self-assessment • Situational awareness • Troubleshooting or diagnosing problems • Sales skills	• Leverage multimedia elements. • Provide nuanced choices. • Build in reflection points. • Keep branching as simple as possible (but not too simple).	• Create a setting environment and characters. • Create correct path first. • Create reflection points.
Live Interactive Experiences	• Building organizational culture and understanding • Immediate clarification of gray areas or misunderstandings • Peer networking • Shared experience	• Communication skills • Collaboration and teamwork • Spontaneity and improvisation • Hands-on practice and experience	• Think-pair-share • Construct activity • Interactive narrative • Problem-based learning	• Review content to determine the right exercises. • Train facilitators and provide appropriate support. • Create necessary collateral.

Type	Why It's Effective	What It Can Teach	The Mechanics	Key Points for Designers
Augmented Reality	• Reduction in learning curve • Making the invisible, visible • Changing of perspective of scale • Visualization of abstract concepts	• Empathy and understanding • Step-by-step procedures • Orientation and tours • Safety instructions and emergency responses • Understanding complex concepts	• Include haptic and sound-based cues. • Develop a safety protocol. • Go bold with colors and contrast. • Determine your AR orientation.	• Create the appropriate AR assets and content. • Develop with safety in mind. • Prototype and test. • Set up a deployment plan.
Virtual Reality	• Multiple senses are engaged. • Group collaboration across distances • Safe space for trial and error • Infinite resources and scenarios	• Technical expertise • Grace under pressure • Teamwork • Leadership and management skills • Dealing with critical incidents	• Field trip and scavenger hunt • Conceptual orienteering • Critical incident • Operational application • Social simulation	• Determine the desired visual environment. • Analyze and select the appropriate technology • Create or gather the 3D assets.
AI-Powered Coaching	• Personalized learning • Immediate, targeted real-time feedback • Engagement and motivation • Exception driven initiatives	• Goal setting and achievement • Professional development • Self-analysis and reflection • Technical skills • Wellness skills	• Be interactive. • Include motivational elements. • Be visual. • Track and report learner's progress.	• Select an AI platform. • Request help for legal compliance and ethical issues. • Design an intuitive user interface. • Design effective, motivational feedback.

Tool 12-2. Action-First Learning Plan Worksheet

1. Name the action-first learning experience.

2. What business need is driving this action-first learning experience?

3. What is the desired learning outcome? What do you want the learners to do after the experience?

4. Indicate which type of action-first learning approach you want to use.

☐ Card game   ☐ Live learning experience
☐ Board game   ☐ AR experience
☐ Escape room   ☐ VR experience
☐ Instructional comic   ☐ AI-powered coaching
☐ Branching scenario   ☐ Other

5. Why do you want to use this action-first learning approach?

6. What key mechanics do you need to include in this action-first learning experience?

7. What technology or materials will you need?

8. Are there any constraints or parameters you need to consider?

9. Describe the process you'll use to build the action-first experience.

10. What is your plan to encourage learner reflection?

11. Who will help you design this action-first learning experience?

12. Additional notes

Tool 12-3. Learner Feedback Worksheet

1. Name the action-first learning experience.
2. What one word best describes your experience with this action-first learning event?
3. What did you learn?

4. How engaging was the experience?				
1	2	3	4	5
Not engaging				Very engaging

5. What, if anything, did you find confusing or hard to understand?
6. What information or knowledge do you wish you had before undertaking this action-first experience?
7. Was there anything you didn't like about the experience? What was it? How would you change it?

8. How effective was the reflection portion of the experience?

9. Do you have any final comments? What else should we know?

Recommended Resources

General

For those of you who would like to incorporate action-first learning in your organization, you'll need to understand the competitive advantage of L&D programs in general. I've created a few LinkedIn Learning courses (which are all found at linkedin.com/learning) to help:

- "Designing a Training Program: Setting Goals, Objectives, and Mediums"
- "Setting and Managing Realistic Expectations for Your L&D Program"
- "Your L&D Organization as a Competitive Advantage"

Note: My other LinkedIn Learning courses are listed with the appropriate topic.

Card Games and Board Games

Try this digital card game platform:

- Enterprise Game Stack (enterprisegamestack.com)

These websites will help you create analog card and board games:

- Print and Play (printplaygames.com)
- The Game Crafter (thegamecrafter.com)
- Make Playing Cards (makeplayingcards.com)

The Game Crafter offers card games teaching a variety of skills, including:

- **Zombie Instructional Design Apocalypse**—a scenario-based card game for practicing instructional design skills
- **Zombie Sales Apocalypse**—a scenario-based card game to build sales skills
- **Zombie Financial Sales Apocalypse**—a scenario-based card game to build sales skills specific to the retail financial industry

My YouTube series *The Unofficial, Unauthorized History of Learning Games* highlights the value of classic learning games like *The Oregon Trail, The MIT Beer Distribution,* and *The Lost Dutchman's Gold Mine.*

Escape Rooms

If you'd like to go to a physical escape room with friends, you'll find many options at theescapegame.com. The Training Arcade offers a tool called "The Detective" that you can use to create your own online escape room training program, or check out Rachel Arpin's work on "The Leadership Escape Game" at rachelarpin.com.

Here are a few board games and tabletop games that follow the escape room format:

- **Unlock! Short Adventures: The Secrets of The Octopus by Space Cowboys** is a game in which players follow clues through a narrative adventure.
- **The Werewolf Experiment by Mattel Games** is a cooperation game in which players must solve 19 puzzles and locks before a mad scientist turns them into werewolves.
- **EXIT: The Professor's Last Riddle by Inka and Markus Brand of Kosmos Games** is a game in which players travel the world trying to unravel the mystery of an archaeology professor's legacy.

Instructional Comics

Three tools that can help you create interactive, online comic-style learning experiences are:

- Vyond (vyond.com)
- VideoScribe (videoscribe.co)
- PowToon (powtoon.com)

Branching Scenarios

For an introduction to branching scenarios, try my LinkedIn Learning course, "Scenario-Based Learning." If you're looking for playable examples of branching scenarios, check out Short Sims at shortsims.com/house.

Christy Tucker (christytuckerlearning.com) has produced dozens of posts related to designing and developing scenarios, including examples of branching scenarios using a range of tools, recommendations for writing scenarios, and tips for working with SMEs. She also has a collection of recorded webinars and presentations about scenario-based learning that are free to access (but may require registration).

For tools to develop your own branching scenarios, try:
- BranchTrack (branchtrack.com)
- Near-Life (near-life.tech)
- Genially (genially.com)
- Twine (twinery.org)
- The Regis Company (regiscompany.com)

More general authoring tools that include branching scenarios are:
- Articulate (articulate.com)
- Adobe Captivate (adobe.com/products/captivate.html)
- Lectora (elblearning.com/create-learning/lectora)
- CenarioVR, which offers 360-degree video branching (hub.elblearning.com/cenariovr-course-authoring-ppc)
- iSpring (ispringsolutions.com)

Interactive Learning

Check out my LinkedIn Learning courses that are focused on interactivity and action-first learning:
- "Learning How to Increase Learner Engagement"
- "Increasing Learning Engagement: A Skills-First Approach"

I've found these audience response tools helpful for live, interactive learning experiences:
- Poll Everywhere (polleverywhere.com)
- Kahoot! (kahoot.com)
- Mentimeter (mentimeter.com)

Augmented and Virtual Reality

My LinkedIn Learning course, "Designing Learning Experiences in the Metaverse," will introduce you to using virtual reality for action-first learning.

Metaverses you may enjoy exploring include:
- Decentraland (decentraland.org)
- Meta Horizon (horizon.meta.com)
- Second Life (secondlife.com)

I recommend these tools for developing AR and VR learning experiences:
- Zapworks (zap.works)
- Meta Spark (spark.meta.com)
- Unity (unity.com)
- Unreal (unrealengine.com)
- LearnBrite (www2.learnbrite.com)

AI-Powered Coaching

In addition to AI tools such as ChatGPT and Claude, which chat with users about any topic, there are many AI-powered coaching tools that help create effective instruction. Two that I recommend are:
- **Centrical** (centrical.com), which is a platform that personalizes the employee experience through AI-driven performance, coaching, quality management, and personalized microlearning.
- **UMU** (umu.com), which offers a platform that supports interactive dialogue exercises with UMU's virtual AI conversation practice coach. It helps employees learn effective communication skills and practice deliberately in real-world simulations with feedback that analyzes keywords, gestures, and eye contact.
- **Presentr** (thepresentr.me), which is an AI-powered coaching tool for learning how to present.
- **Coach Amanda** (leadx.org/hr-ai-chatbot-coach), which is an AI-powered leadership coach.

Accessibility

If you'd like to explore topics related to accessibility in learning, you may find these resources helpful:

- The World Wide Web Consortium's Web Content Accessibility Guidelines (W3C's WCAG; w3.org/TR/WCAG22)
- Penn State University's Simplified Guide to WCAG (accessibility.psu.edu/guidelines/wcaglist)
- Michigan State University's Tutorials and Guides to Accessibility (webaccess.msu.edu/Tutorials)
- Accessibility Guidelines for Video Games Developed Through a Collaborative of Game Makers and Academics (gameaccessibilityguidelines.com/basic)
- 3DPlayMedia's Recommended Resources for Higher Education and eLearning Accessibility (3playmedia.com/blog/online-education-accessibility-policy-building)
- Microsoft's Accessible Mixed Reality (microsoft.com/en-us/research/project/accessible-mixed-realityanast)
- Web Accessibility in Mind (WebAIM), a nonprofit that offers accessibility training, consulting, evaluation, and certification (webaim.org)

Recommended Books

I recommend these books on the diverse topics we've covered:

- *S.* by J.J. Abrams and Doug Dorst (an escape room book)
- *Short Sims: A Game Changer* by Clark Aldrich (for branching simulations)
- *Play to Learn: Everything You Need to Know About Designing Effective Learning Games* by Sharon Boller and Karl Kapp
- *Journal 29* by Dimitris Chassapakis (an escape room book trilogy)
- *Scenario-Based E-Learning: Evidence-Based Guidelines for Online Workforce Learning* by Ruth Colvin Clark and Richard E. Mayer
- *The Visual Language of Comics: Introduction to the Structure and Cognition of Sequential Images* by Neil Cohn
- *The Modern Learning Ecosystem: A New L&D Mindset for the Ever-Changing Workplace* by JD Dillon
- *Escape Room: Getaway From the Dungeons* by EnigmaAction Ed
- *Learning in 3D: Adding a New Dimension to Enterprise Learning and Collaboration Software* by Karl Kapp and Tony O'Driscoll
- *The Do-It-Yourself Escape Room Book* by Paige Ellsworth Lyman
- *Understanding Comics: The Invisible Art* by Scott McCloud
- *Making Comics: Storytelling Secrets of Comics, Manga, and Graphic Novels* by Scott McCloud
- *Handbook of Augmented Reality Training Design Principles* by Laura G. Militello, Christen E. Sushereba, and Sowmya Ramachandran
- *The Future of AR and VR Technology: Navigating the AR and VR Revolution, Exploring Opportunities, Training, Gaming, Applications of Augmented and Virtual Realities for the Next Generation of Professionals* by Raymond Russell
- *Unflattening* by Nick Sousanis (comics)
- *The CEO's Guide to Training, eLearning & Work: Empowering Learning for a Competitive Advantage* by Will Thalheimer

- *Design for All Learners: Create Accessible and Inclusive Learning Experiences* edited by Sarah Mercier
- *Instructional Story Design: Develop Stories That Train* by Rance Greene

References

Agarwal, A. 2019. "Three Reasons Why Active Learning Will Drive
the Workforce of Tomorrow." *Forbes*, July 9. forbes.com/sites
/anantagarwal/2019/07/09/three-reasons-why-active-learning-will
-drive-the-workforce-of-tomorrow/?sh=5381227f8f93.

Allen, M.M. 2024. "Pearls: Desirable Difficulty—Make Learning Harder
on Purpose." *Clinical Orthopaedics and Related Research* 482(1): 27–28.
doi.org/10.1097/corr.0000000000002926.

Arik, S., and M. Yilmaz. 2020. "The Effect of Constructivist Learning
Approach and Active Learning on Environmental Education: A Meta-
Analysis Study." *International Electronic Journal of Environmental
Education* 10(2): 44–84.

Cohn, N. 2018. "Visual Language Theory and the Scientific Study of Com-
ics." In *Empirical Comics Research: Digital, Multimodal, and Cognitive
Methods*, edited by Alexander Dunst, Jochen Laubrock, and Janina
Wildfeuer. New York: Routledge.

Cohn, N., and J.P. Magliano. 2020. "Editors' Introduction and Review:
Visual Narrative Research: An Emerging Field in Cognitive Science."
Topics in Cognitive Science 12(1): 197–223.

Deslauriers, L., L. McCarty, K. Miller, K. Callaghan, and G. Kestin. 2019.
"Measuring Actual Learning Versus Feeling of Learning in Response
to Being Actively Engaged in the Classroom." *Proceedings of the
National Academy of Sciences* 11(39): 19251–19257. doi.org/10.1073
/pnas.1821936116.

Ericsson, K.A., and A.C. Lehmann. 1996. "Expert and Exceptional
Performance: Evidence of Maximal Adaptation to Task Constraints."
Annual Review of Psychology 47:273–305. doi.org/10.1146/annurev
.psych.47.1.273.

França, R. 2020. "edX Review: Is edX Certificate Worth It In 2021?"
Classpert, June 2. classpert.com/blog/edx-review.

Freeman, S., S.L. Eddy, M. McDonough, M.K. Smith, N. Okoroafor, H. Jordt, and M.P. Wenderoth. 2014. "Active Learning Increases Student Performance in Science, Engineering, and Mathematics." *Proceedings of the National Academy of Sciences of the United States of America* 111(23): 8410–8415. doi.org/10.1073/pnas.1319030111.

Hollier, S. 2019. "Augmented Reality and Accessibility. Research Questions Task Force Wiki." W3C Web Accessibility Initiative, August. w3.org/WAI/APA/task-forces/research-questions/wiki/Augmented_Reality_and_Accessibility#Interface_design.

IPC-S (The International Playing-Card Society). n.d. "Games." i-p-c-s.org/wp/games.

iSeatz. 2022. *State of Loyalty: 2022 Hospitality Ancillary Report*. iSeatz, May. iseatz.com/blog/the-2022-state-of-loyalty-hospitality-report.

JAIST (Japan Advanced Institute of Science and Technology). 2023. "Scientists Explain Why Card Games Are So Addictive." Newswise, January 12. newswise.com/articles/scientists-explain-why-card-games-are-so-addictive?channel=.

Kalra, A., N. Subramaniam, O. Longkumer, M. Siju, L.S. Jose, R. Srivastava, S. Lin, S. Handu, S. Murugesan, M. Lloyd, S. Madriz, A. Jenny, K. Thorn, K. Calkins, H. Breeze-Harris, S.R. Cohen, R. Ghosh, and D. Walker. 2022. "Super Divya: An Interactive Digital Storytelling Instructional Comic Series to Sustain Facilitation Skills of Labor and Delivery Nurse Mentors in Bihar, India—A Pilot Study." *International Journal of Environmental Research and Public Health* 19(5): 2675. doi.org/10.3390/ijerph19052675.

Kozanitis, A., and L. Nenciovici. 2022. "Effect of Active Learning Versus Traditional Lecturing on the Learning Achievement of College Students in Humanities and Social Sciences: A Meta-Analysis." *Higher Education* 86:1377–1394. doi.org/10.1007/s10734-022-00977-8.

Martella, A.M., R.C. Martella, J.K. Yatcilla, A. Newson, E.N. Shannon, and C. Voorhis. 2023. "How Rigorous Is Active Learning Research in STEM Education? An Examination of Key Internal Validity Controls in Intervention Studies." *Educational Psychology Review* 35(4): 107. doi.org/10.1007/s10648-023-09826-1.

Steil, A.V., D. de Cuffa, G.H. Iwaya, and R.C. dos Santos Pacheco. 2020. "Perceived Learning Opportunities, Behavioral Intentions, and Employee Retention in Technology Organizations." *The Journal of Workplace Learning* 32(2): 147–159. doi.org/10.1108/jwl-04-2019-0045.

Thykier, C. 2023. "3 UX Considerations When Designing Augmented Reality." The Drum, February 22. thedrum.com/opinion/2023/02/22/3-ux-considerations-when-designing-augmented-reality.

Whiting, J. 2020. "Comics as Reflection: In Opposition to Formulaic Recipes for Reflective Processes." *The Permanente Journal* 24(1). doi.org/10.7812/TPP/19.134.

Willis, V.J. 2004. "Inspecting Cases Against Revans's 'Gold Standard' of Action Learning." *Action Learning: Research and Practice* 1(1): 11–27. doi.org/10.1080/1476733042000187592.

Zuckerberg, M. 2021. "Founder's Letter, 2021." Meta, October 28. about.fb.com/news/2021/10/founders-letter.

About the Contributors

Jessica Angove is the vice president of experiential learning at Tipping Point Media. She has more than a decade of instructional design expertise, and has dedicated most of her career to crafting innovative and technically advanced training and marketing solutions for the healthcare and life science industries. At Tipping Point Media, Jessica oversees the design and delivery of award-winning, experiential learning solutions.

Anders Gronstedt, PhD, is a pioneer in extended reality training simulations. As president of The Gronstedt Group, he leads the development of high-fidelity simulations that accelerate learning at scale for the world's largest employers, including the US Navy, Walmart, Pfizer, Novartis, Takeda, and Bristol Myers Squibb. Anders, a former marketing professor at the University of Colorado, is a thought leader in the industry and regularly contributes to conferences and publications.

Amy Pape, MSIT, is an instructional designer with 20 years of experience in both the public and private sectors. She began designing for greater accessibility as a public sector contractor, creating digital learning materials for warfighters and civilians to meet Level AA Section 508 compliance. For Amy, accessibility became less of a requirement and more of a foundational principle after seeing how well-aligned accessibility guidelines and good design practices can benefit every learner.

Natalie Roth is a recognized employee engagement and experience expert. As a senior director at Centrical, she equips L&D, HR, and operations leaders of global brands across a variety of sectors—including banking, travel, healthcare, and consumer technology—with innovative solutions to elevate the frontline employee experience. These technologies result in measurable improvements in employee engagement and performance.

Kevin Thorn, EdD, is an award-winning e-learning designer and developer, and owner of NuggetHead Studioz. Kevin integrates technology, instructional design, illustration, graphic design, animation, video, and educational comics to create innovative learning solutions. Kevin is also a well-known speaker and trainer in visual communication and design workflows.

Index

In this index, *f* denotes figure.

digital twins, 212
See also spatial computing
disability barriers and countering
considerations, 258
See also accessibility
diversity and inclusivity, 262–263
See also cultural relevancy
Dorst, D., 73
dry runs, 167
See also pilot programs; testing
dyslexia, 39, 117

E

EGS (Enterprise Game Stack), 43
email lists, 167–168
emergency responses and safety
instructions, 184–185, 201, 203
See also critical incidents; safety
protocols
empathy, 109, 134, 181–182, 257
engagement and motivation
AI-powered coaching and, 231, 237
AR and, 192, 195
comics and, 105, 106
escape rooms and, 78
live interactive experiences and,
171–172, 174
Piaget on, 19
See also ARCS Model of Motivation
Enterprise Game Stack (EGS), 43
environment, setting, and character
development, 140
environmental analysis, 115, 214
See also art design
ergonomic problems, 186
Ericsson, A., 231
Escape Room: Getaway from the Dungeons
(EnigmAction Ed.), 73
escape rooms, 7, 73, 75–98, 253,
255–256, 260–261, 265–266, 281
ethical considerations, 240
Eurogames, 56–57, 59
evaluation, of pilot courses, 278–279,
286–287
exception-driven initiatives, 231–232
Explore the Eye, 193–194

F

facilitators
card games and, 69
escape rooms and, 85
live interactive experiences and,
166, 167
metaverse for learning and, 215
See also game masters
feedback
AI-powered coaching and, 230–231,
240
artificial, 141
augmented reality (AR) and,
195–196
branching scenarios and, 141, 147,
148–150
delayed and immediate, 140
escape rooms and, 88
learner worksheet, 286–287
live interactive experiences and,
158, 163–164, 171–172
metaverse for learning and, 205,
206, 209, 216, 220
for pilot programs, 277
user testing, 221
See also self-reflection
fidelity, 222
See also real-life challenges
field trips, 210–211
flowcharts, 86
See also storyboards
follow-up strategies, 167–168
See also maintenance/update plans;
monitoring and evaluation
frustration avoidance, 87

G

Galileo app, 233
game controllers, 217, 219, 220, 221
game masters, 62, 69, 86, 87
See also facilitators
glasses, AR, 177, 179, 182, 183, 186
goal setting and achievement, 232–233
grayboxing, 196
Gronstedt, A., 217

nursing simulation training case study, 118–124

O

onboarding case studies, 25, 27, 253, 255–256
onboarding plans, 44, 216
operationalizing applications, 212
organizational culture, 157–158
orientation specific information, AR and, 183–184, 187

P

Pandemic, 50, 58
participation, equality of, 59
participation, real-time, 158
passive learning, v, 9
personalized learning, 230
personal space experiences, 187
perspective changes, AR and, 181
philosophy, defined, 13
Piaget, J., 19
pilot programs, 274, 276–279, 286–287
planning worksheets, 274–275, 284–285
platform analysis and selection, 214–215
play-based learning principles, 3–4
playtesting, 38, 61, 62, 68–69
    See also testing
Pokémon Go, 177, 197–198
practice activities, 241
    See also deliberate practice
pressure, 78–79, 208
problem-based learning, 164
problems. *See* diagnosing and trouble-shooting problems
production and distribution, 39–40, 62–63, 69, 124, 214–215
    See also deployment plans
progress tracking, 143, 231, 238, 241
proposals, 273
prototypes, 36, 189, 193, 196, 239, 259
public space experiences, 187
puzzles and challenges, escape room design and, 86–87

Q

QR codes, 195

R

Ready Player One (Cline), 204
real-life challenges, 132
    See also setting, environment, and character development
real-time participation, 158
reflection. *See* after-action review; self-reflection
reflection points, 141–142
relatedness, 155–156
relationships, highlighting, 52
    See also social connection; systems thinking and connections
research
    action-first learning, 19–20, 21
    audience analysis, 239
    on comics, 123
    cultural relevancy, 106, 124
    customer loyalty, 242
    needs for, 4
    play-based learning, 3
    See also audience analysis
resistance, steps to counter, 273–274
    See also learning objections, options to defeat
resource management, 55–56
    See also trade-off nuances
resources, 207, 289–293, 295
Revans, R., 11–12, 19
role creation and parameters, 60–61
role-playing, 35–36, 38, 42–44
Roth, N., 242
rules, 38, 61

S

safe environments, 78, 206–207
    See also mistake making, safely
safety protocols, 184–185, 186, 189
    See also emergency responses and safety instructions
sales case studies
    AI-powered coaching, 242–249

About the Author

 **Karl M. Kapp, EdD,** is a professor of instructional design and technology at Commonwealth University in Bloomsburg, Pennsylvania, where he teaches classes related to interactive learning, game design, and gamification. Karl serves as the director of Bloomsburg's Institute for Interactive Technologies, which works with government agencies, nonprofit organizations, and private corporations to create interactive, engaging, and meaningful instruction. His work explores the research, theoretical foundations, and application of research to the design of engaging, meaningful instruction that changes behaviors and makes a difference.

Karl has written 10 books and literally wrote the book on the gamification of learning and instruction: *The Gamification of Learning and Instruction*. He co-authored its companion, *The Gamification of Learning and Instruction Fieldbook*, as well as the well-known book *Play to Learn: Everything You Need to Know About Designing Effective Learning Games* (which he co-wrote with Sharon Boller).

Karl has created a dozen LinkedIn Learning courses, and he's been a TEDx speaker. He created the popular YouTube video series *The Unofficial, Unauthorized History of Learning Games*, in which he explores the history, development process, and outcomes of games designed to help others learn. He scratches below the surface and digs up "lessons learned" that you can apply to your own development of learning games.

He is a frequent international keynote speaker, headlining conferences in Brazil, Belgium, China, England, and France. Karl has won numerous awards, including being named one of LinkedIn's Top Voices in Education and a Guild Master by the Learning Guild. He's also received the ATD Distinguished Contribution to Talent Development Award.

Karl's passion is to help others create instruction that make a difference. Subscribe to his LinkedIn Learning newsletter *L&D Easter Eggs* or explore more of what Karl is up to on his website, karlkapp.com.

About ATD

The Association for Talent Development (ATD) is the world's largest association dedicated to those who develop talent in organizations. Serving a global community of members, customers, and international business partners in more than 100 countries, ATD champions the importance of learning and training by setting standards for the talent development profession.

Our customers and members work in public and private organizations in every industry sector. Since ATD was founded in 1943, the talent development field has expanded significantly to meet the needs of global businesses and emerging industries. Through the Talent Development Capability Model, education courses, certifications and credentials, memberships, industry-leading events, research, and publications, we help talent development professionals build their personal, professional, and organizational capabilities to meet new business demands with maximum impact and effectiveness.

One of the cornerstones of ATD's intellectual foundation, ATD Press offers insightful and practical information on talent development, training, and professional growth. ATD Press publications are written by industry thought leaders and offer anyone who works with adult learners the best practices, academic theory, and guidance necessary to move the profession forward.

We invite you to join our community. Learn more at **TD.org**.